SELECTED WRITINGS OF *Jotirao Phule*

Edited, with annotations and introduction, by

G.P. Deshpande

LeftWord

First published January 2002
Seventh impression, twentieth anniversary edition, January 2022
Digital print edition, January 2022

LeftWord Books
2254/2A Shadi Khampur
New Ranjit Nagar
New Delhi 110008
INDIA

LeftWord Books and Vaam Prakashan are imprints of
Naya Rasta Publishers Pvt. Ltd.

ISBN 978-81-87496-88-5

Visit website

For
all the shudratishudras of various colours and hues
including the organized ones!

Contents

Acknowledgements

I did the first systematic reading of the complete works of Phule in 1990. The occasion was the seminar on Phule in Surat on the occasion of his death centenary. I spoke there on the basis of notes. For various reasons I could not write out my presentation there in full although some points did figure here and there in my writing. The introduction to this volume draws very heavily on those notes.

The second time I turned to Phule was when Jana Natya Manch, a theatre group in Delhi, asked me to write a play on Phule. The play, called *Satyashodhak*, was about the life and times of Jotirao Phule, and. It has since been published in Marathi.

I must thank the editorial board of LeftWord Books for providing me with this opportunity of revisiting Phule the third time. Over the last year or so I have been in the company of Phule, a pleasant but by no means easy job. I must thank my fellow-translators Maya Pandit, Urmila Bhirdikar and Aniket Jaaware. It is not easy to translate Phule. But they have worked hard. We hope that at least some flavour of Phule's Marathi comes across in our translations. They gave me complete freedom in editing their translations. Ram Bapat read the Introduction and made incisive comments. Moloyashree Hashmi read the entire manuscript with diligence and care, and helped improve the translation. She also helped prepare the index. Members of LeftWord staff worked hard to produce this elegant volume. Lastly, thanks are due to Sudhanva Deshpande of LeftWord for his supervision of all details of this volume, and his untiring editorial work. But for his interest and dedication this volume would never have been ready.

G.P. Deshpande

Note on the Selection

In this volume we have included the major prose writing of Jotirao Phule. At the centre of his writing and thought are *Gulamgiri* and *Shetkaryacha Asud*. The full text of both has been translated and published here. *Sarvajanik Satya Dharma Pustak* repeats some of the themes that appear in his two major books, we have therefore not included the entire text of this work, but only some selections. Minor editing has also been done in *Satsar*. Portions left out are indicated by [. . .]. There are several short pieces which he wrote from time to time in response to specific questions of immediate import. We have not included those pieces as well. Further, there are some personal writings, his will for instance, which again do not find a place in this selection.

All his poetry has been excluded from this selection. There are several reasons for this. One, of course, is the cost factor: we wanted a volume that is affordable for the lay reader. Then there is the problem of translation. Phule is very hard to translate, even when he writes prose, because he uses language politically (for more on this, see our Introduction). His poetry is, understandably, even more difficult to translate. Quite apart from the difficulties of translation, a deep familiarity with the seventeenth-century poet Tukaram is called for to relate to Phule's poetic work. As in the case of Bhakti poetry, his poems are also meant to spread a message at a popular level. The message, clearly, is that which is articulated in *Gulamgiri* and *Asud*. The same is true of his play. It is intended to be an enactment at a popular level of his otherwise serious theses. All this does not mean, of course, that these works need not be translated. *All* of Phule should be translated and made available in English. And, hopefully, one day he will be.

There are some texts that Phule wrote in English. They are reprinted here in the original form (including original spellings, capitalization, etc.) and indicated as such. Where there are missing words in the English original, these are indicated in square brackets. The other texts are translations done for this volume from *Mahatma Phule Samagra Vangmaya* (*Collected Works of Mahatma Phule*), Mumbai: Maharashtra State Publication, first edition edited by Dhananjay Keer and S.G. Malshe, 1969; fourth edition edited by Y.D. Phadke, 1991. In the rare instance where a minor discrepancy was observed in the text of the two editions, the 1991 edition has been followed. The translator of each individual piece is identified. To indicate Marathi words, italicization has been done on the following principle: all words that appear in several Indian languages, and are therefore likely to be understood by most Indian readers appear in roman, while all words that are more or less unique to Marathi are italicized. Thus, for instance, *vari* is italicized, but not yatra. Also italicized are words that may be confused with English words: thus, *gram* (village) is italicized. Caste names are not italicized: thus sutar, when it refers to the caste, appears in roman.

Each text in this selection is prefaced by a short introduction by the editor which places the text in context. The texts are chronologically arranged.

There are two sets of notes that appear in these selections. The notes by Phule himself appear as footnotes at the bottom of the page. The notes and annotations by the editor and translators appear as a separate series in the left and right margins. Within these, translators' notes are identified as such; the unidentified notes are by the editor.

Of Hope and Melancholy

Reading Jotirao Phule in Our Times

G.P. Deshpande

I

Let us begin with Jotirao's name, or more precisely, its spelling. His name is a Marathi or Prakrit form of the Sanskrit word jyoti (light or flame, also a star). The classical, or brahmanical if you will, spelling would be Jyotirao. He, however, always spelt it Jotirao.[1] (Rao is an honorific in Marathi, presumably a South Indian influence.) He is also often referred to as Jotiba, with the 'ba' being an affectionate suffix. His father was called Govindrao, and that, following Maharashtrian custom, became his middle name. His last name is spelt differently in different places. The cover of his book *Shetkaryacha Asud* (*Cultivator's Whipcord*) has Phuley. His deposition before the Hunter Commission is signed Phooley (with the 'oo' as in book and not as in moot). The *Sarvajanik Satya Dharma Pustak* (*The Book of the True Faith*) spells it as Fule. This is clearly wrong, since the first letter is 'ph' rather than 'f'. But this work was published posthumously, and the spelling is probably Yashwantrao Phule's (Jotirao's adopted son and publisher of the book). Jotirao himself has used both Phuley and Phooley. His biographer, Dhananjay Keer, has used Phooley. But much of subsequent writing on him (including that by Rosalind O'Hanlon)

[1] See Dhananjay Keer and S.G. Malshe, Introduction, *Mahatma Phule Samagra Vangmaya*, Mumbai: Maharashtra Rajya Sahitya ani Sanskriti Mandal, 1969, p. xxxii. This was the first edition; the fourth edition, edited by Y.D. Phadke, appeared in 1991. There has appeared another edition since. We have, however, used the 1991 edition as the basis for our translations.

uses Phule, and since that is the spelling that seems now to have become standardized, that is what we shall be using here.

The original name of the family, however, was not Phule, but Gorhe. This family was from a small, insignificant village, Lalgun, in Satara district. A dramatic development forced Phule's great grandfather to flee Lalgun. The family were victims of oppression by the brahman revenue official of the area. When the oppression crossed all limits, it appears that Jotirao's ancestor murdered the official and the family ran for its life. They settled down near Pune and took to horticulture which was, in any case, their caste-profession. They belonged to the mali (gardener) caste, taken to be one of the shudra castes in Maharashtra. They became florists by appointment to the brahman ruler of Pune, the Peshwa, who gave them some land just outside the city of Pune. This florist family then acquired the name Phule (after phul, flower).

Jotirao's date of birth is uncertain. An old lady close to the family has recorded that Jotirao used to say that he was born a day before the devastating fire in the Shanivar Vada (the palace of the Peshwas). If that is true, his birth date would be 20 February 1828. This, however, cannot be confirmed. The editors of Phule's *Collected Works*, as well as his biographer Keer, accept 1827 as the year of his birth, and claim that this is traditionally accepted. But the tradition does not seem to be decisive. Acharya Javadekar, for instance, states in his history of modern India[2] that he was born in 1828, and does not even mention 1827 as a possible date.

There is almost no good biography of Phule. What biographical writing exists is for the most part hagiography and propaganda material.[3] Consequently, Phule's writings, the movements he led, and the organizations he created are to be treated as his biography.

It is generally believed that Jotirao had passed the matriculation examination. This probably means no more than saying that he

[2] Acharya Javadekar, *Adhunik Bharat* (first published 1938), Pune: Continental Prakashan, 1979.

[3] The exception, of course, is Keer's biography, first published in Marathi (in 1964) and then in English, and the interested reader can look at it for virtually all the known details of Phule's life. Dhananjay Keer, *Mahatma Jotirao Phooley: Father of Indian Social Revolution*, Bombay: Popular Prakashan, 2000.

successfully completed his middle school education. When he left school in 1848, there was no matriculation examination. Bombay University, which conducted this examination, was set up only in 1857. By 1848, when Phule completed his secondary school education, his father had become a successful building contractor. Jotirao did not need a job. The family business gave him enough financial support. He read Thomas Paine's *Rights of Man* in 1847. The deep and lasting connection between English reformism and Indian social reformers/revolutionaries is too well known to need comment or elaboration here. One point, however, may still be made. With the exception of Phule, as we shall see, virtually all other social reformers/revolutionaries stayed constrained by the limits imposed upon them by the rather weak English branch of European liberalism, exemplified most of all by Mill and Spencer.

Phule established the first school anywhere in India for shudratishudra[4] girls in 1848. His father Govindrao was shocked, and feared, not unreasonably, high-caste backlash. Jotirao and Savitribai, whom he had married in 1840 and who taught in this school, had to leave Govindrao's house. Jotirao, however, was not one to cave in tamely. In 1851, he established another school, this time for girls of all castes. This was followed by an evening school for working people in 1855. By now, Jotirao's activities were causing a furore. An attempt was made on his life in 1856. Phule's activities extended beyond the field of education. The drinking water tank in his house was thrown open to untouchables. This would be considered a brave act even today. In 1868, it was revolutionary. No high caste or *bhadralok* reformer had ever done such a thing. Phule was not one for empty rhetoric. He believed that revolutionary thought has to be backed by revolutionary praxis. Further, none among the nineteenth century reformers had so sensitively thought about the gender question. That is the reason why his first school was for shudratishudra *girls*. He followed it up in 1860 with a campaign for widow remarriage. For most other reformers of his time, this was a matter of theory and reform. For Phule, it was a matter of praxis and revolution. His writing from

[4] Shudra and atishudra. Atishudra would be 'dalit' in contemporary language. Gandhi's term for atishudra was 'harijan' (God's people).

1869, starting with *Shivaji Powada*,[5] concentrated on working out the theoretical basis for his activity. The best-known of his works, *Gulamgiri* (*Slavery*) was published on 1 June 1873. The theoretical excursus on slavery was followed by setting up the organization which he hoped would smash it in practice. The Satyashodhak Samaj (Society of the Seekers of the Truth) was established on 24 September 1873. Phule was a nominated member of the Pune Municipal Council from 1876 to 1882. He was also the first Indian to have actively worked for prohibition. He thereby anticipates two important planks of the Gandhian programme: reassertion of truth as a value in a degenerate, oppressive society, and prohibition in the context of the well-being of the working masses. There is another instance of Phule anticipating Gandhi: on 11 May 1888, a big public meeting in Pune, in recognition of the impact of his theoretical–instructional and agitational–organizational work, fondly conferred on him the title Mahatma. By now, however, he was nearing the end of his life. He wrote his last work *Sarvajanik Satya Dharma Pustak* (*The Book of the True Faith*) in early 1889. He had suffered a stroke in the meanwhile, which rendered the right side of his body practically useless, but he laboured with his left hand to finish the book on 1 April 1889. He died the following year on 28 November 1890. *The Book* was not published in his lifetime. It was published by his adopted son in 1891.

The late nineteenth century was the time when a number of socio-religious and socio-political organizations were formed by various reformers and reform movements. Gail Omvedt gives the following useful table in her book[6]:

Organization	Date of founding
Socio-religious organizations	
Brahmo Samaj	Calcutta 1828
Paramahamsa Mandali	Bombay 1849
Prarthana Samaj	Bombay 1867

[5] *Powada*: ballad or long poem.

[6] Gail Omvedt, *Cultural Revolt in a Colonial Society: The Non-Brahman Movement in Western India, 1873 to 1930*, Bombay: Scientific Socialist Educational Trust, 1976, p. 99.

Satyashodhak Samaj	Pune 1871
Arya Samaj	Lahore 1877
Socio-political organizations	
Sarvajanik Sabha	1871
Indian National Congress	1885

A supplementary note to this table is perhaps in order. The Sarvajanik Sabha, to which Phule makes not very complimentary references, was founded by Ganesh Vasudev Joshi. He was the activist of the Sabha. Justice Ranade was the brain behind it. One should add that Ranade also made a half-hearted attempt to establish a Samajik Parishad (Congress for Social Issues). The idea was that this Congress should meet along with or immediately after the annual session of the Indian National Congress to discuss issues of social change. This did not quite succeed because from Naoroji to Tilak everybody opposed the idea of mixing up political–organizational issues with campaigns for social change. Similarly, the Marathi Granthottejak Mandali (Society for Promotion of Books in Marathi – obviously on new and secular subjects), founded in 1878, did not quite work as Ranade's biographer Phatak would have us believe.[7] For more on this, see Phule's letter on it in this volume.

There were, then, several organizations that were formed in the late nineteenth century. Some of them were more successful than others. Phule, as we noted, founded the Satyashodhak Samaj in 1873, and remained associated with it till his death in 1890. Phule's achievement was that he widened the very idea of a social organization, which Bombay and Calcutta had restricted to being an upper-caste *bhadralok*, or, to use the Marathi word, *pandharpesha*, phenomenon. Phule and the Samaj began their activity at the lower end of the social spectrum. This activity took Phule to all corners of western Maharashtra addressing meetings of shudras. Unlike many *bhadralok/pandharpesha* reformers and their organizations, Phule's vision, and the scope of the Samaj's activity, was broad,

[7] N.R. Phatak, *Nyayamurti Mahadev Govind Ranade Yanche Charitra*. This biography, easily the best available for Ranade, was published by the author in 1924 in Bombay.

sweeping. There was virtually no aspect of social life that did not engage his attention. At a meeting held in Bombay in 1885, for instance, Phule was at pains to emphasize that the lower castes should organize their ritualistic and religious activity themselves, so that the role of the brahman priest becomes redundant. His co-speaker at this meeting was Narayan Meghaji Lokhande. It was under Lokhande's leadership that the Satyashodhak Samaj launched (in Bombay) the first labour organization in India. From revamping their ritual life to organizing themselves as labourers, Phule exhorted the shudratishudras to turn the world upside down.

Let us then turn to Phule's world of ideas which enabled him to have this broad sweeping vision and become the system-building activist that he was.

II

In many ways, dharma and caste are at the centre of Phule's thought. His opposition to brahmanism did not relate only to the varna system. It also related to almost everything within the Hindu system. Phule rarely uses the term Hindu or Hinduism. He refers to brahmanism instead. In his view Hinduism as we know it originates in the Shrutis (the Vedas) and the Smritis.[8] He was convinced that these books were a part of the brahmanical attempt at creating texts which would rationalize and perpetuate their dominance. The brahmanical position claimed the chaturvarnya system (the division of society along the lines of the four varnas) to be god-given and eternal, and therefore unassailable. As such, brahman superiority had divine origins.

Phule rejected this pseudo-religion along with the texts that upheld it. And this rejection, as the writings compiled here will make clear, was total. Phule was not interested in tinkering with this or that aspect of the brahmanical structure to make it a little more humane. He argued for its complete rejection and destruction. In its place, he sought to create dichotomous conceptions of

[8] Codes of individual and inter-varna behaviour. There are several Smritis, the *Manusmriti* being the best-known.

the Hindu social structure. A dichotomous conception of social structure, according to a leading sociologist,

> is a generalization for the entire society of a two-term asymmetric relation in which one side is the privileged at the expense of the other. In this conception society is divided into two correlative and diametrically opposed classes in such a way that each of these classes is characterized by the relation of its members to the members of the opposed classes.[9]

Ossowski is talking here of class societies. But he also cites the example of the *Purusha Sukta* in the tenth *Mandal* of the *Rig Veda* as an example of dichotomous conception of society. Phule's formulation is very similar except that he does not use the term class. He calls the opposed groups by their varna names: brahman and shudratishudra.

It was clear to Phule that brahmanism was a religious, or more accurately *dharmik*, order which perpetuated, rationalized, and made sacrosanct the dominance of the brahmans in this dichotomous conception. Phule's attack on brahmanism is essentially as ideology of brahmanical dominance (*brahmanache varchaswa* or *brahmanvarchaswavadi*). This view of brahmanism, interestingly enough, was not held by Phule alone. Vishnushastri Chiplunkar, Phule's contemporary, bitter adversary, and as staunch a defender of brahmanism as any, actually admitted this dichotomous relationship of opposition:

> Whether in religion [Chiplunkar uses the word dharma], in everyday practice, or in politics and administration, everybody is at war with everybody else. Big fish swallow small fish.[10]

9 Stanislaw Ossowski, *Class Structure in the Social Consciousness*, London: Routledge, 1973, p. 31.

10 Vishnushastri wrote two articles in *Kesari* (Pune) on 15 and 22 March 1881 entitled '*Jyacha Tyacha Brahmanavar Kataksha*' ('Everyone attacks the brahman'), wherein he argued this social Darwinist position. See Rajendra Vora's article on Chiplunkar in *Adhunikta ani Parampara*, edited by Rajendra Vora, Pune: Pratima Prakashan, 2000, p. 220.

The implication is quite clear: this opposition or conditions of conflict and war are laws of nature, just as big fish swallow small fish, and no one can or even should oppose the laws of nature.

For Phule, brahmanism was historical, constructed over time, and since it was the ideology of oppression and dominance, it had to be opposed and ultimately smashed. There was nothing sacred or divine about it. But because it presented itself as divinely ordained, it was necessary to oppose this system in its entirety. The bulk of Phule's writing on religion therefore consists of a fierce polemic against brahmanism. The *Nyaya Sutra* talks of sixteen ways of knowing the existent (*sat*). *Vitanda* (destructive criticism)[11] is one of them, and Phule's attack on brahmanism belongs to this class. He is ferocious and unforgiving in his attack on brahmanism. Open any page of this selection, and the ferocity will be apparent.

Phule also attacks the avatarakalpana. The thesis that the god Vishnu took different forms at different times is in many ways a central thesis of Hindu theology. It is also a way of dissolving the apparent contradiction between polytheistic ritual practice and monotheistic metaphysical positions. Phule's was not the first attack on the avatarakalpana in Marathi. In the thirteenth century the Mahanubhava sect had rejected all the avataras of Vishnu, except Krishna. And even Krishna was not given the status of one of Vishnu's avataras, rather he was *the* God, the *only* godhead. Between the Mahanubhava and the Varkari sampradaya (who worshipped Vitthal of Pandharpur) there was a grand movement to turn the Maharashtrian masses into monotheists.[12]

Phule attacks the avatarakalpana. He heaps utter scorn on the various godheads. His analysis of the various avataras, however, may not stand the scrutiny of either history or even plain reason. But that is perhaps not the issue. His attempt was to subvert the brahmanical structure of ideas and beliefs so that a new, more

[11] This category is used here strictly in the *Naiyayika* epistemological sense and it does not carry any negative connotations.

[12] To pose the contrast between monotheism and polytheism like this is a little questionable. Classical Hinduism/brahmanism thinks of these categories, as also saguna (with qualities) and nirguna (qualityless) as a progression, a continuous process. I have used these categories more for convenience of discussion.

equitable order can emerge. His is a shudratishudra rewriting of history. It is not scientific as much as it is subversive. That is its purpose: subversion and destruction. His writings on the brahmanical gods and on the history of the Aryan race have to be understood in terms of their purpose. Whether the Aryans constitute a race at all, or whether they came from Iran or anywhere else, is beside the point. Phule was *not* writing history. He was rejecting brahmanical history from a shudratishudra perspective. If we keep this in mind, we can make sense of his polemic, and see its historical necessity and inevitability.

A further point may also be made. It is important to see Phule's critique of avatarakalpana historically. A decade or so after Phule's death, S.V. Ketkar[13] formulated the idea of jamat (community or tribe) and jati (caste). This distinction was similar to Weber's, but Ketkar's formulation predates Weber's. Ketkar argues that a community becomes a caste when it adopts brahman priests as its own, and starts worshipping brahmanical godheads.[14] This is of relevance to us not so much because Phule articulated a formulation quite as clear as this, but because his attack on brahmanism seems to flow from a similar understanding. In that sense, he anticipates the Ketkar position.

However, Phule did not look upon brahman orthodoxy or brahmanical religion as 'the ultimate cause of the deprivations of lower castes'. This remained 'a matter of private disagreement between himself and his colleagues'. This point is made by Rosalind O'Hanlon, who analyses Phule's play *Tritiya Ratna* (*The Third Eye*) to conclude that 'he rejected decisively the view that the sufferings of lower castes was the product of a social system supported by all except untouchable castes'.[15]

13 S.V. Ketkar (1884–1937), was a US-trained sociologist and the editor of the first encyclopaedia in Marathi. He was among the pioneering teachers of sociology and taught at the Calcutta University not long after the first department of sociology in India was opened there in 1908.

14 See Y.D. Phadke's useful article 'Dnyanakoshakar S.V. Ketkar' in *Maharashtratil Jatisamstha-vishayak Vichar* edited by Sumant and Punde, Pune: Pratima Prakashan, 1988, pp. 179–80.

15 Rosalind O'Hanlon, *Caste, Conflict and Ideology: Jotirao Phule and Lower Caste Protest in Nineteenth Century Maharashtra*, Cambridge: Cambridge

The dichotomous structure that Phule created by pitting brahmans against the shudratishudras at one level accepted the position of high brahmanism, though of course in a negative sense, by putting brahmanical theory on its head. It was argued at that time that in the Kaliyuga (the last of the four epochs according to brahmanical Hinduism, and the one in which we live), there are only two varnas, the first (brahman) and the last (shudra). This was of course supposed to be a sign of the degeneration that society had suffered. Phule turned this notion into a dichotomous structure, in order to emphasize the bipolarity of society. It will be recalled that Marx did something similar in his analysis of capitalism, by emphasizing the bipolarity of modern society between the bourgeoisie and the proletariat.

Emphasizing the bipolarity of the varna system had two other implications. One, it meant that Phule was not looking at it as a system of endlessly regressing hierarchy, where there is always someone, somewhere, who is lower than the lowest. In other words, his main emphasis is to demonstrate the basis on which the oppressed can come together and unite, rather than on the divisions and schisms amongst them. Two, he rejects the centrality of the pollution principle. This does not of course mean that Phule was blind or indifferent to the pollution principle. His attack on brahmanical dharma necessarily involved rejection of the notions of pavitra and apavitra (pure and polluted), sprishya and asprishya (touchable and untouchable), and so on. He also attacked the moral degeneration of brahmans under the Peshwai (Peshwa rule). On these scores, his attack on brahman hypocrisy is unforgiving. But the main thrust of his attack is on the exploitative and oppressive nature of brahmanism.

Equally unforgiving is his position on *karmavipaka*, the doctrine of karma, which traces all suffering, including individual suffering and, more importantly, social (caste) status, to the karma of previous births. This doctrine, again, is in many ways central to the social system and metaphysics of brahmanism, for the brahman's preeminent position derives its authority from it. Naturally then, Phule trains his polemical gun on this doctrine

University Press, 1985, p. 122.

as well. Curiously, however, he does not discuss punarjanma (rebirth) at any length, even though it is closely connected with *karmavipaka* and sustains the metaphysics of caste.

Phule's thinking on religion cannot be separated from his thinking on caste. His method in the analysis of caste was not to separate jati from varna. In fact, the term jati hardly makes an appearance in his writings. He constructs a *dvaivarnik* (two-varna) structure, with the brahmans and the shudratishudras forming its two poles, in place of the traditional chaturvarnya (four-varna) structure. As the brahmanical system derived its authority from the Vedas, and especially from the *Purusha Sukta* in the *Rig Veda* which asserted varna superiority, it was necessary to develop a counter-discourse to it in varna terms. In any case, there could not be a jati without a varna. As such the institution of jati derived its authority and legitimacy from *varna*. Further, in the dichotomous structure if the brahman derived his authority not from his *jati* but from his varna, it was important for the rest to realize that they could fight this dominance only if they asserted their shudratishudra status, which was, to use the fashionable jargon of our times, the 'Other' of the brahman. Phule does, occasionally, use words like kshatriya vamsha. But that usage does not quite warrant Bharat Patankar's conclusion that Phule referred to all workers as kshatriya.[16] Patankar's position comes closer to the position of the Society of the Maratha Caste for Putting Forward the Dharma of Kshatriyas. A useful summary of their argument has been given by Rosalind O'Hanlon.[17] Patankar's view misses Phule's central point that the brahmanical system is bipolar, and this bipolarity is represented by the brahmans and the shudratishudras. Therefore, caste or varna is a relationship of power and dominance, and has to be attacked at that level. To construct his discourse around a *dvaivarnik* system was thus crucial for Phule, since the Smritis and the Vedas talked essentially in those terms. If the caste system itself had to be destroyed, it had to be done by attacking this central element of the system.

[16] Bharat Patankar, *Mahatma Phule ani Sanskritik Sangharsha*, Mumbai: Lok Vangmaya Griha, 1998, p. 5.

[17] Rosalind O'Hanlon, *Caste, Conflict and Ideology*, pp. 295–301.

Phule thus saw caste both as a category in the productive process, and as something that facilitated the dominance of the brahmans in the ideological sphere. Caste, then, for him, was a category both of the base and the superstructure of Indian society. To be sure, Phule does not use these terms. They were not available to him. But his emphasis on understanding caste in terms of the agrarian productive process as also in terms of power and dominance is unmistakable.[18] He contrasts Baliraja, the mythical shudratishudra king, with Vamana, the brahmanical avatara who put his foot on Bali's head and crushed him deep into the earth. He returns to this myth which in his view was central to all subsequent history. If that terminology were available to him, he may almost have said that all recorded history is the history of Vamana–Baliraja struggle. Indeed, he does describe Jesus as Baliraja.

Phule's reception of Christianity and of missionaries was based on this understanding. That the missionaries themselves did not see their and their religion's role in India quite in these terms is of course obvious. It is possible to argue, in fact, that Phule never fully realized the distance separating his position from the missionary position. Phule has of course been attacked, in his lifetime as much as later, as being soft on the missionaries. The Gandhian Javadekar, for instance, says that Phule never really understood the missionary 'game' (*kava*).[19] Perhaps there is a point here. However, let it also be noted that Phule's position on conversion was perhaps a little more nuanced than is sometimes conceded. A case in point is his defence of Pandita Ramabai, a Chitpavan brahman scholar, who converted to Christianity. She was attacked viciously by both orthodox and reformist brahmans. She also soon

[18] Among his contemporaries in Europe there were some – like Ludwig Kazywicki, the Polish Marxist – who were uncertain of the relationship between base and superstructure. He, for example, in an article on 'An Outline of Social Education' which appeared in *Glos* in 1887 wrote that new productive forces did not always succeed in breaking up old societies, as witness India, where the caste system had proved stronger than other factors and condemned the country to centuries of stagnation. Cited by Kolakowski, *Main Currents of Marxism*, (3 volumes), Oxford University Press, 1978, Vol. 2, p. 200.

[19] Javadekar, *Adhunik Bharat*, p. 132.

found herself in deep conflict with the colonial and racist attitude of the contemporary Anglican church.[20] Phule defended her right to conversion. However, more than Christianity offering salvation, it represents for him an *escape* from oppressive brahmanism. Thus, more than justifying conversion, Phule seems to defend this escape. That Christianity did not represent for him the promised land is also clear from the fact that he himself refused to convert, though it was a more than real option available to him.

This last point is important, since both during his lifetime as well as later, he has been attacked as a semi-Christian, as a hater of Hinduism, etc. The Sangh parivar, in particular, has been arguing this about him off and on through its various papers and journals for some time now.[21] The parivar attack on Phule is no less vicious than the ones he faced from sanatani brahmans in his lifetime, though it may well be shallower and sillier. As such we have no cause to be detained by it. Let us only note the simple fact that Phule himself was firmly against any notion of revelation. By rejecting the very idea of revealed truth and/or divine sanction, he had moved away from the very basics of Christianity or Islam.

There is however one aspect of this question that we may spend some time considering. Phule did not seem to have given much thought to what impact his ferocious attack on brahmanism might have on his people and followers. Both Lokhande and Bhalerao, his close associates and comrades-in-arms, felt that Phule's critique was much too '*kadak*' (hard, vitriolic). After the first two chapters of *Cultivator's Whipcord* were published in *Dinbandhu*, the weekly paper of the Satyashodhak Samaj, Lokhande declined to publish any further chapter. When the book was finally published, Phule, in a private letter to Mama Parmanand in June 1886 said: 'We had prepared a volume called Whipcord. But then there are cowards among us shudra publishers. We had therefore decided not to publish it for a while.' It was clear that Phule could not carry some

[20] See Uma Chakravarti, *Rewriting History: The Life and Times of Pandita Ramabai*, New Delhi: Kali for Women, 1998, especially p. 322.

[21] For example, nearly a century after Phule's death, a Marathi journal called *Sobat*, edited by a self-confessed Hindutvavadi, the late G.V. Behare, carried such an attack in its columns on 4 and 11 December 1988.

of his more prominent colleagues with him because they thought that Phule's critique was 'overstated beyond necessity [*vazvipeksha phajil*] and I [Lokhande] thank the Lord that there were difficulties in its publication'. Phule's critique, then, had raised an important question. On the one hand, it was becoming apparent that the roots of brahmanism went deeper, and its hold was more tenacious, than he had thought. On the other, it raised the question of how radical can or should a critique of religion or dharma be in a pre-revolutionary situation. To be sure, this is not an easy question to answer, and in a sense, the revolutionary movement in all predominantly agrarian societies has had to face this question. The split within and the later decline of the Satyashodhak Samaj was due to several factors, and we cannot go into that question in our limited space here. But it is well worth asking if the Samaj's failure to evolve a coordinated strategy in attacking and revolutionizing the religious belief systems of the masses (and of the cadres) was not one of them.

To Phule's credit, however, it must be said that he was aware of the need to do so. Destructive criticism was not the only aspect of his critique of brahmanism. He also formulated his ideas on what the dharma of the shudratishudras should be like. Earlier in the nineteenth century too efforts had been made to reformulate the tenets of brahmanism. G.H. Deshmukh (known as Lokahitavadi) proclaimed a sixteen-point charter of reforms in June 1849. Pradip Gokhale, in his analysis of Lokahitavadi's position argues that it was limited by his 'brahman identity' (*brahmani asmita*).[22] While there is some truth in what Gokhale argues, one must also see that 'reform', by its very nature, begins from the top. It is necessarily a top-to-bottom process. Lokahitavadi seriously believed that the reform of brahman consciousness was a necessary condition for any successful change in Hindu society at large. His position may therefore have less to do with *brahmani asmita* than with the very logic of reformism. Phule, in this sense, was not a reformist.

[22] Lokahitavadi's article '*Dharmasudharna*' ('Reforming Religion') appeared in *Prabhakara* on 17 June 1849. See Pradip Gokhale, 'Lokahitavadi Gopal Hari Deshmukh' in *Maharashtratil Jatisamstha-vishayak Vichar*, edited by Sumant and Punde, Pune: Pratima Prakashan, 1988, especially p. 20.

He was closer to arguing for a revolutionary social change by concentrating on the contradictions in a dichotomous structure. Most other nineteenth-century thinkers did not think in terms of polar opposites. Phule did.

As a result, Phule attempted to supplant the belief structure of brahmanism with an alternative understanding and praxis. This is the thrust of his work *Sarvajanik Satya Dharma Pustak*. This work is not as well organized as *Gulamgiri* or *Asud*. It was written towards the end of his life, when he was debilitated by paralysis. Phule's central concern here is to dethrone the brahman from his preeminent position of being the go-between between God and man. Phule coined a new word for God. He called him *Nirmik* (the Creator). His formulations on dharma are simple and straightforward, and create in a sense a republic of equalitarian dharma. It may sound paradoxical, but his conception of *satya dharma* is rather secular. If such categories of analysis and discourse had been available to him, he may have, a bit like Ernst Bloch, argued that he was rescuing (Hinduism and) secularism from (brahman) philistines.

III

We have dealt at some length with Phule's perspective on dharma and varna. But someone interested in building a movement of the shudratishudras would also naturally be interested in agriculture and peasants. And Phule, as the selection here will testify, was deeply interested in this question. It is not possible in this short space to survey his voluminous writing on agriculture and production conditions in India. Ashok Chausalkar[23] has provided a useful account of Phule's plans and suggestions for improvement in agriculture and in the lot of the poor cultivator. We summarize below Chausalkar's account, with some comments of our own in parentheses.

1. Phule laid considerable emphasis on proper breeding of cows and oxen, since they are the main beasts of burden in agriculture.

[23] Ashok Chausalkar, *Mahatma Phule ani Shetkari Chalwal*, Mumbai: Lok Vangmaya Griha, 2001.

He also argued in favour of a ban on cow-slaughter. (His position is partly similar to Gandhi's. His plea for the ban on cow slaughter is not related to factors of religiosity, but to his concern for the village economy. Thus, his demand for a ban on cow-slaughter is an economic demand.)

2. Phule advocated building small bunds (*bandhara*) which would prevent the rainwater and natural fertilizers from being washed away and wasted. (Much of Maharashtra is a rain-shadow area, and Phule's suggestion of small bunds remains a possible answer to the eternal problem of drought.)

3. Phule wanted the army personnel to build these bunds. (This suggestion would remind one of Mao Zedong's emphasis on the People's Liberation Army having a symbiotic relationship with the civil masses, especially the peasantry and the working class. And like Mao, again, he includes the local police force – the People's Militia in China – in this task force.)

4. Peasants themselves must ensure that the water supply does not dry up because small waterways to the farms are in disrepair. Water being available in the area but not reaching an individual plot of land has to be avoided. (It is now generally accepted in development discourse that while it is the job of the government to provide water, the local community should be involved in its distribution. In this sense, Phule was the first to have argued for participatory development.)

5. Wherever water can be tapped, wells should be constructed. A map of water resources of each village should be prepared. The government should suitably pay those who build such wells on their own initiative.

6. Grazing lands of the villages have been made parts of the forest land. Such forest land should be returned to peasants. While the forest department should ensure that timber wood is not indiscriminately cut and taken away, the sources of ordinary wood should remain open to peasants.

7. A plan for breeding high quality sheep and lamb must be put into operation.

8. Cultivators' children should get professional training as carpenters, ironsmiths, and the like. (Phule is here proposing a

sort of vocational or professional education which would combine the jobs of at least two or three caste-groups.)

9. Bureaucrats and administrators connected with agriculture are being overpaid. There is a case for revising their salaries.

10. Peasants' children must get their school equipment free. Peasants themselves must get some scientific education about agrarian production and operations.

11. There should be agricultural schools.

12. Phule emphasized the role of the state in the improvement of agriculture. He believed firmly that unless the government wakes up to the production conditions in Indian agriculture and works towards reforms, the peasants will continue to suffer. (In effect, Phule's reform meant increased role of the state rather than its opposite.)

Thus it is clear that Phule had emphasized two or three main aspects of the peasants' question. They relate to: the actual production process; what the state can and should do for the peasantry; and the brahman conspiracies to deprive the peasantry of its meagre income in the name of one ritual or the other. He does not speak of any exploitation inherent in the production process itself. In fact, he takes an undifferentiated view of the peasantry. This is hardly surprising because for him the entire peasantry was shudratishudra, victim of the dichotomous socio-religious structure. He does not speak of landlords or any such categories which would indicate the distinction *within* the shudratishudras. Western Maharashtra, in any case, is not a region of great landholdings. But if Phule is to be believed, there was no rich peasantry in Maharashtra. This seems inaccurate. But neither Phule nor the Satyashodhak movement could have taken any other view, since, in their view, the peasantry was an undifferentiated mass of shudratishudras. They seemed to concentrate more on production conditions, rather than production relations.

Nevertheless, Phule was the first social activist who made agriculture, and the production conditions therein, amongst the main subjects of his concern. In 1875, there were peasant uprisings in the Deccan (mainly in the Pune and Ahmednagar districts). These uprisings were not against the British. They were against the *savkars* (moneylenders). This was a period of considerable agrarian unrest in western Maharashtra. In this context, it is really quite amazing that hardly anyone amongst the major thinkers or social reformers seems to have been agitated over the agrarian question. Nobody seems to be bothered about peasants, their economic problems, or the abysmally low productivity in agriculture. Amongst the exceptions to this, one can count M.G. Ranade and G.V. Joshi.[24] Phule's writing on caste and varna is well known, but little has been written on his understanding on agriculture. The exception to this is perhaps Sharad Joshi, leader of the Shetkari Sangathana (Peasants' Organization), who published his analysis of *Shetkaryacha Asud* in 1989.[25] Even though it is more in the nature of a tribute than serious analysis, it made the basic point that the peasantry is at the centre of Phule's thought and concerns. There is, then, a case for studying Phule's work on agriculture more seriously and extensively.

IV

Phule is the first shudra thinker – as he himself would have liked to be described – to have thought about the gender question. The reformers of the so-called Indian Renaissance were content to take a basically humanist view of the problem. Their approach was liberal, progressive, and historically necessary. But their upper-caste biases were apparent in much of what they did or advocated. In this respect, again, Phule is more radical than his contemporaries.

Manu's system treats women – *all* women irrespective of varna – as shudra or *dasa*. Accordingly, Phule included women, all women, in his notion of shudratishudra. The first school he established, in 1842, was for girls. In 1863, he set up a home for widows who were often forced to abort or kill their children

[24] For a discussion of Joshi's ideas, see Aruna Pendse's article in *Adhunikta ani Parampara*, pp. 304–27, and B.N. Ganguly, *Indian Economic Thought: Nineteenth Century Perspectives*, New Delhi: Tata McGraw Hill, 1978.

[25] Sharad Joshi, *Shetkaryacha Asud – Ha Shatakacha Muzra*, Alibag: Shetkari Prakashan, 1989.

because they lacked social legitimacy. Phule himself adopted the son of a brahman widow as his own. He played an active role in the remarriage of a Sarasvat brahman widow in 1864. The brahmanical practice then was that widows were made to shave off their heads. Phule organized a barbers' strike against this inhuman custom. He was the only one who raised his voice against the near-hysterical reaction to Tarabai Shinde, who had published in 1882 what could be called in today's language a feminist tract on *A Comparison Between Women and Men* (*Stree Purush Tulana*).[26]

Phule did not think of the women's problem in terms of brahman or shudratishudra. In his *Satya Dharma Pustak*, he talks of '*sarva ekandar stree-purush*', all women and men together. Gail Omvedt has pointed out that Phule does not use the common word '*manus*' (human being), but insists on using '*stree-purush*', thus emphasizing gender differentiation, while pleading for equal and common human rights for women and men. He is the first to do so in India.

Phule does not talk of patriarchy. Nor does he give us a theory of man–woman inequality. He relates some aspects of women's position to the Arya-*bhat*[27] social order. Though he does not say so explicitly, he seems to imply that the end of the Arya-*bhat* domination would ensure man–woman equality. To that extent, subordination of women is a part of the larger process of the subordination of the shudratishudras. He would therefore not quite have approved of the present-day tendency towards organizing women in separate caste-based movements. For him, a brahman woman was as much shudratishudra as a dalit woman. In that sense, it was a remarkably modern, and gendered view, which saw gender itself, not varna, as the basis for the oppression that women faced.

Phule felt that the family, being at the centre of the organization of society, was also the centre of oppression in society. Its roots are to be traced to the jati system. Phule's thought has place for varna, but none really for what we know today as patriarchy and

[26] *A Comparison Between Women and Men* by Tarabai Shinde, translated and edited by Rosalind O'Hanlon, New Delhi: Oxford University Press, 1994.

[27] *Bhat*: literally priest, more generally brahman.

its relation to gender inequality and oppression. Nevertheless, one should perhaps add that unlike several groups and movements (including those that argue for caste-based reservation for women) in contemporary India, he did not believe in divisions in the gender consciousness. The women's question was of course a central concern in the nineteenth century. Widow remarriage, banning child marriage, banning the custom of sati, ensuring women's right to education – all these issues were taken up by a large number of people in the nineteenth century, Phule amongst them. But Phule also takes the question farther than anyone else. He is the first one to draw attention to the fact that the labour of the young bride is used as bonded labour (*veth-bigar*) by the family the girl marries into.

Phule was convinced that the family and the marriage system must be reformed, if not transformed altogether. The *Satya Dharma Pustak* reviewed and revised the traditional marriage rites. Gail Omvedt has pointed out that marriage rites were a principle concern of several reformers since Phule. Ramaswamy Periyar made 'swabhiman-vivaha' a part of his swabhiman (self-respect) movement. And during the nationalist movement as well, there were Gandhi *vivahas* (marriages) in certain parts of the country.

We have discussed above Phule's defence of Pandita Ramabai and her conversion to Christianity. This defence had a gender aspect to it. Phule does not seem to have been particularly in favour of conversion *per se*. But he certainly was in favour of all movement *away* from brahman orthodoxy. That a woman had asserted her right to move away from brahman orthodoxy and oppression was important for him. He saw it as a shudra revolting against brahmanism. The assertion of gender rights is for Phule a fundamental part of the struggle of the shudratishudras.

V

Most historians of Marathi literature do not refer to Phule. This is strange and sad. Phule's prose, his use of nineteenth-century colloquial speech, his system of argumentation, his ferocious polemics, his poetry (greatly influenced by the seventeenth-century Bhakti poet Tukaram), his assessment of various Bhakti poets which amounts to the beginning of Marathi socio-literary criticism, all these are aspects of his work which hardly, if ever, get discussed. Those who do refer to some of these things do so mainly to make the point that the brahmans do not take Phule seriously as a writer or to assert that Phule wrote the first political and discussion play in Marathi, *Tritiya Ratna*. Apart from Bhalchandra Nemade's essay on Phule's creative writing,[28] there exists very little by way of serious commentary. This is a lacuna, and one that needs to be filled at least in Marathi. While that is a task which we cannot fulfil here, some brief observations may still be in order.

Phule was very fond of the dialogue form. He wrote a play, of course, but also a lot of his other writing (some of which appears on the following pages) is in this form. The use of the dialogue form connected him with the western, specifically Greek tradition on the one hand, and, though he may not have liked it, to the Upanishadic tradition on the other. One should add that the Bauddhas had a strong dialogic tradition as well. The other major Indian work in this form to follow Phule is of course Gandhi's *Hind Swaraj*, published in 1909.

Phule's language itself is remarkable, and, for his times, unique. It is impossible to translate the vigour and ruggedness of his Marathi. It is a measure of the courage of our translators that they have even undertaken this exercise! There is much in his Marathi that comes from the spoken, rather than literary, language. Phule was trying to build a movement of the oppressed, and was trying through his writings to first and foremost reach out to those masses. It is then only to be expected that he speaks their language when he addresses them. But Phule goes a step further. His use of Marathi remains unconventional (for his times) even when he does not write for mass circulation. In a sense, Phule seems to be remoulding the language itself, and asserting that the real Marathi is not the Sanskritized Marathi of the brahmans, but that which

[28] See Nemade's essay in *Mahatma Phule Gaurav Granth*, edited by Hari Narke, Mumbai: Maharashtra State Government Publication, 1982.

draws from the language of the masses. In this connection, an interesting observation can be made. The poor Muslim peasant or artisan does not figure in Marathi writing of the nineteenth century at all, with the solitary exception of Phule. Every once in a way, Phule uses an expression or phrase that is typical of how the poor Marathi Muslim spoke. An example of this from the following pages is the last line of his letter to Ranade: '*Sadhe hoke buddheka yeh pahla salaam lev*' ('In any case accept the salute of this old man'). Phule also wrote a poem about Prophet Muhammad. While the poem itself may not pass the very stringent theological tests that fundamentalists of our times seem to subject everything to, Phule's admiration for the Prophet and for the liberal, progressive potential of Islam is clear.

Contemporary Marathi literary criticism has ignored Phule, and the loss has been entirely its own.

VI

What Phule tried to do, then, was build a system of ideas that could look at contemporary social reality in its entirety. He takes in his sweep, as any system-builder would, the past and the present. He tried to understand the *dvaivarnik* system with a view to overthrowing it. In his enthusiasm, however, he ignored certain things. For instance, he did not see that the contemporary missionaries were reactionary and conservative, just as the brahmans were. He did not ask the question that Pandita Ramabai faced: why and how were missionaries racist and colonial?

In *Tritiya Ratna* there is a strong polemic against idol-worship. Phule has turned a Christian missionary into an iconoclast (who destroys Hindu, though not Christian, icons). Curiously, however, Phule ignored the Bhakti movement, and its position on idol worship. Dnyaneshwar, whom Phule has attacked in some of his writings, has written *abhangas*[29] against idol worship. Phule did not relate his argument to a tradition which was clearly closer to the hearts of the Marathi shudratishudras. This is probably the

[29] A popular poetic form used by the Bhakti poets. Phule himself also wrote *abhangas*, but coined a new word for them: *akhanda*.

result of Phule's rather one-sided understanding of missionary activity. And this, in turn, is probably linked to his understanding of colonialism and imperialism.

This is a question that needs careful assessment. In today's Maharashtra, there is virtually no discussion of imperialism. Indeed the word hardly ever finds a place even in the discourse of socially radical movements and thinkers. Phule's understanding of British rule in India compares at least partially with that of Karl Marx. Marx wrote in 1853 that 'England has to fulfil a double mission in India, one destructive, the other regenerating – the annihilation of old Asiatic society, and laying the material foundations of Western society in India.'[30] Marx was writing about the future of British rule in India. Phule was thinking about the future of India under British rule. He welcomed the coming annihilation of the brahmanical system which he hoped that British rule would bring about. He also hoped that British rule would lay the material and institutional foundation of a modern, equalitarian society. One says 'hopes' because Phule was not certain it would actually come about. There is some evidence in his writing that he occasionally found the British response to people's needs and demands exasperatingly slow. There is a degree of duality in his attitude to British rule. The important thing was the annihilation that Marx and Phule both, though from different perspectives, hoped for. In that sense one can argue that his view of imperialism was historicist.

But Phule did not see imperialism dialectically. He did not see that the British ruling classes were not kind to the lower classes in Britain. The British legal system, in which he had invested his faith, was no less exploitative and unjust when it had to deal with the British peasantry and the working class. His enthusiasm for British rule made him sceptical of even the shudratishudra uprisings against British rule in his own time, for instance the uprising led by Umaji Naik. It also prevented him from seeing the material basis of what he would brand as 'brahman' nationalism. Strangely even

[30] Karl Marx, 'The Future Results of British Rule in India', *Collected Works*, Moscow: Progress Publishers, Vol. 12, pp. 217–18. Reprinted in Karl Marx and Fredrick Engels, *On the National and Colonial Questions*, edited by Aijaz Ahmad, New Delhi: LeftWord, 2001.

Gail Omvedt has this understanding when she talks of 'brahman national elites'. B.T. Ranadive in his review of her book asks: 'Is this a Marxist analysis?', a legitimate question since Omvedt identifies Marxism as a source of understanding and describes it as 'the most accurate theory for both understanding and affecting human society'.[31] A much broader question can, however, also be asked. How can the 'brahman' elite be national? Even if one agrees with this categorization, 'brahman' elite, one will have to see if this elite had on its side other classes and the toiling masses. Phule did not see, for instance, the significance of Vasudev Phadke, a brahman, working with the ramoshis. The result was that Phule and his comrades and followers ended up taking softer and softer positions on British imperialism and ultimately lost ground to the nationalist movement.

We are still witness to this phenomenon, except that the situation is even worse today. We live in times when the national elite is 'globalized' in its concerns and *weltanschauung* (worldview). It has joined hands with the international elite. Phule's view of the 'fair people of light eyes', i.e. brahmans, can still be useful. Local brahmans have now aligned with the international brahmans. But there has been a weakening of the concern about imperialism amongst the shudratishudras, and the elites in any case do not view imperialism as a problem. To speak in *dvaivarnik* terms, the local brahmans are playing the game of the Washington brahmans, and the shudratishudras have decided to go along with this game by pretending that the alliance between the local brahmans and international brahmans just does not exist. The social and political movements which speak on behalf of the shudratishudras have worked themselves into a bind. It is therefore necessary to see that Phule's system will be useful and productive only if it can have a new, extra input of a theory of imperialism.

The same can be said of the relationship between social movements (especially in Maharashtra) and the organized Left. It seems at times that Phule (and Ambedkar) is being used to establish the irrelevance of the Left. Sharad Patil, who sought to combine

[31] B.T. Ranadive, *Caste, Class and Property Relations*, Calcutta: National Book Agency, 1982, p. 38.

Marx, Phule, and Ambedkar, quite often gives the impression in his writing that the real problem in our society is what he would call leftist orthodoxy rather than rightwing chauvinism. He rarely talks of imperialism. In fact, that is true of any number of socio-political groups today in Maharashtra.

These approaches miss one crucial point. How does one relate to a system builder? One can do so only by interpreting the system in terms of today's problems. You cannot creatively interpret Phule without moving away from his clearly soft position on imperialism.

The truth of the matter is that all forces which desire and need a fundamental transformation of our society are today's shudratishudras, and those who oppose them are the brahmans. If this is understood, errors like branding nationalist leaders as brahmans, or communists as brahman communists, can be avoided.[32] This is increasingly necessary because all movements will traverse the path of increasing irrelevance if they do not see the coming impasse. Phule must be progressively and creatively read.

All system builders should be read in that manner. Phule's canvas was broad, his sweep majestic. He identified and theorized the most important questions of his time – religion, the varna system, ritualism, language, literature, British rule, mythology, the gender question, the conditions of production in agriculture, the lot of the peasantry. This list, already formidable, can be extended as well. No other Indian figure of the nineteenth century comes to mind who displayed this sort of range. Was Phule then a social reformer? The answer will be 'no'. A social reformer is a liberal humanist. Phule was more of a revolutionary. He had a complete system of ideas, and was amongst the early thinkers to have identified, in a manner of speaking, classes in Indian society. He analysed the *dvaivarnik* structure of Indian society, and identified the shudratishudras as the leading agency of a social revolution. And the shudratishudras will lead the revolution on behalf of the whole society, to liberate the entire people from the shackles of brahmanism. What they will lead, then, is not a movement for some reform in the present structure, some tinkering here and there, but

[32] Ibid., p. 47.

a total smashing up of the entire oppressive structure, ideological and material. Phule was the only thinker of the nineteenth century who insisted that this is both necessary and possible.

In his article 'The British Rule in India', Marx talks of England having imparted 'a particular kind of melancholy to the present misery' of the Indian people.[33] Phule, too, was concerned about this misery and melancholy of the Indian peasantry. And like Marx, again, Phule's life work involved analysing this melancholy in order to find a way out of it. In other words, a system of ideas is not complete till there is a principle of hope that underlies it. Marx's did. So did Phule's. To actualize that hope is our responsibility.

[33] Karl Marx, 'The British Rule in India', *Collected Works*, Vol. 12, p. 126; *On the National and Colonial Questions*, p. 62.

Slavery

1873

Translated by Maya Pandit
Preface written in English by the author

Slavery (*Gulamgiri*) and *Cultivator's Whipcord* (*Shetkaryacha Asud*) are Phule's most seminal and important works, and both are included in this volume in their entirety, barring a brief *powada* (ballad), with which *Slavery* concludes. *Slavery* was first published in 1873. Its publication heralded the founding of the Satyashodhak Samaj (Society of the Seekers of Truth), the movement launched by Phule later in the year on 24 September 1873. *Slavery* was in a manner of speaking its manifesto.

The second edition of *Slavery* came out in 1911, was sold out, was reprinted in 1912, and again in 1921. After that, *Slavery* became a rare book. L.K. Vichare, the general secretary of the Satyashodhak Samaj, republished the work forty years later, in 1961. The editors of the *Collected Works* of Phule (in Marathi) tell us that the 1921 text was a reprint of the 1911 edition, which has been used in this volume. The Preface was written by Phule in English. The editor of the second edition, Shri Ramayya Ayyavaru, had stated in his preface:

> We have retained the original text in its entirety, nothing has been deleted or added. The original text was in a language which was not easy to understand. We have therefore made it a little easy to understand with attention to the correct and incorrect forms of words.

In any case there is no reason to disbelieve the authenticity and the thrust of the 1911 text. The blunt, polemical style of Phule is unmistakably there.

The work is seminal. It seeks to identify the main contradiction in Maharashtrian society which is centred around the slavery of the shudratishudras. It poses the problem of slavery in historicist terms. Hindu mythology talks of Lord Vishnu and his ten incarnations (avataras). Phule looks upon avataras as a mythologized and sublimated account of the oppression and exploitation of the peasantry. For Phule, all recorded mythology is the history of varna struggle. He sees a two-fold division of society: the brahmans, and the shudratishudras. The latter group has to forge a unity going beyond their respective castes. 'All slaves must unite; they have nothing to lose but their chains': one could thus summarize the message of this stirring manifesto.

Dedicated
to
the good people of the United States
as a token of admiration for their
sublime disinterested and
selfsacrificing devotion
in the cause of Negro Slavery; and with
an earnest desire, that my countrymen
may take their noble example as their guide
in the emancipation of their Sudra Brethren
from the trammels of Brahmin thraldom.

The Author

Preface

'The day that reduces a man to slavery takes from him the half of his virtue.'

Homer

'Our system of Government in India is not calculated to raise the character of those subject to it, nor is the present system of education one to do more than *over-educate the few*, leaving the mass of the people as ignorant as ever and still mere[1] at the mercy of the few learned; in fact, it is an extension of the demoralizing Brahmin-ridden policy, which, perhaps, has more retarded the progress of civilization and improvement in India generally than anything else.'

Col. G.J. Hally – *On Fisheries in India*

'Many ages have elapsed since peculiar resources were afforded to the Brahmins; but the most considerate cosmopolite would hesitate to enroll them amongst the benefactors of the world. They boast of vast stores of ancient learning. They have amassed great riches, and been invested with unbounded power, but to what good end? They have cherished the most degrading superstitions and practised the most shameless impostures. They have arrogated to themselves the possession and enjoyment of the rarest gifts of fortune and perpetuated the most revolting system known to the world. It is only from a diminution of their abused power that we can hope to accomplish the great work of national regeneration.'

Mead's *Sepoy Revolt*

Recent researches have demonstrated beyond a shadow of doubt

[1] This is probably a typographical error; perhaps the word is 'more'. But both 1969 and 1991 editions of the *Collected Works* have 'mere'. [—*Ed.*]

that the Brahmans were not the aborigines of India. At some remote period of antiquity, probably more than 3000 years ago, the Aryan progenitors of the present Brahmin Race descended upon the plains of Hindoo Koosh, and other adjoining tracts. According to Dr. Pritchard, the Ethnologist, they were an off-shoot of the Great Indo-European race, from whom the Persians, Medes, and other Iranian nations in Asia and the principal nations in Europe like-wise are descended. The affinity existing between the Zend, the Persian and Sanskrit languages, as also between all the European languages, unmistakably points to a common source of origin. It appears also more than probable that the original cradle of this race being an arid, sandy and mountainous region, and one ill calculated to afford them the sustenance which their growing wants required, they branched off into colonies, East and West. The extreme fertility of the soil in India, its rich productions, the proverbial wealth of its people, and the other innumerable gifts which this favoured land enjoys, and which have more recently tempted the cupidity of the Western nations, no doubt, attracted the Aryans, who came to India, not as simple emigrants with peaceful intentions of colonization, but as conquerors. They appear to have been a race imbued with very high notions of self, extremely cunning, arrogant and bigoted. Such self-gratulatory, pride-flattering epithets as आर्य, भूदेव, etc., with which they designated themselves, confirm us in our opinion of their primitive character, which they have preserved up to the present time, with, perhaps, little change for the better. The aborigines whom the Aryans subjugated, or displaced, appear to have been a hardy and brave people from the determined front which they offered to these interlopers. Such opprobrious terms, as (शूद्र) Sudra 'insignificant', महारी 'the great foe', अंत्यज, चांडाळ, etc. with which they designated them, undoubtedly show that originally they offered the greatest resistance in their power to their establishing themselves in the country, and hence the great aversion and hatred in which they are held. From many customs[2] traditionally handed down to us, as well

[2] A most remarkable and striking corroboration of these views is to be found in the religious rites observed on some of the grand festivals which have a reference to Bali Raja, the great king who appears to have reigned once

as from the mythological legends contained in the sacred books of the Brahmins, it is evident that there had been a hard struggle for ascendancy between the two races. The wars of Devas and Daityas, or the Rakshasas, about which so many fictions are found scattered over the sacred books of the Brahmins, have certainly a reference to this primeval struggle. The original inhabitants with whom these earthborn Gods, the Brahmins, fought, were not inappropriately termed Rakshas, that is the protectors of the land. The incredible and foolish legends regarding their form and shape are no doubt mere chimeras, the fact being that these people were of superior stature and hardy make. Under such leaders as Brahma, Purshram and others, the Brahmins waged very protracted wars against the original inhabitants. They eventually succeeded in establishing their supremacy and subjugating the aborigines to their entire control. Accounts of these conquests, enveloped with a mass of incredible fiction, are found in the books of the Brahmins. In some instances they were compelled to emigrate, and in others wholesale extermination was resorted to. The cruelties which the European settlers practised on the American Indians on their first settlement in the new world, had certainly their parallel in India on the advent of the Aryans and their subjugation of the aborigines. The cruelties and inhuman atrocities which Purshram committed on the Kshetrias, the people of this land, if we are to believe even one tenth of what the legends say regarding him, surpass our belief and show that he was more a fiend than a God. Perhaps in the

....

in the hearts and affections of the Sudras and whom the Brahmin rulers displaced. On the day of *Dushara*, the wife and sisters of a Sudra, when he returns from his worship of the *Shumi Tree* and after the distribution of its leaves, which are regarded on that day as equivalent to gold, amongst his friends, relations and acquaintances, he is greeted, at home with a welcome इडा पिडा जावो आणि बळीचे राज्य येवो 'Let all troubles and misery go, and the kingdom of Bali come.' Whereas the wife and sisters of a Brahmin place on that day in the foreground of the house an image of Bali, made generally of wheaten or other flour, and when the Brahmin returns from his worship of the *Shumi Tree* he takes the stalk of it, pokes with it the belly of the image and then passes into the house. This contrariety, in the religious customs and usages obtaining amongst the Sudras and the Brahmins and of which many more examples might be adduced, can be explained on no other supposition but that which I have tried to confirm and elucidate in these pages. [—*J.P.*]

whole range of history it is scarcely possible to meet with such another character as that of Purshram, so selfish, infamous, cruel and inhuman. The deeds of Nero, Alaric or Machiavelli sink into insignificance before the ferocity of Purshram. The myriads of men and defenceless children whom he butchered, simply with a view to the establishment of his coreligionists on a secure and permanent basis in this land, is a fact for which generations ought to execrate his name, rather than deify it.

This, in short, is the history of Brahmin domination in India. They originally settled on the banks of the Ganges whence they gradually spread over the whole of India. In order, however, to keep a better hold on the people they devised that weird system of mythology, the ordination of caste, and the code of cruel and inhuman laws, to which we can find no parallel amongst other nations. They founded a system of priestcraft so galling in its tendency and operation, the like of which we can hardly find anywhere since the times of the Druids. The institution of Caste, which has been the main object of their laws, had no existence among them originally. That it was an after-creation of their deep cunning is evident from their own writings. The highest rights, the highest privileges and gifts, and everything that would make the life of a Brahmin easy, smooth-going and happy-everything that would conserve or flatter their self-pride, – were specially inculcated and enjoined, whereas the Sudras and Atisudras were regarded with supreme hatred and contempt, and the commonest rights of humanity were denied them. Their touch, nay, even their shadow, is deemed a pollution. They are considered as mere chattels, and their life of no more value than that of meanest reptile; for it is enjoined that if a Brahmin, 'kill a cat or an ichneumon, the bird Chasha, or a frog or a dog, a lizard, an owl, a crow or a Sudra' he is absolved of his sin by performing the चांद्रायण प्रायश्चित, a fasting penance, perhaps for a few hours or a day and requiring not much labour or trouble. While for a Sudra to kill a Brahmin is considered the most heinous offence he could commit, and the forfeiture of his life is the only punishment his crime is considered to merit. Happily for our Sudra brethren of the present day our enlightened British Rulers have not recognized these preposterous, inhuman and unjust penal enactments of the Brahmin legislators. They no doubt regard them more as ridiculous fooleries than as equitable laws. Indeed, no man possessing even a grain of common sense would regard them as otherwise. Any one, who feels disposed to look a little more into the laws and ordinances as embodied in the *Manava Dharma Shastra* and other works of the same class, would undoubtedly be impressed with the deep cunning underlying them all. It may not, perhaps, be out of place to cite here a few more instances in which the superiority or excellence of the Brahmins is held and enjoined on pain of Divine displeasure:

The Brahmin is styled the Lord of the Universe, even equal to the God himself. He is to be worshipped, served and respected by all.

A Brahmin can do no wrong.

Never shall the King slay a Brahmin, though he has committed all possible crimes.

To save the life of a Brahmin any falsehood may be told. There is no sin in it.

No one is to take away anything belonging to a Brahmin.

A king, though dying with want, must not receive any tax from a Brahmin, nor suffer him to be afflicted with hunger or the whole kingdom will be afflicted with famine.

The feet of a Brahmin are holy. In his left foot reside all the तीर्थ (holy waters at places of pilgrimages) and by dipping it into water he makes it as holy as the waters at the holiest of shrines.

A Brahmin may compel a man of the servile class to perform servile duty, because such a man was created by the almighty only for the purpose of serving Brahmins.

A Sudra, though emancipated by his master, is not released from state of servitude; for, being born in a state which is natural to him, by whom can he be divested of his natural attributes?

Let a Brahmin not give temporal advice nor spiritual counsel to a Sudra.

No superfluous accumulation of wealth shall be made by a Sudra, even though he has the power to make it, since a servile man who has amassed riches becomes proud, and by his insolence or neglect he gives pain even to Brahmins.

If a Sudra cohabits with a Brahminee adultress, his life is to be taken. But if a Brahmin goes even unto the lawful wife of a Sudra he is exempted from all corporal punishment.

It would be needless to go on multiplying instances such as these. Hundreds of similar ordinances including many more of a worse character than these can be found scattered over their books. But what can have been the motives and objects of such cruel and inhuman Laws? They are, I believe, apparent to all but to the infatuated, the blind and the selfinterested. Anyone who runs may read them. Their main object in fabricating these falsehoods was to dupe the minds of the ignorant and to rivet firmly on them the chains of perpetual bondage and slavery which their selfishness and cunning had forged. The severity of the laws as affecting the Sudras, and the intense hatred with which they were regarded by the Brahmins can be explained on no other supposition but that there was, originally between the two, a deadly feud, arising as we have shown above, from the advent of the latter into this land. It is surprising to think what a mass of specious fiction these interlopers invented with a view to hold the original occupiers of the soil fast in their clutches, and working on their credulity, rule securely for ages yet to come. Anyone who will consider well the whole history of Brahmin domination in India, and the thraldom under which it has retained the people even up to the present day, will agree with us in thinking that no language could be too harsh by which to characterize the selfish heartlessness and the consummate cunning of the Brahmin tyranny by which India has been so long governed. How far the Brahmins have succeeded in their endeavours to enslave the minds of the Sudras and Atisudras, those of them who have come to know the true state of matters know well to their cost. For generations past they have borne these chains of slavery and bondage. Innumerable Bhut writers, with the selfsame objects as those of Menu and others of his class, added from time to time to the existing mass of legends, the idle phantasies of their own brains, and palmed them off upon the ignorant masses as of Divine inspiration, or as the acts of the Deity himself. The most immoral, inhuman, unjust actions and deeds have been attributed to that Being who is our Creator,

Governor and Protector, and who is all Holiness himself. These blasphemous writings, the products of the distempered brains of these interlopers, were received as gospel truths, for to doubt them was considered as the most unpardonable of sins. This system of slavery, to which the Brahmins reduced the lower classes is in no respects inferior to that which obtained a few years ago in America. In the days of rigid Brahmin dominancy, so lately as that of the time of the Peshwa, my Sudra brethren had even greater hardships and oppression practised upon them than what even the slaves in America had to suffer. To this system of selfish superstition and bigotry, we are to attribute the stagnation and all the evils under which India has been groaning for many centuries past. It will, indeed, be difficult to name a single advantage which accrued to the aborigines from the advent of this intensely selfish and tyrannical sect. The Indian Ryot (the Sudra and Atisudra) has been in fact a proverbial Milch Cow. He has passed from hand to hand. Those who successively held sway over him cared only to fatten themselves on the sweat of his brow, without caring for his welfare or condition. It was sufficient for their purposes that they held him safe in their clutches for squeezing out of him as much as they possibly could. The Brahmin had at last so contrived to entwine himself round the Sudra in every large or small undertaking, in every domestic or public business, that the latter is by custom quite unable to transact any concern of moment without his aid.

This is even true at the present time. While the Sudra on the other hand is so far reconciled to the Brahmin yoke, that like the American slave he would resist any attempt that may be made for his deliverance and fight even against his benefactor. Under the guise of religion the Brahmin has his finger in every thing, big or small, which the Sudra undertakes. Go to his house, to his field or to the court to which business may invite him, the Brahmin is there under some specious pretext or other, trying to squeeze out of him as much as his cunning and wily brain can manage. The Brahmin despoils the Sudra not only in his capacity of a priest, but does so in a variety of other ways. Having by his superior education and cunning monopolized all the higher places of emolument, the ingenuity of his ways is past finding out, as the reader will find on an attentive perusal of this book. In the most insignificant village as in the largest town, the Brahmin is the all in all; the be all and the end all of the Ryot. He is the master, the ruler. The Patell of a village, the headman, is in fact a nonentity. The Koolkurnee, the hereditary Brahmin village accountant, the notorious quarrel-monger, moulds the Patell according to his wishes. He is the temporal and spiritual adviser of the ryots, the Soucar in his necessities and the general referee in all matters. In most instances he plans active mischief by advising opposite parties differently, so that he may feather his own nest well. If we go up higher, to the Court of a Mamlutdar, we find the same thing. The first anxiety of a Mamlutdar is to get round him, if not his own relatives, his castemen to fill the various offices under him. These actively foment quarrels and are the media of all corrupt practices prevailing generally round about these Courts. If a Sudra or Atisudra repairs to his Courts, the treatment which he receives is akin to what the meanest reptile gets. Instead of his case receiving a patient and careful hearing, a choice lot of abuse is showered on his devoted head, and his prayer is set aside on some pretext or other. Whereas if one of his own castemen were to repair to the Court on the self-same business, he is received with all courtesy, and there is hardly any time lost in getting the matter right. If we go up still higher to the Collector's and Revenue Commissioner's Courts and to the other Departments of the Public Service, the Engineer, Educational, etc., the same system is carried out on a smaller or greater scale. The higher European officers generally view men and things through Brahmin spectacles, and hence the deplorable ignorance they often exhibit in forming a correct estimate of them. I have tried to place before my readers in the concluding portions of this book what expedients are employed by these Brahmin officials for fleecing the Coonbee in the various departments to which business or his necessities induce him to resort. Any one knowing intimately the workings of the different departments, and the secret springs which are in motion, will unhesitatingly concur with me in saying that what I have described in the following pages is not one hundredth part of the rogueries that are generally practised on my poor, illiterate and ignorant Sudra brethren. Though the Brahmin of the old Peishwa school is not quite the same as the Brahmin of the present day, though the march of Western ideas and civilization is undoubtedly telling on his superstition and bigotry, he has not as yet abandoned his time-cherished notions of superiority or the dishonesty of his ways. The Beef, the Mutton, the intoxicating beverages stronger and more fiery than the famed *Somarasa*, which their ancestors once relished, as the veriest dainties, are fast finding innumerable votaries among them.

The Brahmin of the present time finds to some extent, like Othello, that his occupation is gone. But knowing full well this state of matters, is the Brahmin inclined to make atonement for his past selfishness? Perhaps, it would have been useless to repine over what has been suffered and what has passed away, had the present state been all that is desirable. We know perfectly well that the Brahmin will not descend from his self-raised high pedestal and meet his Coonbee and low caste brethren on an equal footing without a struggle. Even the educated Brahmin who knows his exact position and how he has come by it, will not condescend to acknowledge the errors of his forefathers and willingly forego the long cherished false notions of his own superiority. At present, not one has the moral courage to do what only duty demands, and as long as this continues, sect distrusting and degrading sect, the condition of the Sudras will remain unaltered, and India never advance in greatness or prosperity.

Perhaps a part of the blame in bringing matters to this crisis may be justly laid to the credit of the Government. Whatever may have been their motives in providing ampler funds and greater facilities for higher education and neglecting that of the masses, it will be acknowledged by all that in justice to the latter this is not as it should be. It is an admitted fact that the greater portion of the revenues of the Indian Empire are derived from the Ryot's labour – from the sweat of his brow. The higher and richer classes contribute little or nothing to the state's exchequer. A well informed English writer states that,

'Our income is derived, not from surplus profits, but from capital; not from luxuries but from the poorest necessaries. It is the product of sin and tears.'

That Government should expend profusely a large portion of revenue thus raised, on the education of the higher classes, for it is these only who take advantage of it, is anything but just or equitable. Their object in patronizing this virtual high class education appears to be to prepare scholars. 'Who, it is thought, would in time vend learning without money and without price.' 'If we can inspire,' say they, 'the love of knowledge in the minds of the superior classes, the result will be a higher standard of morals in the cases of the individuals, a large amount of affection for the British Government, and an unconquerable desire to spread among their own countrymen the intellectual blessings which they have received.'

Regarding these objects of Government the writer, above alluded to, states that:

'We have never heard of philosophy more benevolent and more utopian. It is proposed by men who witness the wondrous changes brought about in the Western world, purely by the agency of popular knowledge, to redress the defects of the two hundred millions of India, by giving superior education to the superior classes and to them only.' . . . 'We ask the friends of Indian Universities to favour us with a single example of the truth of their theory from the instances which have already fallen within the scope of their experience. They have educated many children of wealthy men, and have been the means of advancing very materially the worldly prospects of some of their pupils; but what contribution have these made to the great work of regenerating their fellowmen? How have they begun to act upon the masses? Have any of them formed classes at their own homes or elsewhere, for the instruction of their less fortunate or less wise countrymen? Or have they kept their knowledge to themselves, as a personal gift, not to be soiled by contact with the ignorant vulgar? Have they in any way shown themselves anxious to advance the general interests and repay philanthropy with patriotism? Upon what grounds is it asserted that the best way to advance the moral and intellectual welfare of the people is to raise the standard of instruction among the higher classes? A glorious argument this for aristocracy, were it only tenable. To show the growth of the national happiness, it would only be necessary to refer to the number of pupils at the colleges and the lists of academic degrees. Each wrangler would be accounted a national benefactor; and the existence of Deans and Proctors would be associated, like the game laws and the tenpound franchise, with the best interests of the Constitution.'

Perhaps the most glaring tendency of the Government system of high class education has been the virtual monopoly of all the higher offices under them by the Brahmins. If the welfare of the Ryot is at heart, if it is the duty of Government to check a host of abuses, it behoves them to narrow this monopoly, day by day, so as to allow a sprinkling of the other castes to get into the public service. Perhaps some might be inclined to say that it is not feasible in the present state of education. Our only reply is that if Government look a little less after higher education and more towards the education of the masses, the former being able to take care of itself, there would be no difficulty in training up a body of men every way qualified and perhaps far better in morals and manners.

My object in writing the present volume is not only to tell my Sudra brethren how they have been duped by the Brahmins, but also to open the eyes of Government to that pernicious system of high class education which has hitherto been so persistently followed and which statesmen like Sir George Campbell, the present Lieutenant Governor of Bengal, with broad and universal sympathies, are finding to be highly mischievous and pernicious to the interests of Government. I sincerely hope that Government will ere long see the error of their ways, trust less to writers or men who look through high class spectacles and take the glory into their own hands of emancipating my Sudra brethren from the trammels of bondage which the Brahmins have woven round them like the coils of a serpent. It is no less the duty of such of my Sudra brethren as have received any education to place before Government the true state of their fellowmen and endeavour to the best of their power to emancipate themselves from Brahmin thraldom. Let there be schools for the Sudras in every village; but away with all Brahmin school-masters! The Sudras are the life and sinews of the country, and it is to them alone and not to the Brahmins that the Government must ever look to tide them over their difficulties, financial as well as political. If the hearts and minds of the Sudras are made happy and contented the British Government need have no fear for their loyalty in the future.

1st June, 1873 Joteerao Phooley

Introduction

This treatise has been written with a specific objective in mind. Since hundreds of years, the shudras and the atishudras have suffered innumerable tribulations and lived in wretched conditions under the yoke of the brahman rule. They have had to endure abject poverty and severe afflictions for ages. The sole intention of this treatise is to direct the attention of all these oppressed people towards their own plight and make them consider their situation properly so as to enable them to free themselves from the slavery of the brahmans, from their oppression and injustice. It has been conjectured that the brahmans have ruled this country for more than three thousand years. They had come originally from distant lands, outside India, invaded it, attacked the original inhabitants of this land, conquered and forcibly turned them into slaves and oppressed them in several different ways. Then, after their memories had somewhat been blunted and blurred, the brahmans, very skilfully, concealed from them all the true facts: that they themselves had come from outside, defeated the original inhabitants and turned them into slaves. The brahmans also employed several means by which they impressed their superiority upon the minds of these people and sought to protect their own interests. They were eminently successful in this endeavour for two reasons: firstly, the original inhabitants had already been conquered and deprived of their freedom; secondly, the brahmans had reduced them to a pitiable state of ignorance by depriving them of all knowledge. Therefore they were simply unable to understand the trickery and scheming designs of the brahmans. The brahmans established their domination over these people and, in order to eternally perpetuate that domination, they composed several treatises which they claimed to have obtained directly from God. Thus they managed to thoroughly convince the poor ignorant people that their slavery was justified even in the eyes of God. In these treatises, the brahmans wrote that God had deliberately created the shudras for the sole purpose of providing eternal service to the brahmans. It was the decree of God, they wrote, that the shudras should diligently serve them and try to please them throughout their lives. Only then, they wrote, would their lives be fulfilled and their birth itself would be justified.

Now even a cursory glance at these treatises immediately reveals that this claim, that the brahmans had obtained the treatises directly from God, is absolutely untenable. Such treatises do nothing but demean the omnipotence of the just God, the Creator of this whole universe and all the objects in it. And this is the wisdom of these 'learned' brothers of ours, the brahmans! We are simply ashamed to call them our brothers! They heaped miseries on the shudras in the past and still continue to do so through the power of religion that they wield over them. To harass somebody is not the spirit of brotherhood. Still we have to call them our brothers as the great God who created us also created them. If the brahmans think impartially and objectively, without selfish interests, even they will have to admit this. Why, even our learned friends – the English, French, German, American and others – agree that these treatises are extremely self-serving and have deliberately been written to proclaim the superiority of the brahmans over the others and to impress upon them the greatness of the brahmans, so much so that the brahmans are portrayed as superior to even God! Among the several learned friends cited above, several English scholars have already produced books on history where they have stated that the brahmans have turned the shudras and the atishudras into their slaves. How the glory of God has been maligned by the brahmans through their books which claim them to be superior to God! God created this world and everything in it; he gave freedom to all people, including the shudras and atishudras, to enjoy all the things he created in this world. Yet the brahmans wrote untruthful books in the name of God and confiscated the rights of all others except themselves and became all-powerful. Now some of our brahman brothers well may ask us: if the books are untruthful, how come the ancestors of the shudras and atishudras believed in them in the past? And also, how do people believe in them even today? The answer to that question may be given by way of an example. See, everybody is allowed to express his or her thoughts quite freely in the somewhat progressive times today. Nobody is restricted from doing so. Now suppose a scoundrel procures a false letter under the name of a respectable citizen and approaches a gentleman with that. Undoubtedly, the gentleman, however wise he may be, will trust the scoundrel and believe the letter to be authentic, and will be thus easily deceived by the scoundrel. If this is what happens today, it is not at all surprising that the shudras and the atishudras fell prey to the deception of the brahmans in the past. The brahmans had oppressed them so much and reduced them to such a state of ignorance that when they cunningly showed them the books and told them that they were written by God himself, they immediately believed it to be true and fell prey to the trickery of the brahmans. This continues even today as a lot of shudras and atishudras believe in the brahmans and are deceived by them. This is exactly like the example given earlier. The brahmans earn their livelihood by quoting from their selfish books everywhere, all the time, before the poor ignorant shudras who believe everything that they say and are thus made to respect them so much that they feel great reverence for the brahmans, which should be felt for God alone. This is not a small thing. One day, the brahmans will have to answer God for this. The arguments of the brahmans have been imprinted so firmly on the minds of the shudras that they, like the Negro slaves in America, oppose the very people who are willing to fight for them, and free them from the chains of slavery. It is very surprising that the oppressed people choose to remain resigned to their despicable state of existence; they proclaim that they have no complaints about their circumstances and resist the very people who are willing to help them and fight for their rights. Not only do they reject the offer of help, they are willing to fight those very people who want to help them. Now their friends do not stand to gain anything by fighting for the downtrodden. On the contrary, they have to sacrifice hundreds of their own people and endanger their own lives as well in the struggle for the oppressed. What is the purpose behind their altruism? It is the principle of freedom. It is very essential for human beings to be free. When man is free, he can clearly convey his thoughts to people through writing or speech. But if he does not have freedom, then he is unable to communicate his thoughts, however beneficial they might be to the others, and consequently, they just evaporate into thin air. A free man will never hesitate to claim his rights which are granted by God to all humans and which are snatched away by some selfish people to achieve their own selfish ends. He rests happy only when he gets his rights back. Similarly, the purpose behind the free man's struggle against slavery is to liberate the slaves from the tyranny of oppression and injustice of the oppressors, restore their freedom to them and make them happy. This is the goal for which he faces dangers and risks his life. Oh, what a great philanthropic deed is this! No wonder this noble goal was blessed by God with success! We fervently pray to God that he may grant them success in all such worthy tasks to be undertaken by them in future as well. In the continents of Africa and South America, there was in existence the heinous custom of capturing people from distant lands to be sold as slaves which, indeed, had brought shame to all the progressive countries in Europe and elsewhere in the world. Several generous people, like the English and the Americans, strove hard to abolish this cruel custom with total disregard for their own lives and restored several slaves to their loving parents, brothers, sisters, children and friends from whom they had been cruelly estranged. They had given up all hope of ever seeing them again and were helplessly awaiting death in a highly degenerated state of mind and body when they were reunited with their near and dear ones and their joy must have known no bounds on the happy occasion. Oh what a great task did the good Americans perform, indeed! If they had not taken pity on the poor orphaned slaves, they would have perished without setting their eyes on their near and dear ones even once. Did their owners ever treat them kindly? Oh no. Never. Even the most hard-hearted man would not have been able to prevent his tears, had he heard the heart-rending accounts of the misery and pain inflicted on the slaves by their owners. The owners always treated the slaves as beasts of burden, raining kicks and blows on them all the time and starving them. Sometimes, they would harness the slaves as bullocks and make them plough the fields in the blazing sun. The slaves would be whipped mercilessly for the slightest mistake. The owners did not even feed them well. The slaves were starved most of the times. They were thrown a few morsels on which they had to survive. The food was hardly nourishing as it used to be of a very low quality. They were made to work hard in the day till they vomited blood. And at night, they used to be thrown into dungeons or stables to sleep where the poor souls sank into death-like slumber but could hardly have any rest. And how could they? Firstly, they used to be in mortal dread of their owner's call; secondly, the excruciating pangs of hunger would deprive them of any sleep; thirdly, the smarting wounds on their bleeding bodies, caused by the continuous whipping, could result only in a very tormented and disturbed sleep; fourthly, the thought of their loved ones, disconsolate because of the forced estrangement, brought tears to their eyes. They would continually pray to God to have mercy on their souls, to deliver them swiftly from their dismal lives of unparalleled distress. They would pray to God to at least grant them deliverance through death, as death alone could free them from their suffering. Thus were there nights spent! All the sad words in the lexicon will not be able to express the agony of their woebegone existence. The Americans put an end to the cruel custom of slave trading which had existed for hundreds of years, delivered the poor orphaned slaves from their life of misery, freed them from the clutches of their tormentors and enabled them to lead a happy life. The shudras and atishudras will really appreciate this more than anyone else as they have a direct experience of slavery as compared to the others who have never experienced it so. Only slaves can understand what it is to be a slave and what joy it is to be delivered from the chains of slavery. Now the only difference between them and the slaves in America is that whereas the blacks were captured and sold as slaves, the shudras and atishudras were conquered and enslaved by the *bhats*[3] and brahmans. Except for this difference, all the other conditions in which they lived were the same. There is simply not an iota of

[3] Literally priest, more generally brahman. [—*Ed.*]

difference between them. All the calamities suffered by blacks were endured by the shudras and the atishudras who probably suffered more but not less at the hands of the brahmans. The tales of their suffering would not only cause the hardest hearts to shed tears but would also dissolve the hardest layers of rocks on the earth and release streams of tears from within which would drown the whole world. This would lead some brahmans, soft-hearted unlike their callous ancestors, to conjecture that the end of the world had come. Our kind English government simply has no idea how much the shudras and atishudras have suffered and are still suffering at the hands of the brahmans. If they acquire more information about this, they would probably conclude that they have really dropped a very important section from their histories of India. Once they get to know the terrible suffering of these people, they will feel very sorry for them and whenever they have to describe the agony of any oppressed and tormented people, reduced to a pitiable state of existence, they will undoubtedly use the image of the shudras and the atishudras to symbolize it. Where else would a poet, who wants to describe suffering, get so apt an image of suffering? His heart would no doubt be overwhelmed at their distress, yet he would certainly feel relieved that now he does not have to exercise his imagination too hard for creating images of suffering, as in the past, which would have a lasting impact on his readers' mind. It is not at all surprising that the hearts of the shudras and atishudras are virtually torn asunder at the thought of the suffering undergone by their ancestors whose blood flows through their veins. When we think of the terrible calamities faced by them during the brahman rule, our minds are paralysed with fear. And we feel that if merely remembering those calamities causes such intense anguish to our hearts, what must have been the state of mind of those people who actually experienced them? A very good example regarding this can be found in one of the books written by the brahmans themselves. This book describes how Parashuram, one of the chiefs of the brahmans, acted towards the original inhabitants of this country, the kshatriyas. He not only killed several kshatriya men but also snatched from the arms of their orphaned wives their innocent infants and mercilessly sent them to a cruel death. His heart never wavered a bit while doing this dastardly act. However, he did not stop even at this. When he heard of widowed, pregnant and helpless kshatriya women, desperately running away to save the lives of their unborn babies, he chased them like a hunter and captured them. The moment he heard of a boy being born to the unfortunate captive, he would kill the infant instantly. This account has been given in the books written by the brahmans themselves. It must be remembered that the brahmans were the enemies of the kshatriyas. It would be impossible to imagine in our farthest dreams that they would reveal all the true accounts of their cruelty towards the kshatriyas. Undoubtedly they must have deleted considerable parts from their accounts. Obviously, nobody boasts about their own shameful deeds. It is therefore quite surprising that they have described in their books all the gruesome details of the killings of the kshatriya infants discussed above. We feel that the brahmans considered Parashuram's dastardly act of wiping out the kshatriyas from the face of the earth, not only once but twenty-one times, as a great heroic deed; this included the merciless massacre of the young babies and infants as well! And therefore they documented all these deeds in their books. There is a famous proverb which says that you cannot cover the sun with your palm. These massacres were so abominable and so condemned all over, that they could not completely hide all the facts while writing. Therefore they had to record them, however briefly. Even if we ignore all the unreported facts and consider only what the *bhat* brahmans wrote about, the heart bleeds at the horror of the gruesome acts. Just consider what agony the pregnant kshatriya women must have experienced when they were pursued by Parashuram. Womenfolk are not used to running. Besides, most of them belonged to families of good descent and never had the occasion to cross even the thresholds of their houses as they had servants to look after their needs. They were, in short, women who had spent their lives happily in the shelter of their homes and husbands. And these women had suddenly been forced to face a terrible calamity. They had to run for their lives through little known pathways, under the scorching sun, bearing the burden of their unborn babies. This was indeed a most devastating adversity for them. Since they were not used to running, they must have tripped and fallen and dashed against the boulders on the way or the rocky mountains by the sides of the roads and bled profusely through the several wounds caused by the fall on their arms, foreheads, knees and ankles. On hearing that he was in hot pursuit, they must have stumbled on, desperate for their lives; their delicate feet torn by the thorns in the path, and their clothes shred to pieces by the spiky trees. Their bodies, lacerated by the sharp branches, must have left long trails of blood oozing out of the gashes. Their feet must have burnt in the scorching sun and their delicate, lotus-like blue skin burnt crimson. Their mouths must have been parched dry in the burning sun and because of the lack of water and constant running, they must have felt sick. Their mouths must have frothed with fear and the tiny lives inside their bellies must have rolled frantically, causing them unendurable, acute pains. They must have prayed desperately for the earth to open up and swallow them so that they could escape from this merciless pursuit. With their eyes flooding with tears, they must have wailed, 'O Lord, what calamities have you brought down on us! Don't you know we are too delicate to bear such travails? We women lack physical strength, which is why we are called women.[4] Our strength is the strength of our husbands, we are defenceless without them; but this tyrant has destroyed all of that. You know all this. And yet you stretch our endurance to the farthest limits! How can you watch silently while this tyrant kills our husbands, hounds us to death with his deadly weapons and takes pride in the dastardly act? Why don't you punish him? You are omnipotent and yet you do nothing against the injustice done to us?' And while they were thus imploring the Lord, Parashuram must have come upon them, seized them rudely and forced them to go with him. O what agony they must have suffered! How many terror-stricken women must have embraced death! How many women must have fallen at his feet and begged Parashuram for mercy! – saying, 'O Parashuram, we beg you on bended knees, please do not kill our babies when

[4] Phule uses the word 'abala' which literally means devoid of physical strength. [—*Ed.*]

they are born. We pray to you for their life. Kill us if you want but please, o please, spare our babies. You have already killed our husbands and widowed us; we are now deprived of any comforts forever; we will never conceive again; now all that we hope for is the birth of our babies. They are all the happiness that is left in our lives now. Why do you want to kill them and drown us in the ocean of everlasting grief? Please have mercy on us and grant us this favour as you would to a goddaughter of yours. We beg you again and again.' They must have appealed to him thus, repeatedly, yet all their pleas must have fallen on deaf ears. When their babies were born, he must have started to snatch them away to dash them to death, and then, again, the poor disconsolate women, dazed with grief, must have fallen at his feet and beseeched him, trying to cover their babies to protect them from his wrath, 'O Parashuram, if you are bent upon killing our babies, behead us first. Then you can do whatever you want with them. Don't, please don't kill them in front of our very eyes.' But alas! All their fervent pleas went unattended. Our pen just slips through our fingers; it is unable to express the terrible agitation of the unfortunate mothers whose babies were wrenched away from them to be slaughtered. The ruthless tyrant butchered babies in front of their mothers. They must have beaten their breasts, pulled their hair out, rammed their faces into the earth and committed suicide. Or some of them must have perished with grief, and some of them must have gone raving mad, wandering all over the place, calling their sons and wailing loudly. But we should never hope to get this account from the brahmans. Parashuram thus killed hundreds of kshatriyas and reduced their women and children to a most pitiable state. It is really surprising that though Parashuram had wreaked havoc on the kshatriyas by ruthlessly massacring them, the brahmans compelled the shudras and atishudras to address the tyrant as the all-powerful God and as the Creator of the entire Universe. Even after Parashuram's demise, the brahmans continued to torture them to the best of their ability. They used to torture and bury some of these people alive in the foundations of buildings. A detailed account of such things will follow later in this book. They used to consider them as such vermin that if a shudra or atishudra was washing clothes at the riverbank and if a brahman came there, the person had to collect all his clothes, leave his place and go elsewhere for the fear of splashing a few drops of water on the brahman. In spite of these precautions, if he inadvertently splashed a few drops on the brahman's body, or if the brahman suspected that such a thing had happened, he would be inflamed with anger and hit the culprit's head with the pot in his hands. The shudra would collapse bleeding on the ground. Or else, he would have to leave the place quietly with his blood stained apparels. He couldn't even lodge a complaint; whom could he lodge it with? The rulers and the law-dispensing authorities would all be brahmans and the poor fellow would himself get punished for having lodged a complaint. O God! What terrible injustice! Anyway, which grief would one describe when there were so many! During the brahman rule, the shudras and the atishudras had to endure several hardships like this. The shudras, who had to travel a lot in connection with their trade or some other business, had to face several problems on the road. It would be very difficult to walk especially in the early morning. This is the time when shadows are cast long. If the shudra walking on the road saw a brahman approaching, he had to stop walking and sit at the side of the road to avoid casting his shadow on the brahman. He would be so afraid of the brahman's wrath that he would even inconvenience himself. He would resume walking only once he had made sure that the brahman had gone off. In case his shadow fell on the brahman, the brahman would beat him to pulp and then immediately march off to the river to bathe and wash off the polluting effect of the shudra's shadow. The shudras did not even have the freedom to spit on the ground; they had to carry their own earthen spittoons with them while walking through a brahman locality. If ever a brahman caught him spitting on the ground, that was enough! He knew his life was over. The shudras suffered terribly in this manner for a very long time. They were like a prisoner who has been imprisoned for a long time and desperately looks forward to the day when he will be set free and will have the freedom to walk about and meet his friends, relatives and children. And then, as luck would have it, God took pity on them and the British Rule was established in India. The shudras heartily thank the British for this and are exceedingly grateful to them. They will never ever forget the obligations of the British on them. It is the British who have liberated them from the prisons of the brahmans and showed them and their offspring these days of comfort. Had the British not been there, the brahmans would have ground them to dust. Now some people may object by saying that the number of the shudras and atishudras is almost ten times more than that of the brahmans; then how could the brahmans have destroyed them? The answer to that is that one shrewd man can dominate the minds of ten ignorant people through persuasion; secondly, had these ten ignorant people been of one and the same opinion, they would not have allowed one person to dominate them. But since all of them held ten diverse opinions, the wise man had no problem in deceiving them. Similarly, the brahmans came up with a devious and cunning scheme to keep the shudras and atishudras divided. As the communities of the shudras and the atishudras had started expanding, the brahmans were growing apprehensive. They realized that they could sustain themselves and their domination only if they divided the shudras and atishudras and antagonized them against each other. This was how they could make merry and live a life of comfort and luxury, without having to work for it themselves. They wanted to exploit the labour of the shudras and atishudras to sustain not only their own luxurious lifestyle but also that of their future generations. To achieve this devious goal, they created the fraudulent rigmarole of the caste system and wrote several books to legitimize the caste system. Through these books, they influenced the minds of the shudras and atishudras. At that time, a section of these downtrodden people revolted against the brahmans. In order to take revenge on them, the brahmans separated them from the others and dictated that neither they nor their children should ever be touched by other people, called mali or kunbi today. After this, all their trade and commerce ended and they were reduced to a life of abject poverty and had to resort to the practice of eating flesh of dead animals in order to survive. When the other shudras, who proudly called themselves mali, kunbi, sonar, shimpi, lohar, sutar,[5] etc., according to their professions, came to know of this, they started to despise them under the influence of the brahmans. They failed to see the trickery of the brahmans. All the shudras belonged to the same fraternity; but the devious brahmans had deliberately poisoned their minds against a section of their own people who had dared challenge their domination and revolt against them. They failed to see that that was why the brahmans were starving them to death. The brahmans will certainly have to explain a lot before God one day. They poisoned the minds of the shudras against this group of people so much that the shudras now consider them as untouchables, shoo them away when they beg for food even on festival days and charge upon them with sticks in their hands to beat them up. This is how the brahmans have divided the shudras into various castes, punished or rewarded them according to their loyalty, and established their control over them. It has been since this division that the shudras have lost their unity[6] and have come to hold divergent opinions. This has given the brahmans ample time to develop the system as they wanted. There is a famous saying that when two fight, the third profits. The brahmans thus divided the shudras and the atishudras and now are enjoying themselves at the cost of the shudras.

It has already been noted above that the shudras and atishudras have been freed from the physical slavery of the brahmans since the advent of the British. But at the same time we are extremely sad to note that the benevolent British government has ignored the problem of education of the shudras. And as a result, they still remain ignorant and captive in the mental slavery which the brahmans have perpetuated through their books. The shudras do not have the strength even to appeal to the government which fails to notice how the brahmans plunder and exploit them in various government offices. We pray to the all-powerful God and fervently

[5] Mali: gardener; kunbi: small farmer; sonar: goldsmith; shimpi: tailor; lohar: ironsmith; sutar: carpenter. [—*Ed.*]

[6] They now hold antagonistic views and are divided against each other. [—*J.P.*]

hope that the government will look into this problem and liberate the shudras and atishudras from the psychological slavery of the brahmans.

I am very grateful to my friends Shri Vinayakrao Bapuji Bhandarkar and Shri Sa. Rajannalingu for their constant encouragement in the course of writing this book and extend my heartfelt thanks to them.

Part I

About Brahma, origin, Saraswati and Iranians or Aryans

DHONDIBA: The fact that benevolent governments in Europe, like the French, English, came together to prohibit the slave system, demonstrates that they defied the brahman law written in the *Manusmriti*. The book says that Brahma created brahmans from his mouth and shudras from his feet, only to serve the brahmans.[7]

JOTIRAO: You say that the English, French and other governments prohibited the slave system which means they defied the brahman law. But there are so many different people on this earth! Tell me, what does the *Manusmriti* say about their creation? Which limb of the Brahma were they created from?

DHONDIBA: Regarding this, the brahmans, learned as well as the illiterate, say that since people like the English are depraved vulgar sinners, the *Manusmriti* does not mention them.

JOTIRAO: Do you mean to say that there are absolutely no depraved sinners among the brahmans?

DHONDIBA: Actually, there are far more such people among the brahmans than among any other community.

JOTIRAO: Then how come the *Manusmriti* writes about them if they are depraved sinners?

DHONDIBA: This itself proves that the account of the origin of human beings given by Manu is completely wrong, simply because it cannot be applied to all human beings.

[7] This theory of the origin of the varnas actually goes back to the *Purusha Sukta* from the tenth mandala of the *Rig Veda* and as such is much older than the *Manusmriti*. [—*Ed.*]

JOTIRAO: That is why the learned among the English and other such people prohibited slavery because they realized the devious designs of the writers among the brahmans. Had Brahma really been the cause or the origin of all humans, they would not have done so. Manu has written about the origin of all the four varnas. If we compare it with the evolution of nature, it is revealed to be completely false.

DHONDIBA: How so?

JOTIRAO: The brahmans were created from the mouth of the Brahma. All right. But how is it that Manu does not write anything about the original brahman Mother? Which organ of the Brahma was she created from?

DHONDIBA: Probably because she was a depraved vulgar sinner from the perspective of the brahmans. Maybe she should be placed among the mlechhas.[8]

JOTIRAO: How can you say such a thing? Wasn't she the original Mother of the brahmans, the self-appointed kings of the land, who claim themselves to be superior to all others? How do you place her among the mlechhas, eh? How will she stand the stink of liquor and beef there? What you say is not very proper, friend!

DHONDIBA: But you yourself have spoken many a time in packed meetings about how the ancestors of the brahmans used to celebrate people's death anniversaries by killing cows, cooking several delicacies of beef and consuming them. Then how do you say now that their original Mother couldn't have suffered the stink? Just wait for a few days wishing well for the British Raj. You will see that these so-called clean and holy brahmans will not allow even butlers any share from the leftovers of meat from the plates of their bosses, the Residents and Governors. Don't you know that these days most mahar butlers privately grumble a lot about the brahmans? It was Manu himself who did not write about the creation of the original brahman woman. So you must blame him. Why blame me by saying that I speak improperly? All right, go on . . .

[8] Mlechhas: barbarians. In the 19th century this term was occasionally used for the Muslims as well. But it is not clear if Dhondiba is actually suggesting that. See also note 32, p. 275 of the present volume. [—*Ed.*]

JOTIRAO: Ok. Let it be as you wish. Now tell me, is there any written evidence that Brahma's mouth, which gave birth to the brahmans, menstruated every month and that he had to sit in seclusion for four days?[9] – or that he used to powder his body with ash like a lingayat woman to become clean?

DHONDIBA: No. But Brahma is the source of creation of the brahmans. How would he like the advice of a lingayat woman? – the brahmans today despise the lingayats as they do not observe strict rules regarding cleanliness during those four days (of menstruation).

JOTIRAO: Now from this you can observe for yourself that since Brahma had genital organs at four places – mouth, arms, groins and legs (for the four varnas were born out of those four organs according to the *Manusmriti*) – each of them must have menstruated at least for four days each, and he must have sat aside in seclusion, as an untouchable person, for sixteen days in all, each month. If that was so, then who looked after his house during those sixteen days? Does *Manusmriti* say anything about this?

DHONDIBA: No.

JOTIRAO: All right. Does Manu say anything about how the foetus grows right from its conception in the mouth over the next nine months?

DHONDIBA: No.

JOTIRAO: All right. Does it at least say anything about how Brahma fed the infant, the brahman? Did he breast feed it or give it some other milk? How did he grow him?

DHONDIBA: No.

JOTIRAO: Now Brahma had a wife, Savitri. Yet why did he invite the trouble of growing a foetus inside his mouth, giving it birth and developing him on his own head? This is extremely intriguing.

DHONDIBA: What about his other three heads? They were at least free from this bothersome mess. Was that bastard a sissy to like such a game which only little girls play in the house?

JOTIRAO: Now to call him a bastard is a bit problematic as he

[9] It was customary practice in the 19th and early 20th centuries that a woman sat in seclusion during the four days she menstruated. [—*Ed.*]

committed incest with his daughter Saraswati. That is why his other name is Daughter-Fucker. Nobody respects or worships him because of this heinous deed that he committed.

DHONDIBA: Now if Brahma really had four faces, he must have had eight breasts, four belly buttons, four genitals and four anuses. But no reliable information is available about that anywhere. A similar problem can be raised about Sheshashai[10] as well, who had Lakshmi as his wife. Why did he create this child of four mouths if he had a regular wife? We will have to ask the same questions about him as of Brahma.

JOTIRAO: The true facts one arrives upon, after due consideration, are that the brahmans originally inhabited Iran which is located in the region beyond the sea. Several English historians have proved it in their own books that they used to be called Iranians or Aryans then. Initially, the Aryans organized themselves into small armies and invaded the country several times. They disrupted life in the kingdoms of almost all the native kings. After some years, Brahma became their chief after Vamana. He was a bull headed man. He defeated several of the natives, our original ancestors, in the battles and turned them into slaves. He made several laws to permanently distinguish these slaves from his own people. After he was dead, the Aryans called themselves brahmans after him, their original name just forgotten. Leaders like Manu followed Brahma. They were afraid that the rules made by Brahma would be violated. So they composed and spread several strange myths about Brahma. They wanted the slaves to believe that whatever had happened was divinely ordained. So they created another rigmarole of a myth about the god Sheshashai. And after some time, all this writing was conveniently composed in the form of books. The cunning and crafty Narada,[11] their effeminate colleague, constantly surrounded by women, preached this 'gospel' from these books

[10] Lord Vishnu. [—*Ed.*]

[11] The mythical singer-sage who is credited with the authorship of the *Bhaktisutra* (treatise on Bhakti or devotion). Why Phule calls him effeminate is not clear. See the reference to Narada in *Satsar* (p. 272 of the present volume) as well. [—*Ed.*]

to the shudras and dasas and therefore Brahma came to acquire still more prestige. Now, however, if we subject Sheshashai also to a similar scrutiny, it will be a sheer waste of time for both of us. The poor man was thrown on his back and made to give birth to this four-mouthed baby from his navel. And I believe that it would hardly be a manly, valiant deed to pin the already vanquished man to the ground and show him our strength!

Part II

About Matsya and Shankhasura[12]

DHONDIBA: How many troupes of the Aryans from Iran must have entered India before Vamana?

JOTIRAO: Several of them came to India by sea.

DHONDIBA: Did the first one travel in a ship?

JOTIRAO: They didn't have warships then. They came in small canoes, which used to travel fast over the sea. That was probably why the chief of that horde came to be called 'Matsya'.

DHONDIBA: Then how come the brahman historians in their treatises such as the *Bhagawata*[13] wrote that that chief was born of a fish?

JOTIRAO: Now think for yourself. Do you see any similarity between fish and man? They are absolutely different from each other in their physical structure, food, sleep, sexual and procreative habits. Also their brain, liver, lungs, intestines, wombs and sexual organs are completely dissimilar. Man lives on land. He cannot survive in water as he easily drowns in it and dies. On the contrary, fish survive in water only. They cannot survive out of water. Females of the human species give birth mostly to a single child. But the female among the fish lays several eggs and then hatches them. Now if at all there was a human baby in one of the eggs, and she did bring the egg out of water to break it open

[12] Matsya is a fish, supposedly the first of the ten avataras (incarnations) of Lord Vishnu. Shankhasura was a rakshasa. [—*Ed.*]

[13] One of the many puranas (mythical accounts); perhaps the most influential of them all. See also note 39 on p. 98 of the present volume. [—*Ed.*]

and allow the human baby to emerge, how did she survive out of water? Or if she broke the egg in the water itself, how did the human baby survive inside water? Can it be suggested that some expert diver among the humans recognized the egg which had the fish-human baby and dived into the water and brought it out so that the human baby could come out? Granted this is what happened! But which smart man carried out such an awesome task of bringing a human baby out of the egg of a fish? Even in these days of tremendous scientific and medical advancement which has produced brilliant experts in medicine in Europe and America, no doctor, however brilliant, will dare to claim that he can transfer a fish egg onto the land and recover a live fish baby from it. Be that as it may! Which immortal fish came out of water to convey to the diver the whereabouts of that particular egg? And how could the diver understand fish language? The account given in the *Bhagawata* does not provide us with any satisfactory explanations. Therefore we may conclude that some cunning brahmans must have interpolated this fishy myth into the ancient treatise at a later date.

DHONDIBA: All right, where exactly did that chief officer from the ship land with his people?

JOTIRAO: He sailed through the western sea and landed at a port on the western coast.

DHONDIBA: What did the fish do after that?

JOTIRAO: That fish killed a chieftain called Shankhasura and usurped his kingdom. The Aryans continued to rule it till the death of the fish. When he was dead, Shankhasura's people launched a fierce attack on the fish horde.

DHONDIBA: And what was the outcome of that attack?

JOTIRAO: The fish horde was defeated in this attack and they took to their heels. But they were followed relentlessly by Shankhasura's people and therefore had to go and hide themselves in a thicket on the hills. Just then another horde of the Aryans from Iran landed at the port from their boats. These boats travelled slowly like the tortoise because of their size, which was bigger than the canoe. Hence the leader of the people who landed from the boat was called 'Kachcha', that is, tortoise.

Part III

About Kachcha, Bhudev or Bhupati, kshatriya, dvija and King Kashyapa[14]

DHONDIBA: All things considered, the fish and the tortoise do have some differences. But there are quite a few similarities between them, too. For example, both are creatures of water, both lay eggs, both break their eggs open to let out the lives inside. Therefore the historians have noted in their books such as the *Bhagawata*, that Kachcha was born of a tortoise. But if we pursue this line of thinking, the result will be just like that of the fishy tale of the Matsya that we have just seen. That is a sure way of wasting our time. That is why, I'll ask you the next question. What did Kachcha do after getting down at the port?

JOTIRAO: First he drove out the people who had lain a siege on the people of Matsya on the mountain which was close to the port, along with the other original inhabitants of the place. Thus he rescued his people and became the king of the place himself, that is Bhupati, proclaiming his power to all and sundry.

DHONDIBA: All right. But where did all those kshatriyas whom he had driven away go?

JOTIRAO: They were all frightened. Making a great noise that yet another bunch of the Iranians had arrived from Iran, shouting '*dvija aale*',[15] they all followed their leader called Kashyapa to the other side of the mountain. Kachcha pursued them with his troops and descended the mountain behind them. In the mean time, more and more troops kept on arriving from Iran, so he went on harassing them more and more. Later on Kashyapa tried hard to win the mountain back from him but these attempts proved to be quite futile. Kachcha never surrendered even an inch

[14] Bhupati: king of the earth. Dvija: twice-born. The term was used for brahmans, kshatriyas and vaishyas, the first three of the four varnas. Phule however restricts its use to brahmans. The account and criticism of the avataras of Lord Vishnu, which Phule begins here, continues till Part V. [—*Ed.*]

[15] 'The dvijas have come.'—*Ed.*

of the place he had won nor did he budge from there till his death.

Part IV

About Varaha and Hiranyaksha

DHONDIBA: Who became the chief of the dvijas after Kachcha died?

JOTIRAO: Varaha.

DHONDIBA: The historians such as the writers of the *Bhagawata* have written that Varaha was born of a boar. What is your opinion about this?

JOTIRAO: Actually, a little thinking would immediately reveal to us that man and pig are quite different from each other. But to convince you fully about this, let me give you just one example: think how the human female and the female pig behave towards their offspring after their birth. See, the human female, after giving birth to her baby, immediately starts looking after him, protecting him from any possible harm; but the female pig, the sow, devours her first born pup like a bitch and then delivers the other pups. This goes on to prove that the sow or the pig mother who gave birth to Varaha had gobbled up her first piglet which was of the pig species and only then did she give birth to this pig-human. But according to the writers of the *Bhagawata*, Varaha was the incarnation of the omnipotent, Primordial God himself, that is, Adinarayana. Now doesn't this form a blot on his divine knowledge, all-seeing vision and sense of justice and fair play? Shouldn't he have taken care and prevented his pig mother from devouring her first born, that is, his elder brother? How sad that the God himself should make such a grave mistake! This sow, the mother of Varaha, was called Padma. And she committed the crime of infanticide! Yes, killing your own child, of whatever species, amounts to infanticide. But she not only killed her own baby but actually devoured it! No dictionary yields a word which brings out the horror of this deed. Could we call her a ghoul? – but there is a proverb which says that even ghouls do not eat their own offspring. Moreover, there is no evidence available to prove that she took some punishment as atonement for her horrible sin and to save her from the tortures of hell. I really feel very sorry for this.

DHONDIBA: If Varaha's pig-mother was called 'Padma', doesn't it mean that her husband also had some name?

JOTIRAO: Oh yes, her husband indeed had a name – Brahma!

DHONDIBA: So this means that the animals of ancient times gave themselves names, like Brahma, Narada and Manu! But how did these fibbing historians come to know of them? Secondly, the sow, Padma, undoubtedly must have suckled Varaha; but how did she initiate him into the habit of roaming through the lanes of the village in the company of her husband Brahma and teach him how to graze on delicate shoots and foliage? Probably only the Primordial God, the Adinarayana himself, may be able to explain these things! In short, their books do not yield any evidence about any such things. And since there is no evidence, I suspect that all such writing, that Varaha was born of a sow, etc., is nothing but a pack of lies. Wasn't the writer ashamed of himself while writing such things?

JOTIRAO: Bravo! But what about you? You people drink the water with which they and their children wash their feet as holy! So who is more shameless? You or they?

DHONDIBA: All right, all right! But how do you think he came to be called Varaha?

JOTIRAO: Probably because his nature and behaviour was disgusting like a pig's! Wherever he went he wrought havoc. He charged like a pig anywhere and snatched victory. Probably that ridiculous name 'Varaha' was given to him by the kshatriyas, residing in regions of such valiant warriors as Hiranyaksha and Hiranyakashyapu, as a mark of their disrespect for him. And that must have infuriated him. And to take revenge on them, he must have repeatedly launched attacks on their territories, and harassed the residents there. Finally, he killed Hiranyaksha in one such battle. This struck fear in the hearts of all kshatriya chieftains all over the earth (Hindustan) and they were disoriented for quite some time. But then one day, Varaha breathed his last and died.

Part V

About Narasimha, Hiranyakashyapu, Prahlad, *vipra*

DHONDIBA: Who became the chief of the dvijas after Varaha?

JOTIRAO: Nrusimha.

DHONDIBA: How was Nrusimha by nature?

JOTIRAO: Nrusimha was a very greedy, cunning, deceitful, treacherous, scheming, brutal and ruthless man, with a well-built and formidable physique.

DHONDIBA: What did he do?

JOTIRAO: First he started plotting Hiranyakashyapu's assassination. He knew well that he couldn't capture Hiranyakashyapu's kingdom without killing him. To achieve this devious aim, he made his plan carefully, and used one of his dvija teachers as his instrument. This teacher impressed the principles of his religion on the impressionable mind of the young Prahlad, son of Hiranyakashyapu, who then refused to worship their family deity Harhar. Hiranyakashyapu tried hard to persuade Prahlad to worship their god Harhar. But all his attempts proved to be futile since Nrusimha was helping Prahlad from inside. Finally, Nrusimha corrupted Prahlad's mind so much with his lies that he finally consented to even kill his father. But he couldn't muster up enough courage to carry out this heinous task. Therefore Nrusimha sought an opportune time and painted himself as a lion, as the Muslims who paint themselves as tigers in their festival of Muharram, fixed some ferocious-looking fangs inside his mouth, arranged a false mane around his face and made himself up as a lion. Then he draped a fine brocaded sari around his body and pulled the pallu of the sari over his head to hide his visage. Then, moving like a woman of a respectable family, he furtively entered Hiranyakashyapu's palace with the help of Prahlad, stole into his bedchamber and hid himself behind one of the many pillars adorning the room. When Hiranyakashyapu returned to his bed-chamber in the evening, tired after a heavy day's administrative work, and lay down on his bed to rest, Nrusimha quickly removed the pallu from around his head and wrapped it around his waist. Then he emerged from his hiding place and jumped on the prostrate form of the unsuspecting Hiranyakashyapu and thrusting the tiger claws he had fitted on to his fingers into his stomach, tore his body apart. Having accomplished this ghastly deed, Nrusimha swiftly travelled back to his own region along with all the dvijas there. When the kshatriyas realized how Nrusimha had accomplished the ghastly deed by tricking Prahlad, they discarded the name dvija which they had used for the Aryans and started calling them *vipriya*. The name *vipra* used for the brahmans later on is probably a corrupt form of this original word. Later on, the kshatriyas started calling Nrusimha as Naarsimha,[16] an obviously insulting name! Several of Hiranyakashyapu's sons tried hard to capture and punish him for a long time but it was of no use. Naarsimha also lost his hope of ever conquering Hiranyakashyapu's kingdom. Without causing any more trouble, he stayed put in his own place, protecting himself and his kingdom till his death.

DHONDIBA: This goes on to prove that the *vipra* historians were worried that later on, his name and reputation might be tarnished by people because of his heinous crime; and therefore, they concocted several falsehoods – that he was born of a pillar etc. and included those in their so-called historical accounts.

JOTIRAO: Yes, undoubtedly so. Because if we accept that he was really born of a pillar, then who cut his umbilical cord, who gave him cotton dipped in milk to suck on, to save him from a premature death? And how did he grow up without a wet nurse suckling him or without somebody feeding him milk? We cannot accept this fiction as true, because it is contrary to the laws of nature. These fibbing historians not only brought him out of a pillar fully grown, but they also sprouted a thick beard and moustaches on his face and made him a man of such colossal strength that immediately after his birth, he pulled Hiranyakashyapu onto his lap and rent his stomach apart with his savage nails! Alas, that the incarnation of the omnipotent God should thus punish a kind father, who was trying to persuade his erring son

[16] The word used is *bayako*, literally wife. Phule feminizes Narasimha, man-lion, as Naarsimha, female lion. [—*Ed.*]

towards his faith out of real love for him, with nothing less than capital punishment! Why, even the incarnation of an ignorant commoner would not inflict punishment in such a manner! On the contrary, being the incarnation of the Adinarayana, he should have convinced Hiranyakashyapu about who he really was, when he appeared before him; and then he should have reconciled Hiranyakashyapu with his son. But instead of doing any such thing, he simply assassinated him! Isn't this shocking? Now if he was unable to convince Hiranyakashyapu about his being the incarnation of God, how can we call him the giver of intellect to all? It only goes on to show that this Narasimha didn't possess even so much intellect as a certain dung-loving, base prostitute who lives right here in our city, Pune. You know how she has caught one 'scholar', who calls himself a Bruhaspati, in the snare of her sweet words and virtually turned him into her slave. Isn't it amazing that today several American and European missionaries are converting young Indian men to Christianity but not one of them has killed his father!

DHONDIBA: When Narasimha was thus made ridiculous, did the *vipras* attempt in any way to win Prahlad's kingdom?

JOTIRAO: The *vipras* made several secret attempts to win his kingdom but they came to naught because Prahlad had now realized how the *vipras* had tricked him and he had become wise to their real intention. He did not believe them a bit any more but he maintained good relations with everyone on the surface and looked after his kingdom well. After his death, his son Virochana strengthened it further and when he breathed his last, his son Bali came to the throne. He turned out to be a very courageous and brave soldier. First he rescued several small chieftains from the harassment of the various trouble mongers and brought them under his rule. Then he started expanding the frontiers of his kingdom. At that time, Vamana was the chief leader of the *vipras*. He was a greedy, reckless and obstinate man; he did not at all like the growing power of Bali. So in order to win his kingdom, he secretly collected a big army and approached the borders of Bali's kingdom.

Part VI

About King Bali, Jotiba, marathas, Khandoba, Mahasubha, Nau Khandancha Nyayi, Bhairoba, *sat ashrayit*, *tali bharane*, Holy Sunday, Vamana, *paksha ghalane*, *vindhavali*, *ghat basavine*, custom of sati, *aradhis*, *shilanganas*, Bali of rice grains, prophesy of Bali's second coming, Banasura, *kujagiri*, death of Vamana, *upadhye*, Holi, custom of Veer, Bali Pratipada, Bhaubeej, etc.[17]

DHONDIBA: What did Bali do then?

JOTIRAO: Bali immediately dispatched messengers on camels to all noblemen and all the chieftains under his protection, with a strict admonition to immediately proceed to the frontiers with their troops to help him.

DHONDIBA: How big was Bali's kingdom?

JOTIRAO: It was spread far and wide; we may presume that there were several areas under his control in various parts of the country. Besides, he also controlled several islands near the Simhaldweep; because even today there exists an island called Bali. His kingdom included the Konkan region to the south of Kolhapur as well as some parts of the Mawal region. Jotiba was the chieftain there. He used to reside on a mountain called Ratnagiri to the north of Maharashtra. Another region in the south in his kingdom was called Maharashtra. Maratha is probably a corrupt form of this original word. As Maharashtra was a huge region, it was divided into nine divisions (khandas) by Bali. Each division was assigned to an officer called Khandoba. There used to be two assistants under him according to his status. They were called Mallukhan. The Khandoba of Jejuri was one such officer. He used to quell the rebellions of the various wrestlers in the courts of the neighbouring chieftains and bring

[17] *Nau Khandancha Nyayi*: the just of the nine divisions; *sat ashrayit*: the seven protected ones; *tali bharane*: slavish agreement with someone; *paksha ghalane*: observing the rituals after death; *ghat basavine*: the holy earthen pots; *aradhis*: worshippers; *shilanganas*: ritual crossing of frontiers; *kujagiri*: full moon night in the month of Ashwin. [—*Ed.*]

them to their senses. That is why he was also called Malla Ari.[18] Malhari, the name by which he is worshipped today is probably a corrupt form of this word. He was famous for his just warfare. He never attacked any warrior who was running away from the battlefield, from behind. That is why he was also called Martonda.[19] Martanda is the corrupt form of this word.[20] He was also a champion of the downtrodden. He was also a connoisseur of music. He created a raga called Malhar which is famous even today. A famous Muslim singer, Miyan, composed another raga called Miyan Malhar on the pattern of this original Malhar. Bali had also appointed two officers for the task of collecting revenue and dispensing justice, called Mahasubha and Nau Khandancha Nyayi. They used to have several junior officers to assist them. The term Mahasubha seems to have changed to Mhasoba in course of time and that is how we use it today. His job was to assess the agricultural produce of the farmers and charge revenue or grant concessions accordingly. Even today, each maratha family installs a stone in the name of this Mahasubha in some corner of their farm, paints it vermilion, and does not start any work in the field: like sowing, weeding and reaping corn, without burning incense before it and worshipping it. The Muslims also seem to have followed the same procedure of collecting revenue and they probably picked it from Bali, as in those days not only Muslims but even scholars from Egypt came to his kingdom to study. Thirdly, there were some areas near Ayodhya in the Kashi region under Bali's control which was called the tenth division. The chief officer there was called Kalbhairi[21] and he also seems to have been the Kotwal of Kashi for some time. He was so skilled in music that he had composed a new raga called Bhairava. It was so difficult to sing that even famous singers like Tansen thought twice before venturing to

18 The enemy of the wrestlers. [—*Ed.*]

19 The one who attacks only the front, that is the face, '*tonda*'. [—*Ed.*]

20 While Phule's method of deriving Sanskrit words from Prakrit (Marathi) is interesting and probably questionable, it may be mentioned in passing that Martanda is the name of the Sun and as such may have referred to the glory or the *tejas* of Malhari. [—Ed.]

21 Kalbhairava. [—*Ed.*]

sing it. Kalbhairi also created a new musical instrument called daur so intricate in design that even instruments like the tabla and mridanga cannot compete with it in the production of melodious notes. But it did not achieve the fame it deserved as it remained largely ignored. His servant was called Bhairewadi, today known as Bharadi, a corrupt form of the original name. We can see from this account that Bali's kingdom had spread far and wide and was even bigger than that of Ajapal or Dashrath. That is why all the chieftains around used to adopt his policies. Seven among them paid him taxes and accepted being his protégées. That is why Bali was also called the Protector of the Seven. In short then, Bali's kingdom seems to have spread far and wide. There is an old proverb – 'Bali will box your ears'. Whenever Bali had to assign some important task to one of his noblemen, he used to hold court and place some betel leaves in a tray along with a coconut and some turmeric. Then he used to announce that the betel leaves could be picked up only by that nobleman who had the guts to complete that task. Then the nobleman who did have the grit would come forward and, chanting the war cry 'Harhar[22] Mahaveer', pick up the betel leaves with the coconut; then bowing, he would apply the turmeric on his forehead and raising the contents of the tray respectfully to his head, he would collect all the contents of the tray in his pallu. Then Bali would assign the task to that particular nobleman who would decamp his army, and proceed to vanquish the enemy. That is why this ritual was probably called as 'picking up the *tali*'. Of all the great warriors of Bali, however, Bhairoba and Jotiba, along with the nine Khandobas, used to do their utmost to keep their subjects happy. That is why the marathas have always practised this ritual of 'picking up the *tali*' before any auspicious ceremony. They began to consider Bahiroba, Jotiba and Khandoba as gods and include them in the ancient ritual of picking up the tray. They chant 'Harhar Mahadev' and '*Jotibacha chang bhala*', 'Hail

[22] It is logical to assume that the English 'Hurrah! Hurrah!' is a corruption of Harhar. This cry inevitably accompanies the call to arms in the West. The standard expression was 'Hurrah boys! Loose the saddle or win the horse!' [—*J.P.*] [Phule's footnote is in Marathi. The quote is in English. [—*Ed.*]]

the rise of Sadananda' and 'Hail Mallukhan the Proud'. Since Baliraja considered Sunday as the holy day of Lord Shiva, today's marathas, that is the mang, mahar, kunbi, mali and others do not consume any food or even a drop of water unless they have worshipped that family deity every Sunday; first they bathe the idol and then whatever food happens to be in the house serves as the holy offering.

DHONDIBA: What did Vamana do when he came to the frontiers of Bali's kingdom?

JOTIRAO: Vamana charged into Bali's kingdom with all his force and harassing the subjects on his way, arrived near Bali's capital. Bali had no alternative but to fight the intruder even though his armies from various parts of his kingdom had failed to arrive. This was how he fought – Bali began the battle on the first day of the dark fortnight in the month of Bhadrapada, and went on till the fifteenth day of the fortnight. He used to start at daybreak and return to his palace in the evening to rest. That is why it was easy to remember the dates on which various people from both sides died fighting during this fortnight. That is the reason, probably, of the custom of observing a Paksha or Pitrupaksha[23] in the first fortnight of Bhadrapada[24] came into being. Then Bali was so engrossed for the next fifteen days, that is, from the first to the eighth day of the bright fortnight in the month of Ashwin, that he forgot everything and didn't even come back to his palace for rest. Now Bali's queen Vindhyawati got her servants, called the khojas and aradhis, to dig a deep pit and place some firewood at the bottom of that pit. Then she put an earthen pot filled with water nearby and kept vigil near the pit for eight days and eight nights without consuming any water or food, continuously praying to Lord Harhar Mahaveera to ward off the calamity in the form of Vamana. But on the evening of the eighth day, when the news of Bali's death in the battle reached her, she lighted the wood in the pit, jumped into the burning pyre and embraced death. Her maids and servants, that is, the khojas and the aradhis, wrung their hands, beat their breasts

[23] A fortnight of long rituals dedicated to dead ancestors. [—*Ed.*]

[24] The fourth month of the lunar calendar; a monsoon month. [—*Ed.*]

and wailed loudly. They tore off their clothes and threw them into the pyre. They remembered her virtue and ran around the pit, all the time lamenting and wailing loudly, 'O kind queen, the fame of your virtue rings in the world far and wide.' Now to make people forget this terrible event, the unkind *vipra* writers sought to change the pit into a holy fire – 'homa' – and made several other similar changes. After Bali was killed, Banasura valiantly fought Vamana for one day but then had to desperately take to his heels on the next day, that is the ninth day of the bright fortnight of Ashwin. His army also deserted along with him. This success made Vamana so wanton that he just charged into Bali's capital and upon seeing that there were no men to protect it, he plundered all the angans in the city on the morning of the tenth day of Ashwin. The Marathi expression 'gold of the shilangana' is a corrupt form of this expression of looting of the angans. Then he immediately departed for his home. When he reached his house, his wife kept an idol of Bali made from flour on the threshold and jokingly said to him, 'Lo and behold; here is Bali come again to fight you.' So Vamana kicked the flour Bali first and then entered the house. Since that day, the brahman families have had this custom on the day of the Dasara festival,[25] whereby their womenfolk make an image of Bali from flour or rice grains and keep it outside of the threshold and the brahman man first places his left foot on the left side of the image and then pricks his stomach with the twig of the Apta tree and then putting his foot over the image, enters the house. When Banasura's men reached their houses on the tenth night of Ashwin, their women also made Bali and prophesized that Bali will come and establish the kingdom of God on earth again. They stood on their thresholds with lighted lamps in trays which they moved round the faces of their menfolk as a ritual of welcoming them and said 'May the calamities, that is the rights of the dvijas, disappear and may the kingdom of Bali descend soon'. From that day onwards, it has become a custom in the kshatriya families to perform this ritual on the tenth day of Ashwin, that is Dasara day, whereby the womenfolk perform

[25] Dasara is the Marathi word for Vijayadashami, the tenth day. [—*Ed.*]

the ritual of waving earthen lamps around their husbands' faces and wish for the Kingdom of Bali to descend again. Just imagine how excellent the coming Baliraja will be! Oh what a great king! What they did! Their great loyalty! Compare them to these Hindus today! One day they wax eloquent on the occasion of the Queen's birthday at a public meeting in order to curry favours from the British and the very next day, they display exactly the opposite behaviour in newspapers or in their personal talk.

DHONDIBA: All right, but tell me, what happened to those noblemen Bali had summoned? Didn't they at all turn up to lend him a hand?

JOTIRAO: They did come, but they were late. They reached the battlefield with their respective forces and joined Banasura on the fourteenth day of the bright fortnight of Ashwin. On getting this news all the *vipras* in Bali's kingdom took to their heels and went to Vamana. Vamana was so terrified by this news that he collected all the *vipras* together and in order to find some way of saving their lives from Banasura, he kept an all-night vigil in front of his family deity praying for some means of deliverance. Then he proceeded to the border of his kingdom along with his wife and children and his troops, and waited there for Banasura to arrive.

DHONDIBA: What did Banasura do then?

JOTIRAO: Banasura launched a ferocious attack on Vamana, vanquished him and looted all his wealth. Then he harried his soldiers and drove Vamana and his soldiers away from his region to the Himalayas. Then he laid siege to the foothill and cut off their food supply as a result of which Vamana's people started dying of starvation. Finally even Vamana succumbed to death and that was the end of his career. Banasura's followers rejoiced at this news and said that Vamana was indeed one of the greatest afflictions among the *vipras* and his death had finally ended their troubles. So, one may presume that from this time onwards, the *vipras* came to be called *upadhye*, from *upadhi*, meaning affliction.[26] Later on those upadhyas collected all their dead and

[26] This is yet another example of Phulean etymology. *Upadhye* is actually derived from *upadhyaya*, Sanskrit for priest, master of (religious) rituals or

lit a common funeral pyre (which is called Holi today) to burn the corpses. The custom of burning the dead on funeral pyres thus has existed among the *vipras* from ancient times. Similarly, all the kshatriyas, including Banasura, collected the bodies of their dead warriors and on the first day of the dark fortnight of the month of Phalgun, they dressed up as Veers and brandishing naked swords above their heads, they danced to celebrate the heroic deeds of their warriors. Thus the custom of burying the dead is found in the kshatriyas from ancient times. Finally, Banasura left some of his own people for the protection of the remaining upadhyas and returned to his capital, accompanied by his noblemen and held great celebrations for their victory. It is difficult for me to describe them due to constraints of space and time. So I will just narrate them briefly. He counted all his wealth and worshipped it on the thirteenth day of the dark fortnight of the month of Ashwin and then over the next two days, that is on the fourteenth and fifteenth day, which was a moonless night, he gave a great banquet to all his noblemen and indulged in various festivities. Then on the first day of the bright fortnight of Kartika,[27] he bestowed various gifts on his noblemen according to their status and ordered them to resume their duties in their respective regions. This made all the women from all age groups so happy that they cooked festive food for their brothers, fed them to their heart's content and then waved the auspicious earthen lamps around their faces on the second day of the bright fortnight of Kartika and reminded them of the prophecy of the coming of Bali by saying, 'May all evil disappear from here and may Bali's kingdom descend!' From then on, all kshatriya women remind their brothers of this prophecy of Bali's coming and bless them on the Bhaubeej day in the Diwali festival. But of course there is no such custom found in the families of the upadhyas.

DHONDIBA: Oh, so then the Adinarayana took the avatar of Vamana to banish Bali to the nether world! Vamana disguised himself

....

ceremonies. By relating this word to *upadhi*, Phule is attacking the institution of priesthood, rather than establishing etymology. [—*Ed.*]

[27] The tenth month of the lunar calendar. [—*Ed.*]

as a beggar and tricked Bali. He asked Bali for that portion of the earth which he could cover in only three steps. Bali granted him his wish. Then Vamana discarded his disguise and became a man of such monstrous proportions that he covered the whole of the earth and the sky in only two steps and then asked Bali, 'Now where should I keep my third step?' Baliraja, generous to the last degree, answered, 'Keep it on my head.' Then Vamana put his foot on Bali's head and pushed him into the nether world and got his promise fulfilled. This is what the upadhyas have written in books like the *Bhagawata*. But your arguments seem to prove that all of it is false. What do you have to say about this?

JOTIRAO: Now apply your mind to this problem. Consider this – if that monster finished the whole of the earth and the sky in his two steps, how many villages must have been crushed under his foot! If he really put his second step in the sky, consider how crowded the sky must have been, and how many stars must have collided with one another and been ground to dust. Thirdly, if that monster really finished the whole of the earth and the sky in just two steps, where did his torso go? A man can raise his foot upto the height of his navel in the sky. That must have left the sky free from his waist to his head. Now he could have easily put his third step in that space, or put it on his own head and got his agreement fulfilled. Yet he put his foot on Bali's head instead and pushed him down into the nether world. Isn't this treachery? What have you to say about this?

DHONDIBA: Why, that monster claimed to be the incarnation of the Primordial God, didn't he? Then how could he openly trick Bali like this? All those fibbing historians must be denounced for calling such a scoundrel the incarnation of God Himself! Their own writing is witness to the fact that Vamana was nothing but a scheming, treacherous, ungrateful, rascal because he pushed his benefactor into the nether world by deceit.

JOTIRAO: Fourthly, when that monster's head touched the sky and crossed high over the heavens, he must have needed to shout very loudly to ask where he should put his third step as he had covered the entire earth and sky in his two steps; because Bali on earth and the monster's head in heaven must have been separated by innumerable miles. Then how come none of the Russian, French, English and Americans ever heard even a word of his speech? Similarly, Bali was on the earth; so if he did ask Vamana to put the third foot on his head, how did the monster manage to hear that? Bali had surely not turned into a monstrous creature like him! And the fifth point is that it is indeed amazing how the earth did not sink under his weight.

DHONDIBA: Then how else could we have seen these days? I wonder what the monster ate to survive. And when he died, where did they get four men to carry his gigantic corpse to the cremation ground? If we believe that they burned him at the very place he had died, from where did they obtain cow dung cakes[28] or wood sufficient to burn him? And if we accept that they didn't burn him off, what happened to the body? Did the foxes and dogs feast on it for days? In short, then, we can say that if all these doubts are not resolved by the books like the *Bhagawata*, then the upadhyas must have based their so-called historical works on some folktales.

JOTIRAO: My dear, try reading the *Bhagawata* once. I assure you, you will prefer Aesop's Fables!

Part VII

About Brahma, the custom of writing on parchments, magic incantations, origin of Sanskrit, ban on crossing the river Atak, the non-vegetarianism among brahmans, their eating horses etc., the visit, rakshasas, yadnya, Banasura's death, pariwari, the cotton thread, the sacred incantation, mahar, shudra, kulkarni, kulambi, kunbi women, Manu, *bhat-pantoji*[29] teachers, terrible consequences, Prajapati's death, brahmans, etc.

DHONDIBA: Who became the chief of the upadhyas after Vamana's death?

JOTIRAO: There was hardly any time to search for a person from a highly distinguished family and appoint him as the chief. So

[28] Dried cow dung cakes are used as fuel in rural areas to this day. [—*Ed.*]

[29] *Bhat* and *pantoji* are both pejorative terms for brahmans. [—*Ed.*]

a clever clerk called Brahma took the reins of administration in his hands. He was a very cunning person, a turncoat, who could always adapt himself to any situation and achieve his own selfish ends. He was extremely untrustworthy; that is probably why he was called Brahma of the four mouths. In short, he was a man who was exceedingly alert, obstinate, shrewd, audacious and ruthless.

DHONDIBA: What did Brahma do first?

JOTIRAO: He invented the use of nails to engrave letters on parchments. He knew quite a lot of Iranian magic incantations and some silly fictitious tales and he also invented some tales of his own. He composed small poems, like the Persian *bayat*, incorporating the gist of this material in them, in the language Sarvakrit which was used then by all. The name Sanskrit is a form derived from this original word. His fame spread far and wide. The customary belief that the art of magic and fiction originated from the mouth of Brahma seems to have originated from these times. Later, the upadhyas started to die of starvation and they secretly began to escape to Iran. To prevent their escape, Brahma passed an order that nobody was to cross the sea or the river Atak and go beyond.

DHONDIBA: But what did they survive on? What did they eat?

JOTIRAO: They ate anything that they could lay their hands on: fruits, leaves of trees, roots, birds, beasts of the forest; sometimes they had to kill their own horses whose flesh they roasted and ate to survive. That is why their rakshaks (protectors) began to call them bhrashta (corrupted). Later on, the word rakshak became rakshasa and bhrashta became *bhata*. Later still, the *bhats* were ashamed of themselves for having killed and eaten flesh of birds and animals in the difficult times and they attempted to prohibit the custom of non-vegetarianism. But several of them had tasted flesh and liked it. They found it very difficult to give up this habit. So they cunningly established the custom of sacrificing animals and consuming their flesh and calling such occasions by lofty names, like Pashu Yadnya or Ashwamedha, to lend them an aura of respectability. Then they incorporated these rituals in their books.

DHONDIBA: What did Brahma do later on?

JOTIRAO: Later on, when Bali's son Banasura died, there was anarchy everywhere. Everybody behaved as if he were the king of his little empire and indulged in pleasure seeking activities. Seeking this opportunity, Brahma gathered the rapacious crowd of the *bhats* (their parivar, which is pronounced as parivari now as a corrupt form), and attacked the rakshasas (that is, the rakshaks) in the middle of the night suddenly and vanquished them. Then he thought about the future security of the *bhats*. 'Suppose some calamity befalls us,' he thought, 'and we are all scattered and vanquished! There has to be some means by which we can identify and recognize our people and come together.' So he gave each person of the clan a white thread, signifying their caste, which is called as Brahmasutra today, and taught each of them a caste-signifying incantation called Gayatri and made them recite it by heart. He also prohibited them from disclosing this incantation to the kshatriyas. The *bhats* could easily identify their own people with the help of these two signs.

DHONDIBA: What did Brahma do then?

JOTIRAO: Then Brahma took his *bhats* and invaded the kingdom of Banasura and having defeated most of the big and small noblemen there, he won their territories. Then except for the maha-ari people, called mahar today (a corrupt form of the original maha-ari), among the kshatriyas who were putting up a stiff resistance, he captured the others and made them his slaves. Intoxicated with power, he called them *kshudra*,[30] the corrupt form of which is shudra today. Several among them were distributed amongst his own people to work as servants in their houses. And the rest were dispatched to different villages to work as menial labourers in the fields with a *bhat* officer for each village who was appointed to maintain a register of their kulas[31] and provide them with a little food, just enough for them to survive. That is why the officer was called Kulekarni (one who keeps an account of the Kulas). Kulkarni is a corrupted form of this original word. Similarly, the families who worked as menial

[30] The insignificant, ignoble ones. [—*Ed.*]

[31] Kulas: families. [—*Ed.*]

farm labour were called *kulavadi*, the corrupted form of which is *kulambi* or kunbi. Their womenfolk had to go to the houses of the *bhats* as and when the work in the fields was inadequate and they had to work there also. That is why, there is no difference of meaning between the words kunbin and dasi. Later on, drunk with power, the *bhats* became more and more arrogant and insolent and began to consider the shudras as very inferior and ignoble. A full account of their present behaviour will require far more space and that itself would result in an independent book so I will not go into all the details of that; I'll restrict myself only to a brief enumeration of the main points. They are as follows:

Some of the *bhats*, today (though they might be as illiterate as the mahars and mang sweepers), are faced with the prospect of starving to death. To save themselves somehow from that fate, they do not hesitate to deceive the poor ignorant shudras right and left. They have no morality, no sense of good and evil remaining. They go to any length to dupe the shudras. When all else fails, they go from door to door in the shudra locality, chanting some meaningless rabble in the name of religion, and begging for alms and manage to survive somehow. But they never earned a decent livelihood by working. They are ashamed to work in the fields of the shudras. They can't be their servants; they will never tend their cattle; they will never collect the manure and carry it to the dung pit; they will never plough, weed, sow in the fields; they will never carry baskets of manure on their heads and spread it around the plants in the orchards; they will never cut the hay and heap it on the haystack, draw water from the wells to irrigate crops, guard farms at night with sticks in their hands, reap corn from the fields, chafe it and fill it in sacks, carry the sacks to the shudra homes for safe storage, and carry baskets of vegetables on their heads. They are ashamed to do any of these. They are ashamed to work in a shudra house, to brush their horses, to run ahead of them on the way, to carry the shoes of the shudras in their hands, to sweep and clean their houses, to clean their used pots and pans, to clean and light their lamps, to carry baskets of mud and soil to their construction sites, and to work as menial labour for them. Similarly, the *bhatnis* (the *bhat* women) are ashamed of working as maids of the shudra women, of rubbing scented oil in their hair, of bathing them, of combing their hair, of sweeping and cleaning their houses, of making their beds, of pressing their feet, of washing their saris, and carrying their shoes.

What about the *bhats* then! The maha-aris started attacking the *bhats* in order to rescue their brethren from their clutches. As a result, the *bhats* started hating the shudras so much that they wouldn't eat the food cooked by them. Why, they wouldn't even drink the water touched by them! They began the custom of *sowale*[32] to avoid the touch of the shudras. Later on, some of the shudra-hating *bhat* writers became so shameless that flinging all decency to the winds, they increased the importance of their sacred *sowale* so much that they even went to the length of declaring that if a shudra touched a *bhat* in *sowale*, he became polluted. They have written several religious books spreading this belief. They prohibited shudras from receiving any education so as to make them forget their past. They were scared that if the shudras remembered their superiority in the past, they would trample them under their feet. They weren't satisfied by this; they even went on to forbid the shudras from listening to even a word of anyone reading a religious book. Several examples to this effect can be found in the *Manusamhita*. So the *bhats* of today refuse to read a religious text in front of the shudras. Now some of the mercenary *bhat* teachers are unable to declare that they won't teach the shudras for fear of displeasing the Christian British government; yet they can't bring themselves to expose to the shudras all the frauds of their ancestors; they are afraid that once the shudras wisen to their trickery, their importance will considerably diminish. Therefore, instead of teaching the shudras some basic practical knowledge, they fill up their minds with a lot of rubbish about the fake principles of patriotism and turn them into devotees of the English state. And finally, they would influence their young minds with lies about how an ignorant, devout, shudra king like Shivaji freed our country

[32] A brahmanical code which lays down the domains of purity and pollution. *Sowale* is the domain of purity and *owale* is the domain of pollution. [—*Ed.*]

from the Muslims and how he protected and revered cows and brahmans. Thus they turn out students who possess nothing but a hollow pride in their religion; as a result, hardly any students from amongst the shudras come out as real scholars who can shoulder the various 132 responsibilities and positions in society. Almost all government departments are so crowded with *bhats* who oppress the shudras so much that the stories of their black deeds will certainly put the oppressive British indigo plantation owners in Calcutta to shame. Today it is the *bhats* again who rule though under the name of the British. They are not only harming the interests of the shudras but also of the British themselves; and nobody can say that they won't do so in future as well. Not that the 'sensible' British government is not aware of this fact! Yet they deliberately turn a blind eye towards them and function in accordance with their interests. This will have disastrous effects in the end. In short, then, we may say that Brahma was so intoxicated with his victory after having turned the original inhabitants of this region into slaves, that the maha-aris jestingly called him Prajapati. After his death, however, the name of the Aryas, *bhat*, was forgotten and they began to be called brahman after Brahma.

Part VIII

About Parashuram, matricide, twenty-one campaigns, Khanderao seeks refuge with Ravana, Just of the Nine Divisions, Seven Water Maidens, black thread around custom of burying alive mahar in foundations of buildings, prohibition of widow remarriage among the brahmans, killing kshatriya infants, Parashuram committed suicide after his defeat, a challenge to Parashuram the Eternal.

DHONDIBA: Who became the ruler of the brahmans after Prajapati?
JOTIRAO: Parashuram.
DHONDIBA: How was he by nature?
JOTIRAO: Parashuram was a bully; he was an audacious, vicious and barbarous villain. He did not hesitate to behead his own mother Renuka. He was burly and was a skilled archer.

DHONDIBA: What happened during his regime?

JOTIRAO: After Prajapati's death, the remaining maha-aris who had not been captured by the brahmans fought with the brahmans twenty-one times to rescue their brethren from the slavery of the brahmans with such force, that they came to be called *dvaitis*. The word daitya is a corrupted form of this original word. Finally when Parashuram had completely vanquished them, some of the great warriors, extremely frustrated by the annihilation, escaped to the domains of their friends to spend their remaining days. For example, the Khanderao of Jejuri sought asylum with Ravana, the Just of the Nine Divisions and the Seven Protected Ones, all escaped to Tal Konkan[33] and spent their remaining days there in hiding. So the brahmans pejoratively gave them female names; they called the Just of Nine Divisions as Janai of the Nine Khanas (a small section) and the Seven Protected Ones as Seven Water Maidens. All the other maha-aris whom Parashuram had conquered and captured, were compelled to swear that they would never fight the brahmans again and made to tie black threads round their necks as a mark of their humiliation.[34] Then he prohibited their shudra brethren from even touching them. Then he began the custom of calling those great maha-ari kshatriyas by such insulting names as atishudra, mahar, antyaj, mang and chandal and of oppressing them to such an extent that it would be difficult to find a more horrifying example of such behaviour in the whole world. For example, that ruthless villain, in order to take revenge on the poor kshatriyas, established the custom of burying mang people with their wives alive in the foundations of the buildings of the brahmans; he used to pour oil and vermilion down their throats so as to stifle their cries of pain. This horrifying custom gradually died out with the advent of the Muslims in India. Quite a few of Parashuram's people had also died fighting the maha-aris. The brahman widows far outnumbered the brahman men. And it became a problem to

33 The lowlands of the (Konkan) coast of Maharashtra. [—*Ed.*]

34 Some other people also have to wear such humiliating signs: the bharadis have to wear *pungis* [*Pungi* literally means a musical pipe. The precise denotation here is unclear. [—*Ed.*]] and *vaghyas*, a black thread. [—*J.P.*]

take care of them. Finally widow remarriage was completely stopped and this straightened things out a little. But Parashuram was so incensed with the massacre of brahmans, his own people, that he wanted to root out each and every single kshatriya. So he took up a stormy campaign to capture every single pregnant kshatriya woman, widowed in the war and desperately trying to hide herself from him. Some children, however, miraculously survived this genocide and their descendents can be found in communities like the parabhu today. Similarly, there must have been people like ramoshi, jingar, tumbadiwale, kumbhar[35] in the mayhem because they have similar customs and traditions like the shudras. In short, then, he killed every individual who belonged to the family of Hiranyaksha, from his son Bali[36] onwards, and removed them from the face of the earth. This had the effect of firmly entrenching in the minds of all the shudra chieftains the belief that the brahmans were expert in black magic and they were mortally afraid of their magic incantations. However, the number of brahmans also had drastically decreased during this entire foolish endeavour and therefore all the brahmans started cursing Parashuram. Just then, Ramchandra, the son of a kshatriya chieftain, broke Parashuram's bow at King Janak's palace in full court, and Parashuram was so angry that he accosted Ramchandra, who was returning home with his newly won bride Janaki, on his way, challenged him and fought him. But Ramchandra defeated him and this disgraced him so much that, shamefaced, he renounced his kingdom and went to stay in the Tal Konkan region with his family and some followers. There, full of remorse for all his past shameful deeds, he secretly committed suicide without anybody's knowledge. No one knows about the place or time of his suicide even today.

DHONDIBA: All brahmans swear by their holy books and claim that Parashuram was an incarnation of the Adinarayana himself, and that he is immortal; yet you say he committed suicide! How's this?

[35] Jingar: saddle makers; tumbadiwale: apothecaries; kumbhar: potters. [—*Ed.*]

[36] Banasura's daughter Usha was married to Pradyumna, son of Krishna. [—*J.P.*]

JOTIRAO: Two years back, I had written a *powada* on Shivaji in which I had challenged all the brahmans in the very first abhanga[37]; I had said, 'Go. Fetch Parashuram from wherever he is and ask him whether or not the maha-aris, the ancestors of today's mangs and mahars, who had fought Parashuram were kshatriyas or not.' But they did not produce him or his testimony. Had Parashuram really been an incarnation of the Adinarayana, and therefore immortal, the brahmans would have produced him and only convinced me but all the Christians and Muslims in the whole world and would not have hesitated to vanquish the rebellion of the Muslims with the power of their magic incantations.

DHONDIBA: Now I would say, summon Parashuram to appear before you once again. If he is really alive, he will definitely present himself before you. Because however knowledgeable these brahmans may call themselves, Parashuram would have definitely called them corrupt and polluted. If you want evidence of this – these days, some brahmans have ritualistically discarded the habit of eating bitter gourds and secretly taken to devouring carrots of the malis which their shastras forbid them to eat.

JOTIRAO: All right. Let it be so.

To

Immortal Parashuram alias the incarnation of Adinarayana,

O brother Parashuram, according to the brahman books, you are immortal. You never did denounce the custom of eating bitter gourds. You will not have to face the ordeal of creating new

[37] Abhanga: The great warrior son of kshatriya/ Enemy of the Muslims in the Treta Yuga//1// The brave one, fought several battles/ valiantly, for his country//2// The sturdy youth fought Parashuram/ twenty one times, no less//3// Maha-ari, they called the brave one/ The brahman's son trembles at his name//4// After his defeat, brahmans made him untouchable/ started calling him maha-Ari mang//5// Cowards took revenge on their foe/ Vipers, those sons of ungrateful wretches//6// You say he is immortal? Summon him here/ Joti will examine him himself//7//. [Verse written by Phule in the abhanga form. All medieval Bhakti poets used this form. Phule himself wrote many abhangas, which he came to call akhandas. [—*Ed.*]] [—*J.P.*]

brahmans from the corpses of fishermen. Because several of those whom you created out of the corpses have already established themselves as 'Vividh Dnyani'[38] and you will not be required to give them any more knowledge. Just come here and give them the punishment of the Chandrayana Prayashchitta and allow them to perform miracles before the British and the French, with the power of your magic incantations, as you used to do in the past. That is all I want. Don't try to run away now, hiding your face. Present yourself before us within a period of six months; if you do so, then not only me, but people from all over the world will also be convinced that you really are Adinarayana incarnate and will consider you reverently. But if you fail to appear before us, the mahars and mangs here will not hesitate to publicly expose your brahman stooges, who call themselves 'Vividh Dnyani', and who are hiding behind the back of our Mhasoba. Then they will not be able to blow their own trumpet; instead, they will have to beg alms and receive stones from people. And finally, their hunger will drive them to eat the leg of a dog, like Vishwamitra. So appear before me and save the brahmans from this horrible fate.

Waiting to test the veracity of your claims.

Yours faithfully,

Jotirao Govindrao Phule

Date: 1 August 1872

House no 527,

Juna Gunj Peth, Pune

Part IX

Vedic Incantations, power of magic, killing with black magic, being possessed of the Holy Spirit, use of rosary beads, four Vedas, the great confusion of the Brahma, the reign of Narada, new treatises, prohibition on educating the shudras, inconsistencies between the *Bhagawata* and the *Manusamhita*.

DHONDIBA: So! You rubbed their noses into dirt! Now as you say,

[38] Vividh Dnyani: versatile scholars. A dig at the journal *Vividh Dnyana Vistar* run by brahmans, which was very influential in 19th-century Maharashtra. [—*Ed.*]

Parashuram died and dust came to dust! All right. But how do you explain the indelible impression that the brahmans left on the minds of the other kshatriya kings?

JOTIRAO: See, the brahmans in those days used to charge their weapons with their secret magic mantras, and turn them into deadly missiles against their enemies. They used such weapons against Banasura and devastated his subjects, his kingdom and his family. This terrified all the kshatriyas who became mortally scared of the deadly power of the brahman black magic. Let me give you an example. Once a brahman rishi called Bhrugu, kicked Lord Vishnu (according to them the Adinarayana), on his chest. Now, instead of getting angry, the god started massaging Bhrugu's foot, arguing that the kicking must have tired the foot. Now see the cunning! When Lord Vishnu himself could suffer the kick so patiently, why should the shudras complain about the kicks, blows and the murderous assaults of the brahmans? The moral of the story is that the shudras shouldn't utter a word of complaint, even if the very life is beaten out of them.

DHONDIBA: From where do you think these rascals of today have obtained their knowledge of black magic?

JOTIBA: It is difficult to say that these people didn't obtain their knowledge of Bengali black magic of killing and mesmerizing from the Vedas. It is true that the Vedic incantations have undergone a lot of change and are corrupted with time, yet several incantations used by them today are quite similar to the Vedic incantations. For example, they utter a mantra, 'om namo, om namah, om rhim, rhim namha', which is also found in the Vedic mantras. One may surmise from this that the original ancestors of the brahmans must have settled in Bengal after getting into this country. And their magical powers must have spread all over the country from there. That is why it is called the Bengali black art. Not only this. The ancestors of the Aryans, just like the illiterate people of today, made a great show of being 'possessed' by spirits. Their own Vedas provide evidence that they used to consume an alcoholic spirit called somarasa and deceive ignorant folks by claiming that their intoxicated babbling was actually a conversation with the gods. Several

European historians have corroborated this. The cunning brahman *bhats* of today deceive the poor ignorant malis and kunbis with their yapping, i.e., their so called incantations – the magic mantras, – magic bands and other such rituals to earn their livelihood. Yet the poor unfortunate people are unable to expose these dirty tricks as they are too heavily burdened with work. They have to sweat in their fields the whole day to feed their children. On top of everything else, they also have to pay heavy taxes to the government.

DHONDIBA: But then this explodes the brahmans' claim that the four Vedas have sprung from the four mouths of Brahma.

JOTIRAO: Of course it is a blatant lie! How come we find the suktas composed by several brahmarishis and devarishis after Brahma's death in the Vedas, which are supposed to have sprung from the mouths of the Brahma? Similarly, it cannot be said that only one author composed the four Vedas, at one and the same time. Again, several European historians have also argued and proved this conclusively.

DHONDIBA: But when did the brahmans create this supreme confusion?

JOTIRAO: After Brahma's death, the brahmans divided Brahma's writings into three divisions which they called the Vedas. Then several brahmarishis added to these three texts, several stories and myths they knew and also their own concoctions tailored along the lines of these models. Thus they created, after some time, a fourth text, that is, the fourth Veda. In the meantime, Parashuram's destruction of Banasura's kingdom and his subjects struck a terrible fear in the hearts of the kshatriya satraps and they all started believing in the deadly power of the brahmans' magic mantras. The effeminate and eunuch-like Narada exploited this opportunity to the hilt and started paying frequent visits to the royal houses of kshatriyas like Ramchandra and Ravana, Krishna and Kamsa and Kauravas and Pandavas. He used to entertain their wives and children with his stringed instrument, called the veena; he used to sing and dance before them. Making a great show as if he was trying to instruct their minds, he told them innumerable lies, disclosing their secrets to others and poisoning their minds against each other. Naturally, they started fighting with each other. Thus the kshatriyas were weakened and the way of brahmans was cleared. They compiled all their magical incantations, their silly tales together and composed several new books such as the smritis, shastras, puranas, samhitas, etc., out of them. These they forced on the shudras and established their domination over them. They abandoned their traditional warmongering and created a great rigmarole of their religiosity. They did not want the shudras to ever realize how they had been tricked. So they strictly prohibited education of the shudras and made strict rules about this in their books like the *Manusamhita*. Keeping the shudras illiterate also enabled them to make whatever changes in their books they wanted to suit their interests.

DHONDIBA: Was the *Bhagawata*[39] composed during this same period?

JOTIRAO: Had they composed the *Bhagawata* then, it could not have contained the story of Janamejaya, the great grandchild of Arjuna, because he was actually born in a period much later.

DHONDIBA: I think you are quite right. Really, the *Bhagawata* contains such atrocious fictions! The tales of Aesop are a thousand times better! At least they do not contain anything which would corrupt the minds of young children.

JOTIRAO: Similarly it can also be proved that the *Manusamhita* was written much later, after the *Bhagawata*.

DHONDIBA: Really? The *Manusamhita* was composed after the *Bhagawata*? How's that possible?

JOTIRAO: Then think. Manu narrates the story of Vasishtha in the *Manusamhita*, swearing before King Sudaman that he did not commit any murder. This story comes from the *Bhagawata*. Manu narrates it in the eighth adhyaya of the *Manusamhita* in shloka number 110. *Manusamhita* also contains the story of Vishwamitra eating the leg of a dog when he was starving to death in a tough period in his life; this story occurs in the tenth adhyaya of the *Manusamhita*. Several such examples can be quoted from the *Manusamhita*.

[39] See note 13 on p. 70 of the present volume. [—*Ed.*]

Part X

Second Baliraja, the defeat of brahmanical religion, Shankaracharya's cunning, atheism and cruelty, vernacular authors, Work and the Path of Knowledge, Bajirao, hatred of the Muslims, how the Americans and Scottish devastate the brahman stronghold, etc.

DHONDIBA: This is really too much! This fraud is now absolutely clear to me. As you have said in the Introduction of your *powada*[40] on Shivaji, a few brahman authors played great mischief; like a bunch of silly girls cooking up fictitious tales in the inner courtyard of a house.

JOTIRAO: But later on, one great champion of the downtrodden, the holiest of the holy, the great sage and lover of Truth, Baliraja, came into this world. He realized that the great Almighty God, our great Father and Creator, had given us the true and holy knowledge and had granted everyone an equal right to it. He fathomed the Divine Will – that this knowledge be shared by all alike. Therefore he undertook the task of releasing his poor oppressed brethren from the bondage of slavery by wicked, cunning and treacherous hunters like the brahmans and strove to establish the kingdom of God on earth. Thus the prophesy of our ancient women, that one day Bali's kingdom will be established on earth once again, was realized at least to some extent. Millions became the followers of this Baliraja in Europe where he had brought about a tremendous upheaval. All of them began to work ceaselessly for this noble task of establishing God's Kingdom on earth. Ancestors of great scholars like Thomas Paine, became his followers and attained eternal joy. In this country, after there was relative stability, several intelligent Balis exploded the silly games of fraudulent make-believe stories concocted by the brahmans. Rational sages like Shakya Muni[41] rejected all the fraudulent books written by the selfish, presumptuous, licentious and vice-ridden brahmans, who spread superstitious rituals, based on their Vedic incantations

[40] Ballad. [—*Ed.*]

[41] The Buddha. [—*Ed.*]

of black magic, among other people. They hummed and hawed, pretending to be possessed by the Holy Spirit, encouraged the killing of cattle in religious festivals and fairs and enjoyed beef. Shakya Muni brought brahmans, who were lost in the mire of this rigmarole, to their senses and turned them into his followers. But several among the remaining fraudulent brahmans ran away to Karnataka.[42] Now among these people was born a devious and treacherous scholar called Shankaracharya who possessed a twisted and distorted intellect. He could not tolerate the rising fame and popularity of Buddhism and the downfall of brahmanism. He realized that several of his brethren had lost their livelihood and were starving. So he banned the wicked practice of eating beef and consuming alcohol, only two things among the several enjoyed by the brahmans which were denounced by the Buddhists. He also made several alterations in these books and made out as if he was proposing a new atheist[43] philosophy; in point of fact, it is nothing but the same old philosophy of the old brahman books presented in a new form. This is known as the Vedanta or the Dnyana Marga.[44] Then he founded the Shivalinga and assimilated the Turks, who had settled in this country, with the Hindu kshatriyas. Very much like the Muslims, he used the sword of the Turks to get the Buddhists defeated. He thus reestablished the domination of the fraudulent tales from the *Bhagawata* and rigmarole of the Vedic incantations on the ignorant shudras. In the terrible wake of this devastating turmoil, his people killed several of the Buddhists by crushing them in oil presses. They burned down their most precious books except for the *Amarkosha*,[45] which they retained for their own use. Later on, the owl-like disciples of Shankaracharya began to ride in palanquins, carry flaming

[42] Phule means South India. Shankaracharya was not born in Karnataka but in Kerala. [—*Ed.*]

[43] Phule uses the word Nastik. The original meaning of the term is 'someone who denies the authority of the Vedas'. In more recent times the term is used as a translation for atheist. Shankaracharya was not a Nastik in either sense. It is not clear why Phule calls his philosophy (mata) Nastika Mata. [—*Ed.*]

[44] Path of Knowledge. [—*Ed.*]

[45] Dictionary of the Sanskrit language. [—*Ed.*]

torches in broad day light and parade in the streets, dressed like clean-shaven widows. There were several brahman authors like Mukundaraj, Dnyaneshwara and Ramdasa,[46] among the plenty that mushroomed all over, who wasted their talents in composing silly books. None of them dared to even touch the rope of bondage tied around the necks of the shudras. Obviously, they lacked the courage to renounce such wicked practices and deeds openly. So they made a distinction between 'Karma Marga' (the Path of Action) and 'Dnyana Marga' (the Path of Knowledge), assigning every wicked practice to the former and atheist opinion to the latter. Then they wrote heaps of hollow books on these and allowed their selfish brahman brothers to continue robbing the shudras. The brahman ruler Rao Baji[47] used to spend his nights in shameless debauchery but considered it polluting to see a Muslim, a devout servant of God, till late in the morning. But the string of the musical instrument of his debauchery snapped when raga Adi Bhairava[48] began. Because towards the end of his infamous rule, the flag of the great British began to fly high over his kingdom and the oppressive rule of the brahmans came to an end. Several American and Scottish missionaries, followers of the Baliraja in the West, that is Jesus Christ, came to this country, without the least regard for what their governments would say. They preached the true teachings of Jesus among the shudras and freed them from the deceit and slavery of the brahmans. They pulled out the rope of slavery around their necks, tied there by the brahmans and threw it on the oppressors' face. By now most of the brahmans have realized that these missionaries will certainly not allow them to dominate the shudras. Therefore, the wily brahmans intend to drive the British government and the missionaries away from this country before the friendship between the missionaries,

[46] Mukundaraj (13th century) was the author of the work called *Viveksindhu* taken to be the first known book in Marathi. Dnyaneshwar wrote his commentary on the Geeta in A.D. 1290. Ramadasa, a champion of brahmanism, flourished in the 17th century. [—*Ed.*]

[47] The last Peshwa, the brahman ruler of Pune. [—*Ed.*]

[48] The raga, the musical composition is here used as a metaphor for the great benevolent destruction brought about by British rule. [—*Ed.*]

that is, the faithful followers of the Baliraja, and the ignorant shudras matures further. So now they are using their hereditary deceit once again and have started to incite the shudras against the British. The rest of them have acquired various jobs as clerks etc. in government offices and infested the places so thickly that it is impossible to find any office, either government or otherwise, without a brahman in it.

Part XI

Preaching of the puranas, the resultant rebellions, shudra princes, kulkarni, prayer of Saraswati, recitations, observance of religious rituals, offering of money as a token of respect (dakshina) at the temples, organizations with ambitious names, etc.

DHONDIBA: What? You mean, the rowdy ancestors of these ruffian brahmans came to our country from outside, defeated our ancestors and turned them into their slaves. Then they brutally forced the rule of their own kings upon us and ruled the roost with great fanfare. I can't call this dastardly act as great heroism! But just imagine, had our ancestors defeated their (brahmans') ancestors, wouldn't they have meted out the same treatment to these jugglers, the *bhats*? Anyway, let that be. Now tell me, whatever happened when these *bhats* disguised their brutality as religion, and by what trick did they prejudice the minds of the ignorant shudras against the benevolent British government?

JOTIRAO: Several *bhats* started holding nightly meetings in the temple of that heroic god Maruti, in the central square of the villages, outwardly professing to preach religion but really to pollute the minds of the ignorant folks with stupid tales (puranas) from the *Bhagawata*. Were they satisfied with dissuading the shudras from having any contact with the missionaries, the followers of Baliraja? No, not they! On the contrary, at the earliest opportunity, they told similar tales from the puranas to all the other ignorant people and poisoned their minds against the British as well. That is why there have been so many rebellions against the British in this country.

DHONDIBA: Well, that certainly is true! It really would be very difficult to find a single rebellion against the British which did not have a brahman priest in a leading position, instigating it either openly or secretly. See, there was one Dhondopant who was sentenced for life in the rebellion of Umaji Ramoshi; and who were the people in the so-called chapati rebellion of 1857?[49] None other than the deshastha brahmans from the north like Bhatpande, the konkanstha brahman, Nana, Tatya Topya and such others.

JOTIRAO: But you must note that it was the shudra princes like Shinde, Holkar who greatly helped the British. True, they were, in a sense, employed by the brahmans and were somewhat under their obligations. Yet they did not care a bit for that! Anyway, our benevolent government must have got into heavy financial debt in quenching this rebellion of the *bhat* brahmans. Yet on whom did the government enforce heavy taxation to overcome the financial losses? Not on the useless temple-kingdoms. Well, it goes to their credit that they imposed taxes on all subjects, guilty and innocent alike! But to whom did they assign the duty of collecting taxes from the poor, innocent and ignorant shudras? To the same money- sorry, Brahma-worshippers, the *bhat* kulkarnis who were seething with rage that the shudra princes did not help their Nana in his time of need. And they cursed them with no holds barred as if it were the time of the Holi festival! That kind of language and they pretend to become pure after bathing thrice a day! From the moment the government, that original Brahma rakshasa, assigned these *gram* rakshasas (the devils of the village) this duty, they have been hounding the shudras day and night. You know how the Muslim kings had once assigned the task of slitting necks of birds and beasts, to produce halal meat, to people from their own religion, called

[49] Mysterious chapatis are believed to have circulated during the Revolt of 1857; thus 'chapati rebellion'. The 19th century was marked by a number of anti-British rebellions, mostly with a low caste or tribal base. Phule was of the view that these uprisings against the British could lead to a consolidation of brahman power. Thus his somewhat unfair assessment of Umaji Ramoshi and his anti-imperialism. See also note 33, p. 275 of the present volume. [—*Ed.*]

the mulanis. But these expert brahmans have perfected the art of slitting shudra throats to such finesse that they have left the mulanis far behind. Therefore all village people have conferred on them the title of 'pen-wielding butchers', without waiting for the government to do it. That is how they are known all over. Yet this wise government does not transfer them like other employees. On the contrary, it merely seeks their consent and entrusts them with the task of preparing notices to be served to the shudras, regarding the taxes they have to pay. The government consults these kulkarnis again if some notices are to be cancelled and some shudras are to be exempted from paying the taxes. What can one say to this injustice!

DHONDIBA: But how does the kulkarni benefit from this?

JOTIRAO: That he alone can tell! But even if they do not make profit from some adamant lout, they can harass him for a week, force him to pay repeated visits to the revenue office, make him lose wages for that period and reduce him to a wreck! Maybe they do not gain a farthing in such transactions, yet they do their 'official duties' with the cunning of a stork who pounces on a fish in a flash. What loyalty this! See how all the people, from young to old, have started singing the praise of Goddess Lakshmi, like Shankaracharya of yesteryears. 'Oh our official government Goddess Saraswati, how benevolent thou art! You mete out the same justice to those who take bribes and to those who helplessly give them too!' So she is greatly pleased with them and it is rumoured that she had showered money on their houses continuously for some nights. It was the biggest talk of the town. Now if this is true, then it is the duty of the government to investigate into this matter and parade such a beneficiary kulkarni in the streets seating him on a donkey!

DHONDIBA: Oh yes. Some intelligent men had indeed got a few *bhats* arrested for their trickery and handed them over to the prison officials of the Baliraja. But these 'pen-wielding butchers' are now hoodwinking these officials as well, it is said, and their trade is flourishing again. That is why, several *bhats* today are again making merry on the money earned by the shudras by the sweat of their brow. Instead of being grateful to them, they exploit them with their ceremonious bathing and ritualistic praying. They make a great show of being pious and holy, and convince the shudras that their chanting incantations from the Vedas has magical powers. Thus they impress the ignorant shudras. Then to turn them into their followers, they collect subscriptions from them and hold ceremonious worships of the Shivalinga either at the back or in front of the Shadawali Peer in Pune. They make the gullible shudras believe that it was only because of these religious ministrations that it rained well or the plague did not cause havoc. On the last day of such programmes, they keep rice-balls on hand-carts and spin yarns to dupe the shudras with their tricky words. They organize grand fairs to deceive them, arrange sumptuous feasts for their own kind, that is, for the idle rogues, *bhats*. After the brahmans have eaten to their heart's content, they give the leftovers to the various shudras, who are made to sit and wait in long lines for a long time; some are given only a handful of rice, some only a little curry and some are just kicked out with curses. Thus, having fed them with this 'grand feast', the *bhats* bombard them with prattle about the greatness of their Vedic mantras and black art. But why they don't invite the English to such feasts is really a mystery to me.

JOTIRAO: Ha! These *bhat* brahmans, barking mantras, go wagging their tails for a few flecks of rice to any feasts thrown by anyone! But even if they organize innumerable festive worships of Shiva, will they dare to invite the valiant English to their feasts? They won't!

DHONDIBA: That sums it up nicely! A prick to the colt and a sign to the horse is enough of a cue to gallop away. I am convinced! Just like the proverb, once bitten twice shy.

JOTIRAO: All right. As you wish. But let me tell you one thing. Let these enlightened *bhats* of today whitewash their black magic and religious fanfare as much as they want, no one is going to be worse off for that. But do you know how that impotent fool, the *bhat* king Rao Baji, behaved with his master? He imprisoned the Bhonsala king's royal family in the fort at Satara! He amassed a huge fortune by exploiting the toiling shudras, and he favoured Sardar Dhamdhere, that great coward, so much that he bestowed upon him a royal charter of rights! This deed impressed even a just and loyal British officer like First Sorterquand![50] He was thrilled to the core to read the clauses of the charter! Tell me, if that heinous deed impressed him so much, what can we say about the others! These brahman kings have established rich temples like the Parvati.[51] All that occupies their attention is providing sumptuous feasts to their own kinsmen, the idle, slothful, potbellied *bhats*! But they have absolutely no concern for the blind, lame, widows and their orphaned children of any other castes. They have also established the tradition of bestowing every year huge sums of money called dakshina on the *bhats* who study their spurious and cunning religious books. Yet the government has done nothing to prohibit these oppressive practices and allows them to continue. Isn't this a blot on their political acumen and wisdom? All the lavish expenditure incurred on such hollow practices benefits none but the *bhats*! These vagrant bulls, fed on the free meals, have grown such bullies that they bulldoze the poor shudras, their real benefactors, to drink the dirty water with which they have washed their feet as holy, beguiling their minds with silly tales from their religion of black magic. O tell me, how come the ancestors of these orthodox *bhats* dared to commit such gross and indecent deeds, blatantly violating several tenets of their own *Manusamhita* and other religious texts? At least now they should come to their senses and without listening to the credulous government, should immediately establish a Sarvajanik Sabha,[52] a public organization of the *bhats*, to prohibit the *bhats* at places, such as the Parvati, from polishing off food procured by the sweat of the toiling shudras. Only then will their religious texts exert some influence on the organization, for organizing widow

[50] The reference is obscure but presumably a minor British officer in Pune. [—*Ed.*]

[51] Temple atop a hill in Pune, built by the Peshwas. See also note 52 on p. 167 of the present volume. [—*Ed.*]

[52] Sarvajanik Sabha: a reformist organization of the brahman social reformers and liberals. While Phule is perhaps less than fair to the liberal reformers, this critique flows from his scepticism of upper-caste, specially brahman, reformism. [—*Ed.*]

remarriages. Their grandiosely named organizations should not just point out to the shudras the tiny mistakes of the government and instigate them against the British. What they should do instead is to realize and remove their own faults. They should not behave like the proverbial lame cow who refused to graze on the grass because it was near the village. Before rushing on to do anything else, they should first embrace the American, Scottish and English missionaries, the followers of the teachings of the holy Baliraja, who have freed the shudras from the bondage of slavery. Enough of *bhat* mischief! Down with the mysticism of chapatis and dal–rice!

Part XII

Vatandar *bhat* kulkarnis, need for the European colonies, a blot on the face of the Department of Education, about how the European officers are easily duped, etc.

DHONDIBA: All right. You observed earlier that it would be very difficult to find any government or private office without a *bhat* in it. Tell me, who then is the chief *bhat* among them all?

JOTIRAO: The chief *bhat* is the vatandar kulkarni. Many European collectors, taking pity on the shudras who were being duped by the *bhats*, sent report after report to the government about the *bhats*' mischief. They have made provisions in the law to restrict the *bhats* in various ways and reduced their power. Yet these pen-wielding butchers still enjoy great domination over the shudras because of their cunning religion. They sit in their offices and, like the Devil, curse the Christian religion of that Baliraja, from behind the safe screen of their own religion. If we refuse to believe that this is so, then how do the illiterate shudras, who can neither read nor write, ever learn to hate those opinions so much? Do tell me if you have any other explanation! But that is not all. They exploit every opportunity to prejudice the shudras against the government! They probably take some government rule and deliberately distort it in order to instigate the shudras against the government. The shudras are mortally scared of the brahmans; they don't disclose a word of this to the government because all the senior officers are none other than brahmans. Now at least our government should wake up and place at least one English or Scottish preacher in each village, gifting him with one plot of tenantless land for his upkeep, and assign him the task of preaching and submitting to the government at least one report every year on everything that happens in the village. If such a law is made, it will prohibit the *bhats* from organizing a revolt against the government, which they could easily do by organizing religious worships of the Shivalinga in front of the Peers like in Pune, and simultaneously sending word to distant people through their mystic chapatis. They could instigate the shudras to virtually knock the government down and stuff those chapatis down its mouth. The law will prohibit a united front of the kulkarnis from doing this. The shudras will never find a stronger foothold unless this is done! Not only that; when the preaching of the missionaries opens the eyes of the shudras to the true knowledge, they will never be beguiled by these village monsters. Secondly, the government should not assign the administrative work of the patil and kulkarni to one caste alone; instead, they should test people's ability for doing that work and select people through examinations. Like the military, this will easily bring under control the nefarious activities of the *bhats* and also inculcate among the shudras a taste for learning. The government should stop all grants to the Education Department as they do not serve any useful purpose and divert them instead to the Collectorates and compel each European Collector, unlike George Gervis, to impartially select intelligent students from all castes, open schools for them near the Collector's bungalow, provide them with simple food and clothing, impart instruction to them and after they complete their education, conduct examinations for selection to the jobs of patil and kulkarni and appoint them to these posts. If this is done, they will not help the kulkarnis and debauched *bhats* like Nana.[53] Instead, they will see to it that the illiterate shudras are no more swindled or set against each other by the *bhats* who often swindle the shudras

[53] Nana: powerful minister of the Peshwas of Pune. [—*Ed.*]

and acquire their vatan land by the most fraudulent means. Virtually lakhs of rupees have been spent on the Education Department but this has not helped produce a sizable number of learned people among the shudras. Why, it would be difficult to find even one educated person among the mahars, mangs and chambhars. Finding a person who is a university graduate or has a Master's degree is next to impossible. Alas! How the *bhat* teachers have blackened the white face of our Education Department! These bitter gourds were fried in ghee and rolled in sugar[54] by our government but still their bitter taste has not gone.

DHONDIBA: Tell me, how do these *bhats* swindle the shudras and acquire their vatan lands fraudulently?

JOTIRAO: The kulkarnis catch some illiterate shudras who cannot read and write; they lend money to them and, while writing the mortgage deeds, incorporate terrible conditions with the help of their own kinsmen who write these deeds. While these deeds are read out aloud, these conditions are not; or something else is read out instead. The unsuspecting shudras affix their thumb impressions on these documents. After some days, the *bhats* acquire the vatan lands of the shudras on the basis of the horrible conditions deceitfully incorporated in the deeds.

DHONDIBA: All right. Now tell me, how do these 'pen-wielding butchers' set the shudras against each other.

JOTIRAO: By creating various disputes among them regarding their land, the boundaries of their farmlands, plots, etc. One finds several disputes at the times of festivals like Pola or Shiral Sheth,[55] about who is to have the honour of throwing the sweet chapati in the holy fire first! Now can you say with conviction that these disputes are not begun by the *bhats*? Can you cite any examples of disputes where the *bhats* were not at the root?

DHONDIBA: But what do you think the *bhats* gain out of such disputes?

JOTIRAO: Oh, several old and respectable but illiterate shudra

[54] A popular Marathi phrase. [—*Ed.*]

[55] Shiral Sheth: a godhead of the trading community. Pola: festival of the bullock. Both these festivals are non-brahmanical. Brahman intervention in them thus has no authority. [—*Ed.*]

families have been instigated to fight amongst themselves by the *bhats*. Then they are reduced to such a miserable state that they have to survive by taking up repair work of the roofs and houses of these very pen-wielding butchers. It is because of the wily tricks of these butchers that the expenditure of the civil and criminal offices of the government far exceeds the provisions made for them. Most of these brahman clerks, along with the secretaries and the mamledars, have completely forsaken the noble meaning of the Gayatri mantra ('Let's pray to the brilliant Sun who will stimulate our intellect') and now sing the new beggar's song instead ('Throw us a penny please!'). This they have probably learnt from the 'holy' maulavis, the *bhats* among the Muslims.[56] And since then, their broker's commission has increased so much that they ride only in stately coaches, grunting like overfed and rowdy bulls, gallivanting around. Also note how the number of the munsif judges, the veritable nawabs these days, has increased and how they lord over the others, displaying their pomp! But has this helped the poor people to get speedy justice without much cost? Forget it! Now the village people have coined a new idiom. They know from their own everyday experience that the brahmans in all government offices really won't budge unless their palms are greased. So now they say, 'Never stir out of your houses without a lot of grease if you want to get your work done in government offices.'

DHONDIBA: But why don't these shudras from the villages go to the Collector and complain to him in private about such misdeeds?

JOTIRAO: What! You expect the ignorant plaintiff who doesn't even know how to write the letter 'a' to stand before the great officer and present to him his grievances in a systematic way? And suppose, some courageous man does manage to muster all his strength to lodge a complaint that nobody listens to him; just wait till the news leaks out to those butchers, the brahmans! Rest assured that he will be ruined forever! Because they will immediately circulate word about his doing among all their kinsmen, right from the *bhat* secretaries in the Collector's office

[56] By equating the Muslim priestly class with the brahmans, Phule establishes yet again his distrust of the middlemen to God. [—*Ed.*]

to the *bhat* clerks of the Revenue Department and in the courts of justice, and start their beggar's song. Immediately, half of the pen-wielding butchers will arrive with heaps of evidence in favour of the complainant and present themselves as his witnesses and half of them will arrive with evidence against him and testify as the witnesses of the defendant. Then in the ensuing confusion, they will spoil the case so badly that the judge will simply be too confused to distinguish the truth from the falsehood. The poor learned European Collectors and Judges will pour over the case but still will be unable to make any sense of it and so, instead of dispensing justice, they will scold the poor complainant for being a fussy nitwit and send him packing home with a few well-chosen epithets! The poor man will just go home and bawl his soul out! How many such poor people must have committed suicide because they couldn't make their voice heard! And how many must have turned into highwaymen and perished! How many must have gone stark, raving mad because of the frustration raging in their hearts! And how many must have gone half-mad and roamed the streets over with their beards grown wild, telling their woes to all and sundry!

Part XIII

About the mamledar, Collector, revenue, judges and *bhat* employees in the Engineering Department

DHONDIBA: How do the *bhats* dupe ignorant shudras just because they hold the post of a mamledar?

JOTIRAO: Several of the *bhat* mamledars were adjudged guilty because of their criminal dealings and were punished. They used to behave so atrociously and oppressed the poor so much that their black deeds would easily make up a big volume. Do you know, in this Pune, the *bhat* mamledars do not accept the guarantee even of big moneylenders unless it is accompanied by a character certificate by a kulkarni. You can imagine the treatment given to the poor shudras, then! You can very well imagine the rigmarole of black magic the *bhats* must be weaving while issuing such certificates! Similarly, the municipal authorities won't allow a householder to build a new toilet in the place of the old one in his own house unless he produces a letter of approval by the mamledar, who won't issue it in the first place unless it is accompanied by the favourable remarks of the kulkarni of that particular area. The kulkarni has a map of the area. Now there is no provision for adding the names of all new buyers in the area to a register, and no such register is maintained in the Collector's office either; so on what grounds does one accept the kulkarni's remarks regarding any property as true? Yet this is what happens. All of this leads one to suspect that the *bhat* kulkarnis must have initiated and sustained this illegal practice in order to benefit their kinsmen, the pen-wielding butchers. Now reflect on this a little. If the *bhat* kulkarnis are able to play their devilish games successfully in a city like Pune, right under the nose of the neighbouring European residents, and protect the interests of their pen-wielding butchers of kinsmen, what havoc must they be wreaking in villages? If we refuse to believe this, then how do we account for the fact that hordes of illiterate shudras from villages are found running frantically from pillar to post, clutching their revenue records in their arms, complaining against the *bhat* clerks? Are they all liars? One says, 'The *bhat* mamledar never accepted my petition in time because of the interference of the *bhat* kulkarni, and so the opponent caused my witnesses to turn hostile and I had to provide security for my own complaint'; another wails, 'The *bhat* mamledar did accept my petition but has suppressed it till now, but then he promptly accepted the defendant's application the very next day and rejected my claim to cultivate the fields which I had been doing for a long time, and turned me into a pauper.' Then there is yet another who howls, 'The *bhat* mamledar never recorded my statement truthfully when I gave it and then distorted the same in such a way that the whole case went haywire and now I am driven to madness.' And yet another says, 'My opponent, hand in glove with the *bhat* mamledar, challenged my right to cultivate my own land and forcefully sowed seeds there; when I approached the mamledar with my complaint, I folded my hands and bowed before him most reverently. I handed over my petition to him without uttering a single word, and stood at a distance, trembling from head to foot, with the most pathetic demeanour. But the mamledar, just like Yama, the god of Death, looked at me from head to toe and immediately threw my petition on my face with the utmost scorn, and fined me for having committed contempt of court. Since I had no money to pay the fine, I had to stay in prison for quite a few days! In the meantime my opponent has acquired illegal possession of my land, which I had carefully ploughed and made ready for cultivation. But now he has captured it and started cultivating it. So I had to repeatedly submit petitions to the Collector. But the clerk there has just suppressed my applications and now nobody knows where they are. Now what can I do? Some say that he did read out my application to the Collector but deleted the important portion from my application while reading and has managed to get the earlier verdict of the *bhat* mamledar confirmed. Some say that the Collector delivered his judgement in my favour orally, but when the *bhat* clerk wrote it down, he changed the verdict. But when he read it out before the Collector, of course, he took care to read out the Collector's words verbatim though he had not written them down. So the Collector signed the judgement without reading it, believing he was really signing what he had said. When I received the decree from the mamledar, I smote my brow and cried that these brahman clerks won't stop till they get what they want!' And another man says, 'When I could not get justice from the Collector, I sent a couple of petitions to the Revenue Commissioner. But the *bhat* clerks there sent my petitions back to the Collector for his comments. And the *bhat* clerks in the Collector's office manipulated my papers in such a way that the Collector returned them to the Revenue Office with the remark that I was a most cantankerous litigant and the Revenue Commissioner believed it to be so. Now what can one do against such mischief mongering!' Then listen to this. This man says, 'When my case came for hearing, the clerk started interfering. The Hon. Judge admonished him and told him to shut up. But when he started reading the case, what could he understand? All the *bhat* clerks in the Collector's office had acted on the instigation of the kulkarni and changed my case entirely.' Yet another says, 'I had to work according to the contract I had signed with the *bhat* in his room of worship. While working for him ceaselessly for the past so many years to make him rich, I lost all my houses, doors, farms, jute bags, all my possessions and finally even the broken beads of my wife. When we began to starve, my younger brothers started working as labourers on the road works. But the *bhats* were there too. All that they do is to take the roll call, read the Marathi and English newspapers, tell the worker the summary of any item criticizing either the British government or his religion, and go home. The government pays them more than double the amount it pays to the labourer. On top of this, the *bhats* demand money from the workers and, if a worker refuses pay, they report all kinds of lies about him to the senior officer and mark him absent from the very next day. But that is not all. While the worker is returning home after work, the *bhat* will order him to bring some banyan leaves for him, or ask him to cut some wood and deliver it to his house. Another asks him to cut the branch of a mango tree and bring it home. Someone else asks him to bring him betel leaves stealthily without the knowledge of the resident lessee (*tirgul*) of the land. And yet another informs him that he is invited for dinner by a jolly widow and orders him to go home, eat his bread and then immediately go to the brahman's place to keep watch in his absence while his wife and children rest. Then he tells him to be present at the site of work in time next morning as the senior engineer is coming for inspection. My brothers tell me about all such harassment they have to undergo at the hands of the *bhats* when they come home and shed many tears. But tell me, O brother, what I can do. These *bhatjis* call themselves the guru of the eighteen varnas,[57] they may behave in whatever way they like, but the shastras scream from the rooftops that the shudra shall not say even a word of disapproval! Otherwise I would have learned to speak English long back and informed

[57] *Ashtva* (eighteen) varnas or *ashta pagad* (eighteen kinds of headgear) are general expressions meaning the plethora of jatis. [—*Ed.*]

the British officers about their black deeds. That would have brought them to book! And served them right! Apart from this, all the contractors also relate so many tales about the deceits and misdeeds of the brahmans in the Engineering Department that they would fill a whole volume easily. So I will stop here. I will just add that the government should consider it their duty to look into the complaints listed above and take strict action against the *bhats* if the complaints are found to be true.'

Part XIV

About the helplessness of the European officers, the domination of the khots,[58] the need for retired European officers who get pension to keep an eye on the misdeeds of the *bhats* in villages and to inform the government of these, and about religion and the false caste pride

DHONDIBA: Obviously, all such misdeeds and atrocities take place because the *bhats* have infested government offices. But tell me what are the European officers doing? Why don't they report all such malpractices of the brahmans to the government?

JOTIRAO: Because their tables are so heavily laden with files that need looking into, thanks to the skill of the brahman clerks, that they spend most of their time just looking into the most urgent cases and signing only the Marathi papers. Then when could these poor officers take up such cases and report them to the government? Yet there are now reports that most of the European collectors in the Konkan region have indeed started taking up the cases of the illiterate shudras who have been swindled and oppressed by the *bhat* khots, the traditional landlords, with a view to putting an end to that oppression. They themselves file the cases on behalf of the shudras against the *bhats* and become the complainants. But the *bhat* khots have taken a leaf out of the book of American slaveholders and started inciting the shudras against the government, with the help of their devious religion. So the shudras have now turned against the European collectors and appealed to the government to allow them to remain under

[58] Landlords in the Konkan. [—*Ed.*]

the domination of the *bhat* khots. See the devious move of the khot *bhatjis*! They have taken hold of the pawn, the illiterate shudra, trapped the benevolent European collectors in their move of the shudra reaction and checkmated them.

DHONDIBA: What can one do when these illiterate shudras listen to the wily advice of the *bhats* and invite trouble for themselves from all sides! And how much more they will suffer when they lift their hands to strike the government as the *bhats* want them to do! It would be exceedingly difficult for them to get a second chance at liberating themselves from the slavery of the *bhats*. I earnestly request you to apply your mind to this problem! It's no use telling the shudras about this as they won't listen. At least apprise our kind government about the real facts! Of course, what can you do if the shudras are fated to suffer so?

JOTIRAO: I really do not mean to suggest that the government should not appoint *bhats* in their offices at all; but then it should be proportionate with their population. And if the government is unable to obtain adequate number of people from all castes in proportion to their population, then only Europeans should be employed to work on those posts. Then the *bhat* employees will not be able to harm the interests of the government and those of the shudras. Secondly, the government should provide those European collectors, who can speak Marathi well, with pension for their life, and make them stay in the villages among the illiterate shudras, so that they can keep a close watch, through the shudras, on the tricks of the *bhats* and kulkarnis, and send detailed reports to the government on all that happens there. This will expose all the shameless frauds of the *bhats* in the Education Department and check the anarchy there. This will also enlighten the oppressed shudras and true knowledge will enable them to renounce the irrational domination of the *bhats* over them. I am quite convinced that they will never forget the obligations of the Queen, who alone can remove the bond of slavery tied around their necks by the wily brahmans.

DHONDIBA: Then why did you learn *dand-patta*[59] and shooting in your childhood?

[59] *Dand-patta*: martial art of the Marathas. [—*Ed.*]

JOTIRAO: To overthrow our benevolent English government.

DHONDIBA: From where did you get such a wicked idea?

JOTIRAO: From some learned *bhats*! They argue, sitting near the stoves in the kitchen, that most people from the various castes are simply ignorant of the tenets of our ancient and true religion. That is why, there is no unity among them. As a result, they say, our society stays splintered in various castes and we are divided. This is the reason why the English could conquer us. They also say that the English are projecting their own cunning religion as the only great support of the shudras, and pretending to call them their brothers, are destroying the patriotic feelings in our credulous and illiterate people. According to them, unless we, the people from all castes, unite against them, we will not be able to drive them out of our country. And unless we drive them out, we will not be able to compete with the Americans, French and Russians. To achieve this, they say, we have to suitably modify, change and improve our ancient religion. That is what, they claim, will bring unity amongst us. They support their argument with quotations from Thomas Paine and others. As a young boy, I was impressed by the logic of this argument, and I was crazy enough to think along the same lines. But when I reflected deeply upon the same books they quoted from, the hidden meaning of the selfish advice of these so-called enlightened *bhats* dawned on me. They are afraid that if we, the shudras, really become the brothers of the English, we will condemn their wily religious books and then these *bhats* who are so proud of their caste will have to eat dust; the lazy idlers will not be able to gorge themselves on the food produced by the sweat of our brow. And not even the father of their god Brahma will be able to claim that the *bhat* is superior to the shudra. But one should not really be surprised at their distorting the meaning of the word patriotism because even their ancestors were unable to understand the true meaning of the term. The English learnt the word from the Greeks before the advent of their Baliraja. When they became the followers of that Baliraja, their patriotism knew no bounds. No other people from any other religion can match them on this score. Let them, if they so desire, show someone from amongst themselves, who can match George Washington, the American follower of that Baliraja; or if they can't do that, let them produce a match for Lafayette, his French follower. At least then they can avoid being called illogical. Had their ancestors known what patriotism really meant, they would never have described the shudras as inferior to even beasts in their books. These *bhats* claim to become clean after drinking the urine of cows who consume human excreta. Yet they consider the clean spring water in the hands of the shudra as dirty and undrinkable. The ancestors of these so-called enlightened brahmans are supposed to have presented patriotism that is superior to that of the Greeks! But who taught us the true difference between the two? What fool would accept their advice to drive the English, who have rescued us from the slavery of the *bhats*, away from our land? Who would be idiotic enough to raise his hand against his saviour? Let me tell you, the English are here today, but who knows whether they will be here tomorrow? They won't be there till eternity. Therefore, all the shudras should make haste to free themselves from the ancestral slavery of these *bhats*. That would be the sane thing to do. Thank God that He helped the brave English to subdue the rebellion of the *bhat* Nana. Otherwise those enlightened brahmans who worship the phallus would surely have sentenced many mahars for life for tucking their dhotis at one side or for having uttered Sanskrit shlokas in their kirtanas.

Part XV

About the government Education Department, municipality, Dakshina Prize Committee, united front of the *bhat* press, the conspiracy of the *bhats* to prohibit education of the shudra and atishudra children

DHONDIBA: What are the deceitful practices of the *bhats* in the Education Department of the government?

JOTIRAO: Let me tell you about a particular incident. The *bhats* were scared that one particular book[60] recommended by the Education Department would expose all the deceitful practices that their ancestors had indulged in; so they held several private meetings with the government, they wrote various articles in newspapers advising the government on this issue in various different ways and, finally, managed to get the book thrown out of the Department of Education. Now tell me, if our government, which professes to be their disciples, chose to bow before the wishes of these so-called progressive *bhats*, and threw the book out of the schools and the Department, what right do we have to feel indignant that some ignorant officials in the past crucified the very person whose teachings were embodied in that very book, on the insistence of a few corrupt blasphemous leaders?

DHONDIBA: But how is the government at fault here?

JOTIRAO: Well, if we believe that the government is not at fault when it threw the holy book out of their schools, then you may also say that the government would be right to prescribe only those books, written by these very people who opposed the holy book, and to appoint only such people as teachers in the schools for the shudra. Would that be right? Consider the matter in the right spirit. These accusers managed to get the holy book thrown out of the schools. But the government never throws out books written by them; on the contrary, the government not only awards them huge sums of money as prize, but also appoints them as teachers in all the government schools and grants them plenty of time to abuse the holy book before the shudras under the guise of preaching to them. So, if our innocent government is unable to banish those people, those accusers of the holy book, from our schools, then it should close down all schools opened for the shudras and rest at home. At least that would save us shudras the tax we pay for the Education Department. You know, one Chief Executive *bhat* officer in the Education Department has to be paid a monthly salary of six hundred rupees; that means, he pockets seven thousand two hundred

[60] It is not clear which text Phule is referring to. The *Collected Works* edition in Marathi also does not give the details. [—*Ed.*]

rupees per year![61] There is no danger now of any harassment by the government. But just consider, if the gods above decide to wreak havoc on us in the form of a natural calamity, how many shudra families will have to toil in their fields to earn that much money in one year! At least one thousand! Right? Now consider how much money is given to these so-called scholars! How much do the shudras benefit from it really? Do you know, just to get a pittance like four annas, the shudra labourer has to carry baskets of rubble and earth on his head, from early morning till late in the evening. He can't find time to rest for even a minute. But these *bhats*, who get twenty rupees a day, just sit on comfortable chairs in well-ventilated rooms in the schools! Yet he finds enough leisure every morning and evening, to ride in a horse carriage, decked up like a bridegroom of the municipality, to enjoy the cool air outside, to impress people with his pomp, and to roam his eye over the drawing rooms and even toilets of their houses! Have you wondered where he gets that much leisure from? He finds it more important to show off than to awaken the poor ignorant folks to the advantages of education. A missionary earning ten rupees a month is a thousand times preferable to them! At least everybody, from children to old people in the city where he lives, knows him as their preacher. But this strutting *bhat*, he is not even known to his immediate neighbours. All that he does by way of work is teach in the school for a couple of hours when he feels like it, gossip with his European boss, submit a couple of reports to him in a year, and that's what he calls work! And this fellow is called an honest worker and a patriot by a few sycophants! Do you know, it is these 'honest' workers who have swindled the Education Department off lakhs of rupees? Yet, to this day, they have not been able to educate the atishudras nor have they made even a single atishudra a member of the Municipal Council. Think about it! How many of these 'honest' *bhat* teachers have a real sympathy and feeling for the atishudras? And that is not all. Do you know, one of these 'patriotic' *bhats* was the Chief Officer of the Municipality last year when the position of water supply

[61] A huge amount, given the average earnings in 1872. [—*Ed.*]

was very serious; yet he could not make arrangements for the atishudras to draw drinking water from the government tank! That is why there is a great need for at least one of the atishudras to be a member of the Municipality.

DHONDIBA: What you say is right, of course! Yet I have heard that there are quite a few shudras on the Municipal Committee who are so terribly learned that whenever they have to express an opinion, they just nod away mechanically. All yes-men! Can't even sign their names. What can one expect from them, except a big zero? Do you think you can find such people among the atishudras, like these imbeciles who nod away all the time, sitting on comfortable chairs, just putting a few signatures here and there?

JOTIRAO: Of course! There will be several among the atishudras who can read and write a hundred times better than the shudra. But since the spurious religious books of the *bhats* branded the atishudras as untouchables, the poor fellows have had to work hard to eke out an existence and have no time, like the shudra members, to mix among other people and become rich. They have to work like the very donkeys they use at work.

DHONDIBA: What is the community-wise membership of the municipality like? Which community is in majority?

JOTIRAO: The *bhat* community, of course!

DHONDIBA: That is why the *bhats* are in majority in this committee, except for the scavengers and the unskilled labourers. Most of the employees in the Water Supply Department were *bhats*. They used to supply so much water to the *bhat* localities in the scorching summer that everybody there could even wash their clothes and utensils. A lot of water used to be just wasted. But all the areas where shudras live had such water scarcity that a passer-by would find it difficult to get even a little water to quench his thirst, leave alone enough for washing clothes and pots and pans. Apart from this, they have built many new tanks in the *bhat* localities. Now people from areas like Gunj Peth have gone hoarse demanding water from the Committee, but in vain! The committee has a majority of *bhats* so all their requests fell on deaf ears. Finally, last year in the summer, when water was scarce, the mangs and mahars from the Mith Gunj area could endure it no more and went to the Kala Haud,[62] built exclusively for the *bhats*, and began to draw water from it. Then the Committee came to its senses and forced itself to take action. Then they spent so much money on it that it really does not become the wisdom and glory of the chief officer. Anyway, I wonder why Marathi journalists never draw the government's attention to the terrible mismanagement in the Municipal Committee.

JOTIRAO: Come on, obviously all the Marathi journalists are *bhats*. How will they ever lift their pens to write against their own brothers? When a European became the chairman of the Municipal Council, he never allowed the *bhats* to play any mischief. But these rascals then ganged up and raised such a hue and cry against him! They spread all kinds of complaints against him saying people suffered so much because of his policies! They harassed him so much that finally, he tendered his resignation in sheer exasperation and wanted to have nothing to do with the council. Our benevolent government accepted all the trash printed in those selfish newspapers as the truth and even went on to believe that it represented the opinions of the shudras and atishudras. This is a grave mistake of the government. They don't even know that the shudras and the atishudras have never met these journalists even once in their lifetime as far as these matters are concerned. Most of the atishudras haven't even seen a newspaper; they don't know what it means. Then how do these *bhat* journalists claim to understand and represent the opinions of these atishudras who are completely alien to them? How do they know them? I feel that they have just invented this strategy to humour ignorant people, to ridicule the government and to earn some money for themselves. If this is not so, explain one thing to me! Our government departments are infested with *bhat* employees and this has had a terribly adverse impact on the shudras and atishudras. Why don't they find any time to investigate this? Yet they have all the time in the world to find out and report what the Prime Minister of the Queen in London

[62] A drinking water tank in the Shukrawar Peth area of central Pune. [—*Ed.*]

babbled in his dreams about India, though the place is so far from India, beyond the seven seas. Let it pass. One *bhat* member of the Municipal Council has been assigned the task of preparing a summary report of all news in the Marathi newspapers for the government. But tell me, if a converted Marathi Christian writes in his paper that the Committee is completely insensitive to the problems of poor people, do you think the *bhat* member will report such news to the government? Of course he won't; how will he dare write a report to the government against his own kinsmen?

DHONDIBA: But if what you say is true, that the interests of all the other castes are seriously harmed because of this overcrowding of government offices by the *bhats*, I see a way. Why don't you write a small booklet exposing this situation for the Dakshina Prize Committee? At least that would open the eyes of the government.

JOTIRAO: You know, I had written a play about how the *bhat* joshis deceive the shudras with the rigmarole of their self-serving religion, and how the Christian missionaries disseminate true knowledge of their impartial religion among them to lead them onto the path of Truth.[63] And I had submitted this play to the Dakshina Prize Committee, too. This was way back in 1855. But even there, the opinions of the *bhat* members held sway and the European officers could do nothing. So my play was straightaway rejected. This Dakshina Prize Committee is nothing but a younger sister of the Municipal Council. Show me what illuminating work it has done to enlighten and encourage the shudras. I put that play aside for quite a few years. In the meantime, I wrote another book called *The Cunning Craft of the Brahmans*, and published it at my own cost. One of my friends in Pune then suggested to me that I should send letters to some high ranking officers in the Education Department with a request to buy some copies for themselves. I sent those letters

[63] The reference here is to the play *Tritya Ratna* (The Third Jewel) that Phule wrote in 1855. The text of the play was not available till the journal *Purogami Satyashodhak* published it in its April–June issue of 1879. It found its place in the 1988 edition of the *Collected Works* of Phule. [—*Ed.*]

accordingly. But not one of them dared to blacken his name by buying a single copy for fear of offending the *bhats*.

DHONDIBA: Tatyasaheb,[64] do you know, you don't have the skill of projecting yourself in front of people, therefore you can't sell your books.

JOTIRAO: My dear, one should never employ unholy means to attain one's aims, however noble they are. Otherwise the good cause suffers. So what if they did not buy my books? Has God not been kind to me? It is all right then. But I learnt a valuable lesson, didn't I? I never cringed before those people and learnt to rely on the great God, our Father, who created us. I am very grateful to Him for that.

DHONDIBA: Then the government also felicitated you in a public function for your great work of opening schools for girls from the *bhat* and other communities. They felicitated you with a ceremonial shawl at that time. Then you also opened a school for the atishudra people with some commendable *bhat* friends of yours but then when all those schools prospered, you abruptly gave up your work and distanced yourself from it. Afterwards you stopped visiting the houses of your European friends as well. What are the reasons for this?

JOTIRAO: Well, the government did felicitate me with the ceremonial shawl for having started schools for girls from all communities. And when I perceived the need for educating children from the atishudra communities, I also started schools for them too. I achieved this task with the help of quite a few of my enlightened *bhat* friends in whom I entrusted the work of the schools; and almost all Europeans helped me with donations. But among all of them, I will never forget the help rendered to me by Mr Reeves. He didn't help me with generous donations alone. He always found time out of his busy schedule to visit the schools and inquire about the progress of the students. He always encouraged the students in their studies and tried to inculcate in them the zest for education. All the atishudra students will remain eternally indebted to him for his help. How

[64] Tatya: literally, elder brother. Phule was affectionately called thus by many associates. [—*Ed.*]

can they ever pay him back his kindness? Not even with shoes stitched of their skins can they do so. I am exceedingly grateful to the other European gentlemen for their immense help. I was required, at that time, to seek assistance from some *bhat* friends of mine also, who became members. I will tell you the reasons for that some other time. But later on, when I started to expose the hidden cunning in the crafty books of their ancestors, they started to disagree with me. They seemed to think that there was absolutely no need to educate the atishudra students. If at all they have to be educated, giving them the basic literacy skills is not enough. I was of the opinion that we should give them good education, which would give them the ability to discern between good and bad. Why did they feel that they should not be given education? Perhaps they feared that once the atishudras were educated, they would learn to distinguish between truth and falsehood; they would realize that they owed their education to the benevolent government and become loyal servants of the government. The *bhats* were probably worried too, that education would lead atishudras to a true understanding of how the ancestors of the *bhats* had oppressed them and this would probably result in their hating the *bhats*. When our perceptions became so acutely divergent, I decided that the time had come to separate our ways; so I distanced myself from both projects. After a few years, in 1857, the *bhat* rebellion[65] broke out. After that, I began to sense that the European officers were giving me the cold shoulder; they did not speak to me as genially as they used to, and whenever I came across them, they met me with a frown. I then stopped visiting their homes, too.

DHONDIBA: Now this behaviour hardly becomes their reason and judgement! Why, just because of the arrogance of the *bhats*, they began to frown at you! That means they chose to ignore and reject the innocent and side with the guilty! But you, on the contrary, went a long way to help the *bhat* widows who had strayed from the path. Such women had to resort to inhuman

[65] The British saw the Revolt of 1857 as a 'Sepoy Mutiny'. Savarkar (1909) saw it as a war of independence. Phule's view falls between the two both chronologically (1872) and politically. [—*Ed.*]

ways of abortions. To avoid that, you opened a virtual sanctuary in your own house to deliver them of their children safely and in complete secrecy. I know, you have not asked the government for any kind of help for this noble work and haven't enlisted the help of any *bhat* members either. You spend all the money from your own pocket.

JOTIRAO: Our noble government seems to have adopted the policy of trimming their sails to the prevailing wind. You see, because of the prohibition of untouchability, all doors of employment have been closed down for the atishudras. So naturally they resort to theft as a strategy of survival. Now the government has adopted the policy whereby they have to report at the nearest police station, which, by itself, is a sound policy. But the poor widows of the *bhats* cannot remarry because of the social stigma on remarriage. So some of them commit adultery and then they have to resort to abortions and infanticide. Isn't it amazing that the government chooses to turn a blind eye to such things and does not conduct any inquiry into affairs such as these, as is done in the case of the mangs and ramoshis. Why does the government hold the mangs and ramoshis to be more reprehensible than these *bhat* widows who commit abortions and infanticide? Secondly, the *bhats* always blow their own trumpet. What is the point in taking such people as partners in such work when they can't snatch away the razors from the hands of the barbers who shave their young, widowed sisters?

DHONDIBA: Anyway; earlier you said that in general there are several irregularities found in the Education Department. What are they?

JOTIRAO: Well, a detailed description would require a huge volume. So let me just point out only a couple of them here. Firstly, there is terrible apathy towards training teachers for the shudra and atishudra schools.

DHONDIBA: How do you say so? The government, I hear, has established a separate school for training teachers to teach in all the schools. So the government probably has no discriminatory motives.

JOTIRAO: All right; then show me how many atishudra children have been trained so far by these specially trained teachers. Don't avoid me now; give me a straight answer.

DHONDIBA: Well, generally all the *bhat* teachers claim that if the atishudra children are admitted into these schools, that would lead to complete mayhem in India. So naturally the government is afraid.

JOTIRAO: Why, the army recruits people from all castes; that doesn't lead people to create mayhem in India. All this is because of the sheer negligence of the government. When people are recruited in the army, it is the government officers who look after the work themselves. And when teachers have to be trained, they assign that task to some ignoramus, donning ceremonial shawls. He, of course, doesn't have any idea what this work involves. Had he an iota of sense, he would not select so many *bhat* candidates for the training school. But he is not aware of his responsibility and the result is there in front of you.

DHONDIBA: But what can the government do to remedy this?

JOTIRAO: Well, the only remedy for this is that the government must assign this work to the European collectors. Otherwise the project will not succeed. See, these Collectors are in close contact with the shudras and atishudras; so instead of leaving the task to their *bhat* employees, and without depending on the *bhat* kulkarnis, if they personally visit the villages, and explain the advantages of receiving education to all the downtrodden people, from young to old, the villagers will gladly select their intelligent children and entrust them with the Collector to be trained as teachers. I really doubt whether the ignorant *bhat* officers will ever do this. But I feel confident that the Collectors will definitely be able to achieve the goal. There is a proverb that says that any work should be done only by the person who is meant for it. If another tries to step into his shoes, he will make a mess of it. Now think Dhondiba, how essential it is to prepare trained teachers from amongst the shudras and atishudras. Once they are trained, they will be conscious of the problems of their caste. They will be fired with the desire to initiate the young shudra and atishudra children into the pleasures of learning. Generally, in villages, the youngsters are sent to tend cattle as cowherds with sticks. But once they experience the delights of learning, they will run back to the village to learn more from their teacher instead of playing silly games. They could even take turns tending the cattle, but learn they will. Of course, I am aware that it is an uphill task. Even the Americans, who are far more advanced compared to other people, had a tough time rescuing their slaves from the clutches of their own brothers. They had to fight continuously for three years to break down their tough resistance. How can we expect our village *bhat* teacher to impart true instruction and education to the shudras and atishudras to enable them to liberate themselves from the bonds of slavery? Even our government spends too much money on these *bhat* teachers; they could easily get six shudra teachers or nine atishudra teachers for the salary they pay to just one *bhat* teacher! Yet the government so thoughtlessly squanders away money, which is, in fact, earned by the sweat of the shudras. Mind you, it is our duty to appraise the government of this fact. If we don't, we will have only ourselves to blame. Tell me, how many atishudra students would you find in the boarding school run by Mr Chaudhari in his spacious house?

DHONDIBA: Ha! Why ask this question when you know that even shudra students aren't allowed there?

JOTIRAO: Why, just now you were claiming that the government does not have any preferences, weren't you? Now you tell me why this is so!

DHONDIBA: Oh, the reason obviously is the great number of *bhat* employees there! You yourself had shown me proof. Do you remember the *bhat* gentleman working with you then? He used to come and teach in the school for the atishudras and taught all students alike, without bothering about getting polluted by their caste. Yet when the same gentleman left your job and joined that boarding school, he became so acutely conscious of the 'polluting factor' that once he dragged one poor goldsmith to the *chawdi*,[66] because he had committed the 'crime' of drinking water from the school tank in summer to quench his thirst.

[66] *Chawdi*: the place of business or tribunal or a kotwal's office in the village. [*—Ed.*]

JOTIRAO: Then there is this *bhat* celebrity, the songs composed by whom are so popular in this 'new' society; yet he follows the dictates of his hypocritical religion and worships stone idols in his house. He has even built a wall around the water tank in his house so that no shudra can drink water from it. And now he has decided to go to Kashi and stay there permanently. Look at the injustice! In the Shukrawar Peth, people from the tailor caste had built a similar wall around their water tank. Our so-called impartial Municipal Council resolved to bring down that wall. Yet they did not even dream of touching the wall built by the brahman. Why? Obviously because the Municipality is infested with *bhats*. Many *bhatjis* got a small tank built near the old one for their exclusive use and they waste so much water washing their dirty linen which they call their *sowale*. Well, they won't be brahmans worth their salt if they don't indulge in such crafty practices! They would consider their birth wasted otherwise!

Part XVI

Denouncing the tyranny of the Brahma rakshasa

DHONDIBA: All this conversation goes on to prove that the *bhats* have managed to throw dust in the eyes of our credulous government using their crafty religion and their harassing of the shudras and atishudras is worse than that of the Americans torturing their slaves. So why don't you denounce their crafty religion and undertake the task of awakening our ignorant brothers?

JOTIRAO: I have prepared such a letter last evening and given it to one of my friends, with a request to correct all the mistakes of punctuation and spelling in it and then send it to all newspapers, both *bhat* and Christian, for their comments. This is the draft of the letter.

How the shudras can emancipate themselves from the slavery of the Brahma rakshasa

The original (Iranian) ancestors of the *bhats* waged a war against the original inhabitants in this land long, long ago and after defeating them, turned them into their slaves. Later on, intoxicated with their power, they exploited every opportunity to produce crafty and cunning books and built, as it were, a strong fortress of these books in which they imprisoned all the slaves for generations. There they have been torturing them in various ways and enjoying themselves at the cost of the slaves. When the valiant British established their rule in this land, the kind-hearted Europeans and Americans were deeply aggrieved by our misery. So they entered our prisons and asked us, 'Folks, you are human beings just like us. Our Creator[67] and Sustainer are one and the same. You are entitled to have all the rights that we have. Then why do you obey the dictates of these crafty *bhats*?' All these sacred ideas awakened me to my real rights. Then I kicked the crafty brahman prison gates open and fervently thanked the Creator for this deliverance.

Now before pitching my tent in the courtyard of these benevolent European preachers, I solemnly take a pledge:

I denounce all the main books of the *bhats* which decree us their slaves as well as any other books which claim so, and embrace that book (which may have been written by a person belonging to any other country or religion) which propounds that all human beings have a right to enjoy human rights in equal measure. I will deem myself to be the younger brother of the authors of that book since we have all been created by the same Creator and will behave accordingly.

Secondly, there are some people who, on the basis of the authority derived from their arrogant religious beliefs, mercilessly treat other fellow human beings as mean and inferior. I will not blacken the name of our Creator by allowing them this license because it will go against the holy rule of equal rights decreed by Him.

[67] Here Phule uses the term *Utpannakarta*. Later in his *Sarvajanik Dharma Pustak* (published in 1891) he uses the simpler word *Nirmik*. Both the terms, however, mean the same thing, i.e., the Creator. [—*Ed.*]

Thirdly, I will regard all those shudras who, I am convinced, follow the path of righteousness, who believe only in God, their Creator, and who have vowed to behave in a clean and straight manner, as my brothers. I will treat them as members of my family and will eat food with them without any inhibitions whatsoever.

I appeal to my illiterate, suffering shudra brethren, that if any one of them desires to free himself from the slavery of the *bhats*, he should communicate his name to me in a letter. This will immensely strengthen my resolve and I will be extremely grateful to him.[68]

Jotirao Govindrao Phule

5 December, 1872 — Pune, Juna Gunj No 527

DHONDIBA: I am impressed by all the points in this declaration and wholeheartedly approve of them. I have resolved to behave accordingly. I rejoice my release from the age-old prison house of the false and wily *bhats*. In short, your teaching has absolutely convinced me of the fakeness of the Hindu religion. But tell me,

[68] We have received some comments from some newspapers regarding this declaration. We present them here so as to give an idea about their worth:

Lokkalyanechchu [One who desires the well-being of all people. [—Ed.]]

Pune, Saturday, 4 January, 1873.

We have received an article by one Mr Jotirao Govindrao Phule, who considers himself a great scholar, thinker and philosopher, which is full of praise for himself and defamation of the brahmans. Though a well-known scholar recommends the article, we do not consider the article fit for publication in our journal. We hope that Shri Phule understands this.

Shubhavartaman and *Church Sambandhi Nanavidha Sangraha*

Kolhapur, 1 February, 1873

This article has been sent to us because the native journalists in Pune did not allow it to be printed in their newspapers. Since Mr Phule has expressed a desire for the article to be published in our newspaper, we have included it in this issue. Our Hindu friends may find the writing in this article a little offensive. Yet we consider the arguments expressed in it as admirable. When Mr Phule realized that caste distinctions are man-made, he courageously declared his willingness to eat food with anybody. We fervently wish for many such valiant men to be born in this country. [—*J.P.*]

cannot God, in whom we, as well as all the wise men believe, see the plight of us shudras, for He is omnipotent and all-seeing?

JOTIRAO: I'll explain about this some other time and then you will understand.

Memorial Addressed to the Education Commission

19 October 1882

Written in English by the author

Lord Ripon, the Viceroy, had appointed an Education Commission for India under the chairmanship of Sir William Hunter in 1881. It was the first among several such commissions that modern India has known. Phule in his deposition before the commission is mainly concentrating his attention on primary education. He had proposed that primary education till the age of twelve be made compulsory. Not surprisingly, the Hunter Commission did not accept any of Phule's proposals. He, in turn, did not find the recommendations of the Hunter Commission satisfactory. Later in 1891 he even accused Sir William Hunter of total ignorance of the state of shudras and the atishudras. Because of this ignorance 'Huntersaheb is indulging in meaningless and idle loquaciousness [*vachalpana*]'; one of the many examples of Phule's blunt criticism of the English and their administration.

[Education Commission, Bombay, Vol. II, Calcutta, 1884, pp. 140–45.]

A Statement for the information of the Education Commission

My experience in educational matters is principally confined to Poona and the surrounding villages. About 25 years ago, the missionaries had established a female school at Poona but no indigeneous school for girls existed at the time. I, therefore, was induced, about the year 1854,[1] to establish such a school, and in which I and my wife worked together for many years. After some time I placed this school under the management of a committee of educated natives. Under their auspices two more schools were opened in different parts of the town. A year after the institution of the female schools, I also established an indigeneous mixed school for the lower classes, especially the Mahars and Mangs. Two more schools for these classes were subsequently added. Sir Erskine Perry, the president of the late Educational Board, and Mr. Lumsdain, the then Secretary to Government, visited the female schools and were much pleased with the movement set on foot, and presented me with a pair of shawls. I continued to work in them for nearly 9 to 10 years, but, owing to circumstances, which it is needless here to detail, I seceded from the work. These female schools still exist, having been made over by the committee to the Educational Department under the management of Mrs. Mitchell. A school for the lower classes, Mahars and Mangs, also exists at the present day, but not in a satisfactory condition. I have also been a teacher for some years in a mission female boarding school. My principal experience was gained in connection with these schools. I devoted some attention also to the primary education available in this Presidency and have had some opportunities of forming an opinion as to the system and *personnel* employed in the lower schools of the Educational Department. I wrote some

[1] This is a typographical error. The correct date should be 1851. [—*Ed.*]

years ago a Marathi pamphlet exposing the religious practices of the Brahmins, and, incidentally among other matters, adverted therein to the present system of education, which, by providing ampler funds for higher education, tended to educate Brahmins and the higher classes only, and to leave the masses wallowing in ignorance and poverty. I summarized the views expressed in the book in an English preface attached thereto, portions of which I reproduce here so far as they relate to the present enquiry:

'Perhaps a part of the blame in bringing matters to this crisis may be justly laid to the credit of the Government. Whatever may have been their motives in providing ampler funds and greater facilities for higher education, and neglecting that of the masses, it will be acknowledged by all that in justice to the latter, this is not as it should be. It is an admitted fact that the greater portion of the revenues of the Indian Empire are derived from the ryot's labour – from the sweat of his brow. The higher and richer classes contribute little or nothing to the state exchequer. A well-informed English writer states that our income is derived, not from surplus profits, but from capital; not from luxuries, but from the poorest necessaries. It is the product of sin and tears.

'That Government should expend profusely a large portion of revenue thus raised, on the education of the higher classes, for it is these only who take advantage of it, is anything but just or equitable. Their object in patronizing this virtual high class education appears to be to prepare scholars who, it is thought, would in time vend learning without money and without price. If we can inspire, say they, the love of knowledge in the minds of the superior classes, the result will be a higher standard, of morals in the cases of the individuals, a large amount of affection for the British Government, and unconquerable desire to spread among their own countrymen the intellectual blessings which they have received.

'Regarding these objects of Government the writer above alluded to, states that we have never heard of philosophy more benevolent and more utopion. It is proposed by men who witness the wondrous changes brought about in the Western world, purely by the agency of popular knowledge, to redress the defects of the two hundred millions of India, by giving superior education to the superior classes and to them only. We ask the friends of Indian Universities to favour us with a single example of the truth of their theory from the instances which have already fallen within the scope of their experience. They have educated many children of wealthy men and have been the means of advancing very materially the worldly prospects of some of their pupils. But what contribution have these made to [the] great work of regenerating their fellowmen? How have they begun to act upon the masses? Have any of them formed classes at their own homes or elsewhere, for the instruction of their less fortunate or less wise countrymen? Or have they kept their knowledge to themselves, as a personal gift, not to be soiled by contact with the ignorant vulgar? Have they in any way shown themselves anxious to advance the general interests and repay the philanthropy with patriotism? Upon what grounds is it asserted that the best way to advance the moral and intellectual welfare of the people is to raise the standard of instruction among the higher classes? A glorious argument this for aristocracy, were it only tenable. To show the growth of the national happiness, it would only be necessary to refer to the number of pupils at the colleges and the lists of academic degrees. Each wrangler would be accounted a national benefactor; and the existence of Deans and Proctors would be associated, like the game laws and the ten-pound franchise, with the best interests of the constitution.

'One of the most glaring tendencies of Government system of high class education has been the virtual monopoly of all the higher offices under them by Brahmins. If the welfare of the Ryot is at heart, if it is the duty of Government to check a host of abuses, it behoves them to narrow this monopoly day by day so as to allow a sprinkling of the other castes to get into the public services. Perhaps some might be inclined to say that it is not feasible in the present state of education. Our only reply is that if Government looks a little less after higher education which is able to take care of itself and more towards the education of the masses there would be no difficulty in training up a body of men every way qualified and perhaps far better in morals and manners.

'My object in writing the present volume is not only to tell my Shudra brethren how they have been duped by the Brahmins, but also to open the eyes of Government to that pernicious system of high-class education, which has hitherto been so persistently followed, and which statesmen like Sir George Campbell, the present Lieutenant Governor of Bengal, with broad universal sympathies, are finding to be highly mischievous and pernicious to the interests of Government. I sincerely hope that Government will ere long see the error of their ways, trust less to writers or men who look through high-class spectacles, and take the glory into their own hands of emancipating my Shudra brethren from the trammels of bondage which the Brahmins have woven around them like the coils of a serpent. It is no less the duty of each of my Shudra brethren as have received any education, to place before Government the true state of their fellowmen and endeavour to the best of their power to emancipate themselves from Brahmin thraldom. Let there be schools for the Shudras in every village; but away with all Brahmin school-masters! The Shudras are the life and sinews of the country, and it is to them alone, and not to the Brahmins, that Government must ever look to tide over their difficulties, financial as well as political. If the hearts and minds of the Shudras are made happy and contented, the British Government need have no fear for their loyalty in the future.'

Primary Education

There is little doubt that primary education among the masses in this Presidency has been very much neglected. Although the number of primary schools now in existence is greater than those existing a few years ago, yet they are not commensurate to the requirements of the community. Government collects a special cess for educational purposes, and it is to be regretted that this fund is not spent for the purposes for which it is collected. Nearly nine-tenths of the villages in this Presidency, or nearly 10 lakhs of children, it is said, are without any provision, whatever, for primary instruction. A good deal of their poverty, their want of self-reliance, their entire dependence upon the learned and intelligent classes, is attributable to this deplorable state of education among the peasantry.

Even *in towns* the Brahmins, the Purbhoos, the hereditary classes, who generally live by the occupation of pen, and the trading classes seek primary instruction. The cultivating and the other classes, as a rule, do not generally avail themselves of the same. A few of the latter class are found in primary and secondary schools, but owing to their poverty and other causes they do not continue long at school. As there are no special inducements for these to continue at school, they naturally leave off as soon as they find any menial or other occupation. In *villages* also most of the cultivating classes hold aloof, owing to extreme poverty, and also because they require their children to tend cattle and look after their fields. Besides an increase in the number of schools, special inducements in the shape of scholarships and half-yearly or annual prizes, to encourage them to send their children to school and thus create in them a taste for learning, is most essential. I think primary education of the masses should be made compulsory up to a certain age, say at least 12 years. Muhammadans also hold aloof from these schools, as they somehow evince no liking for Marathi or English. There are a few Muhammadan primary schools where their own language is taught. The *Mahars*, *Mangs*, and other lower classes are practically excluded from all schools owing to caste prejudices, as they are not allowed to sit by the children of higher castes. Consequently special schools for these have been opened by Government. But these exist only in large towns. In the whole of Poona and for a population exceeding over 5,000 people, there is only one school, and in which the attendance is under 30 boys. This state of matters is not at all creditable to the educational authorities. Under the promise of the Queen's Proclamation I beg to urge that Mahars, Mangs, and other lower classes, where their number is large enough, should have separate schools for them, as they are not allowed to attend the other schools owing to caste prejudices.

In the present state of education, payment by results is not at all suitable for the promotion of education amongst a poor and ignorant people, as no taste has yet been created among them for education. I do not think any teacher would undertake to open schools on his own account among these people, as he would not be able to make a living by it. Government schools and special inducements, as noted above, are essential until such a taste is created among them.

With regard to the few Government primary schools that exist in the Presidency, I beg to observe that the primary education imparted in them is not at all placed on a satisfactory or sound basis. The system is imperfect in so far as it does not prove practical and useful in the future career of the pupils. The system is capable of being developed up to the requirement of the community, if improvements that will result in its future usefulness be effected in it. Both the teaching machinery employed and the course of instruction now followed, require a thorough remodeling.

(a) The teachers now employed in the primary schools are almost all Brahmins; a few of them are from the normal training college, the rest being all untrained men. Their salaries are very low, seldom exceeding Rs. 10, and their attainments also very meager. But as a rule they are all unpractical men, and the boys who learn under them generally imbibe inactive habits and try to obtain service, to the avoidance of their hereditary or other hardy or independent professions. I think teachers for primary schools should be trained, as far as possible, out of the cultivating classes, who will be able to mix freely with them and understand their wants and wishes much better than a Brahmin teacher, who generally holds himself aloof under religious prejudices. These would, moreover, exercise a more beneficial influence over the masses than teachers of other classes, and who will not feel ashamed to hold the handle of a plough or the carpenter's adze when required, and who will be able to mix themselves readily with the lower orders of society. The course of training for them ought to include, besides the ordinary subjects, an elementary knowledge of agriculture and sanitation. The untrained teachers should, except when thoroughly efficient, be replaced by efficient trained teachers. To secure a better class of teachers and to improve their position, better salaries should be given. Their salaries should not be less than Rs. 12 and in larger villages should be at least Rs. 15 or 20. Associating them in the village polity as auditors of village accounts or registrars of deeds, or village postmasters or stamp vendors, would improve their status, and thus exert a beneficial influence over the people among whom they live. The schoolmasters of village schools who pass a large number of boys should also get some special allowance other than their pay, as an encouragement to them.

(b) The course of instruction should consist of reading, writing Modi, and Balbodh[2] and accounts, and a rudimentary knowledge of general history, general geography, and grammar, also an elementary knowledge of agriculture and a few lessons on moral duties and sanitation. The studies in the village schools might be fewer than those in larger villages and towns, but not the less practical. In connection with lessons in agriculture, a small model farm, where practical instruction to the pupils can be given, would be a decided advantage and, if really efficiently managed, would be productive of the greatest good to the country. The text-books in use, both in the primary and Anglo-vernacular schools, require revision and recasting as much as they are not practical or progressive in their scope. Lessons on technical education and morality, sanitation and agriculture, and some useful arts, should be interspersed among them in progressive series. The fees in the primary schools should be as 1 to 2 from the children of cess-payers and non-cess-payers.

(c) The supervising agency over these primary schools is also very defective and insufficient. The Deputy Inspector's visit once a year can hardly be of any appreciable benefit. All these schools ought at least to be inspected quarterly if not oftener. I would also suggest the advisability of visiting these schools at other times and without any intimation being given. No reliance can be placed

[2] Modi: a running script in which most Marathi correspondence and account-writing used to take place. It was taught in schools till well into the 1940s. See also note 8, p. 157 of the present volume. Balbodh: elementary reading. [—*Ed.*]

on the district or village officers owing to the multifarious duties devolving on them, as they seldom find time to visit them, and when they do, their examination is necessarily very superficial and imperfect. European Inspector's supervision is also occasionally very desirable, as it will tend to exercise a very efficient control over the teachers generally.

(d) The number of primary schools should be increased –

(1) By utilizing such of the indigenous schools as shall be or are conducted by trained and certificated teachers, by giving them liberal grants-in-aid.

(2) By making over one half of the local cess fund for primary education alone.

(3) By compelling, under a statutory enactment, municipalities to maintain all the primary schools within their respective limits.

(4) By an adequate grant from the provincial or imperial funds.

Prizes and scholarships to pupils, and capitation or other allowance to the teachers, as an encouragement, will tend to render these schools more efficient.

The Municipalities in large towns should be asked to contribute whole share of the expenses incurred on primary schools within the municipal areas. But in no case ought the management of the same to be entirely made over to them. They should be under the supervision of the Educational Department.

The municipalities should also give grants-in-aid to such secondary and private English schools as shall be conducted according to the rules of the Educational Department, where their funds permit, such grants-in-aid being regulated by the number of boys passed every year. These contributions from municipal funds may be made compulsory by statutory enactment.

The administration of the funds for primary education should ordinarily be in the hands of the Director of Public Instruction.

But if educated and intelligent men are appointed on the local or district committees, these funds may be safely entrusted to them, under the guidance of the Collector, or the Director of Public Instruction. At present, the local boards consist of ignorant and uneducated men, such as Patels, Inamdars, Surdars, &c., who would not be capable of exercising any intelligent control over the funds.

Indigenous schools

Indigenous schools exist a good deal in cities, towns, and some large villages, especially where there is a Brahmin population. From the latest reports of Public Instruction in this Presidency, it is found that there are 1,049 indigenous schools with about 27,694 pupils in them. They are conducted on the old village system. The boys are generally taught the multiplication table by heart, a little Modi writing and reading, and to recite a few religious pieces. The teachers, as a rule, are not capable of effecting any improvements, as they are not initiated in the art of teaching. The fees charged in these schools range from 2 to 8 annas. The teachers generally come from the dregs of Brahminical society. Their qualifications hardly go beyond reading and writing Marathi very indifferently, and casting accounts up to the rule of three or so. They set up as teachers as the last resource of getting a livelihood. Their failure or unfitness in other callings of life obliges them to open schools. No arrangements exist in the country to train up teachers for indigenous schools. The indigenous schools could not be turned to any good account, unless the present teachers are replaced by men from the training colleges and by those who pass the 6th standard in the vernaculars. The present teachers will willingly accept State aid, but money thus spent will be thrown away. I do not know any instance in which a grant-in-aid is paid to such a school. If it is being paid anywhere, it must be in very rare cases. In my opinion no grants-in-aid should be paid to such schools unless the master is a certificated one. But if certificated or competent teachers be found, grants-in-aid should be given and will be productive of great good.

Higher education

The cry over the whole country has been for some time past that Government have amply provided for higher education, whereas that of the masses has been neglected. To some extent this cry is justified, although the classes directly benefited by the higher education may not readily admit it. But for all this no well-wisher of his country would desire that Government should, at the present time, withdraw its aid from higher education. All that they would wish is, that as one class of the body politic has been neglected, its advancement should form as anxious a concern as that of the other. Education in India is still in its infancy. Any withdrawal of State aid from higher education cannot but be injurious to the spread of education generally.

A taste for education among the higher and wealthy classes, such as the Brahmins and Purbhoos, especially those classes who live by the pen, has been created, and a gradual withdrawal of State aid may be possible so far as these classes are concerned; but in the middle and lower classes, among whom higher education has made no perceptible progress, such a withdrawal would be a great hardship. In the event of such withdrawal, boys will be obliged to have recourse to inefficient and sectarian schools, much against their wish, and the cause of education cannot but suffer. Nor could any part of such education be entrusted to private agency. For a long time to come the entire educational machinery, both ministerial and executive, must be in the hands of Government. Both the higher and primary education require all the fostering care and attention which Government can bestow on it.

The withdrawal of Government from schools or colleges would not only tend to check the spread of education, but would seriously endanger that spirit of neutrality which has all along been the aim of Government to foster, owing to the different nationalities and religious creeds prevalent in India. This withdrawal may, to a certain extent, create a spirit of self-reliance for local purposes in the higher and wealthy classes, but the cause of education would be so far injured that the spirit of self-reliance would take years to remedy that evil. Educated men of ability, who do not succeed in getting into public service, may be induced to open schools for higher education on being assured of liberal grants in-aid. But no one would be ready to do so on his own account as a means of gaining a livelihood, and it is doubtful whether such private efforts could be permanent or stable, nor would they succeed half so well in their results. Private schools, such as those of Mr. Vishnu Shastree Chiploonkar and Mr. Bhavey, exist in Poona, and with adequate grants-in-aid may be rendered very efficient, but they can never supersede the necessity of the high school.

The missionary schools, although some of them are very efficiently conducted, do not succeed half so well in their results, nor do they attract half the number of students which the high school attract. The superiority of Government schools is mainly owing to the richly, paid staff of teachers and professors which it is not possible for a private school to maintain.

The character of instruction given in the Government higher schools, is not at all practical, or such as is required for the necessities of ordinary life. It is only good to turn out so many clerks and schoolmasters. The Matriculation examination unduly engrosses the attention of the teachers and pupils, and the course of studies prescribed has no practical element in it, so as to fit the pupil for his future career in independent life. Although the number of students presenting for the Entrance examination is not at all large when the diffusion of knowledge in the country is taken into consideration, it looks large when the requirements of Government service are concerned. Were the education universal and within easy reach of all, the number would have been larger still, and it should be so, and I hope it will be so hereafter. The higher education should be so arranged as to be within easy reach of all, and the books on the subjects for Matriculation examination should be published in the Government Gazette, as is done in Madras and Bengal. Such a course will encourage private studies and secure larger diffusion of knowledge in the country. It is a boon to the people that the Bombay University recognizes private studies in the case of those presenting for the entrance examination. I hope, the University authorities will be pleased to extend the same boon to higher examinations. If private studies were recognized by the University in granting the degrees of B.A., M.A., &c., many young men will devote their time to private studies. Their doing so will still further tend to the diffusion of knowledge. It is found in many instances quite impossible to prosecute studies at the colleges for various reasons. If private studies be recognized by the University, much good will be effected to the country at large, and a good deal of the drain on the public purse on account of higher education will be lessened.

The system of Government scholarships, at present followed in the Government schools, is also defective, inasmuch as it gives undue encouragement to those classes only, who have already acquired a taste for education to the detriment of the other classes. The system might be so arranged that some of these scholarships should be awarded to such classes amongst whom education has made no progress.

The system of awarding them by competition, although abstractedly equitable, does not tend to the spread of education among other classes.

With regard to the question as to educated natives finding remunerative employments, it will be remembered that the educated natives who mostly belong to the Brahminical and other higher classes are mostly fond of service. But as the public service can afford no field for all the educated natives who come out from schools and colleges, and moreover the course of training they receive being not of a technical or practical nature, they find great difficulty in betaking themselves to other manual or remunerative employments. Hence the cry that the market is overstocked with educated natives who do not find any remunerative employment. It may, to a certain extent, be true that some of the professions are overstocked, but this does not show that there is not other remunerative employment to which they can betake themselves. The present number of educated men is very small in relation to the country at large, and we trust that the day may not be far distant when we shall have the present number multiplied a hundred-fold, and all be taking themselves to useful and remunerative occupations and not be looking after service.

In conclusion, I beg to request the Education Commission to be kind enough to sanction measures for the spread of female primary education on a more liberal scale.

Poona
19th October 1882

Joteerao Govindrao Phooley,
Merchant and Cultivator and
Municipal Commissioner,
Peth Joona Ganja.

Cultivator's Whipcord

April–July 1883

Translated by Aniket Jaaware

Cultivator's Whipcord (*Shetkaryacha Asud*) was written in 1883 but the publication of the entire text was delayed because, as Phule put it, 'We the shudras have amongst us cowardly publishers.'

Aniket Jaaware, our translator, had proposed 'whiplash' as a translation for *asud*. However, Phule himself preferred whipcord, and that is what we have retained.

Asud and *Gulamgiri*, between them, sum up Phule's political and economic philosophy and define his historicist understanding of the varna system. Phule believed that Maharashtrian Hindu society was made of two groups, the brahmans and the shudratishudras. This two-fold division and the historical tension between the two is central to his thought. Here we see Phule analysing history, mythology, language, the social struggle at the core of Maharashtrian society, revolutionary change and its appropriation by the dominant class, in this case the brahmans. Even if one were to read only these two books, one would get the essence of Phule's thought and system.

Cultivator's Whip-cord
by
Jotirao Govindrao Phuley
for the defence of the Shudra (Dasya) Community

For the kind consideration of
His Excellency the Right Hon'ble
Sir Frederick Temple Hamilton Temple Blackwood,
Earl of Dufferin,
K.P., G.C.B., G.C.M.G., F.R.S.D.C.I.,
Viceroy and Governor General of India.

Contents

While I was working on this *Whipcord* many people spoke to me on the proposed book. I present here two typical examples –

The one who calls himself a pure maratha

A shudra sadhu

Prologue

Without knowledge, intelligence was lost, without intelligence morality was lost and without morality was lost all dynamism! Without dynamism money was lost and without money the shudras sank. All this misery was caused by the lack of knowledge.

What we mean is, there are many causes for the abjection of shudra farmers, relating to religion and state, and we have written this book with the intention of discussing some of them at least. Because of an artificial and tyrannical religion, and because almost all the government departments are dominated by brahmans, and because the European workers are lazy, the shudra farmers are ill-treated by the brahman workers. Our intention is that they should be assisted in defending themselves from these, and therefore we have titled this book as *The Cultivator's Whipcord*.

Dear Readers, at present, farmers can be divided into three groups – pure farmers or kunbis, malis and dhangars.[1] Now if we look at how this division came about, we find that originally there were people who depended on farming for their livelihood. These are the *kulavadis* or kunbis. Gradually there emerged people who worked on their farmlands and in the process diversified into cultivating fruits and vegetables. They became the gardeners or malis. Then there emerged a third group who did both these and possessed goats etc. They became the dhangars or shepherds. These differences must have come about because of differences in work. But now these are thought to be three separate castes. At present there is no inter-marriage between these, but there is inter-dining and other relationships.[2] Therefore these (kunbis, malis and

[1] Mali: gardener; dhangar: shepherd. [—*Ed.*]

[2] The clan-god of shudras, Khanderao of Jejuri married two women, Mhalsabai from the shudra kunbis and Banabai from the dhangars, and this proves that in the past there was inter-marriage between kulavadis and dhangars. [—*J.P.*]

dhangars) must have been in the past of a single and same shudra farmer caste. Later people from all the three castes had to give up their original business of farming and take up various businesses for their livelihood. Those who have some energy, have continued to be farmers, though most of them are illiterate God-believers, naked and forever hungry; and those who were totally supportless have left their areas and sought business here and there, wherever they could find it. Some have started a fodder-business, some of wood, some of cloth, and some others have started taking contracts, others to be employed as writers, and finally are proud of themselves with their pensions. Thus they earn money and build estates. But after them, their cavalier sons, who have little love of knowledge, become penniless in no time and blame their fathers (for not having left behind enough). Many there are whose ancestors won whole jagirs and inams on the strength of their soldiery or their wit, and some indeed had become parallel kings like Shinde and Holkar. But at present their descendents, ignorant and illiterate, have either pawned their jagirs and inams, or sold them off outright and are in debt, and many there are, who are penniless and without food. Most inamdars and jagirdars have no conception of the various adventures and achievements of their ancestors or of their various sufferings, and because they are ignorant and in the company of selfish and cunning men and because they are indulging day and night in luxury and addictions, it has become rare to find those whose jagirs are not pawned off and those who are not entirely possessed by debt. Now even among those *samsthaniks*[3] who have no debts and liabilities, the people around them and their brahman administrators are so selfish, cunning and politic that they prevent the *samsthaniks* from acquiring a taste for virtue and knowledge; they are content to believe that their ancestors created this wealth only for their enjoyment. Blinded by religion and incapable of governing their kingdoms on their own, they throw their lot in the hands of fate and depend entirely on their brahman administrators; and generate virtue by donations of cow during the day, and progeny by night.

[3] Rulers of princely states in colonial India. [—*Ed.*]

It is especially possible for such kings and lords to improve the lot of their shudra brothers, but they never think of it and as long as the stupidity of believing that 'the brahman is the one I worship' (*brahmano mama daivatam*) does not leave their heads, however much we might break our heads over it, it would be futile; and even if after this someone is prompted to do so (improve the lot of their brothers, that is), how would they listen to any ideas which go against the selfish religion which has been firmly implanted in their minds from childhood, and think about them? And the administrators close to them will not allow such a self-less person to do anything. But if someone is courageous enough to give me some time and let me explain according to my wit, I will happily present my ideas to him.

Anyway, a comparison of the condition of the shudra God-fearing farmer of Hindustan with all other countries in the world reveals that their condition is worse than farmers in other countries, and is even worse than that of beasts.

It needs hardly to be stated that this book is composed from the abject conditions of contemporary ignorant shudras and atishudras and English, Sanskrit and Prakrit books. It is clear that without such help, it could not have been constructed.

I request the scholarly and discerning reader to ignore the lacunae in the book, forgiving me for them, and taking only the good things from it, since I have written of my discoveries in it according to my limited wit. And if in their perusal, they see parts that are inappropriate or false, or if they find any support (in other books etc.) to strengthen the book, they should write to us through newspapers. We will gratefully acknowledge them and consider their suggestions in the second edition.

Shrimant Sarkar Gaikwad, Senakhaskhel Samsher Bahadur Sayajirao Maharaj has, with great enthusiasm and affection, made me read this book to him and listened to it with great attention, sparing time from all his kingly duties, when I went to Baroda; and the Maharaj has, in his generosity, felicitated me and helped me with money. I am deeply grateful to him.

I have read out portions of this book to several shudra

gentlemen in Pune, Mumbai, Thane, Junnar, Otur, Hadapsar, Vangani, Malyache Kural, etc., and they have sent me signed letters stating that the matter in the book is true and correct.

Chapter First

Because the brahman workers are dominant in all the departments of the government, their selfish relations, *bhat* and brahmans so exploit the ignorant farmer in the name of their greedy religion that the farmer is left without any means of sending his little ones to school, and even if some such one has the means, because of their ill advice, he is without the wish to do so.

Now, the first type of letterless farmer is so exploited by the brahman under the pretext of religion that it would be very hard to find a parallel example anywhere in the world. The ancient and cunning Arya brahman scripture-writers have so smoothly machinated to tie up the farmer in their selfish religion that from even before he is born, when his mother gets her menses and the *garbhadhaan* rituals[4] are performed, till he dies, various things are looted from him. Not only that, but even after he dies, his son has to bear the weight of religion for the *shraadha*[5] and other rituals. For, the moment a farmer's woman gets her menses, in the name of japa and anushthan, the brahmans loot their money, and in the process, under the pretext of brahman-bhojan collect their relatives and friends, create such a confusion of dakshina and ghee and chapati that of the left-over food, not even dal and chapati is left to fill the poor farmer's belly. In the name of pacification of gods that rule the menses, the brahmans pacify their bellies and the moment some dakshina is put into their hands, after blessing the farmer and telling the farmers' women to fast on Saturdays or the fourth day of the month, leave for their respective homes. Later the brahman, on every Saturday or the fourth day, makes the women put necklaces of cotton-leaves on Maruti's neck and grass on Ganapati's head, get foodstuff for themselves and if possible, later, promising fulfilment

[4] To mark conception. [—*Ed.*]

[5] Death rituals. [—*Ed.*]

of these rituals, they extract minor feasts from the farmer. In the meanwhile, in the course of nature, if the farmer's woman gets pregnant, the dedicative vow[6] made in the name of the ghosts of unmarried brahmans, are invoked casually while talking to the farmer, and when the farmers' women are close to delivery, the brahman frequents the farmers' houses, and sweet-talking them into believing themselves the hosts of ceremonies, fulfil all those supposed vows made earlier. Later, when the farmer woman has a son, the line of wealth manifests itself on the brahman's palm. This is how: first the chief priest goes to the farmer's house and asks the exact time of birth to the ignorant women, who count time with threads and shadows; and thus makes the horoscope, fixing that sign under which the most unlucky and ill stars match, so that the joy of having a son is completely taken away by the farmer's anxious fears. Then on the next day, they bring together their own relatives and friends and make them sit for japa and anushthan, and make the farmer give at least enough money for fruits and other things, because they are fasting. If it is summer, they obtain fans; if rains, umbrellas; if winter, white sheets. Moreover, if the chief priest can manage it, he takes oil, rice, coconut, ghee, sugar, fruits and other things as well, for the pooja. In order to impress upon the farmer the love for idol-worship, many of these do not shave or cut their hair during the ritual, some eat only fruit. Thus by cheating the farmer with smooth lies, they extract a lot of money from him. And all of you know what great enjoyment they have at the time of the completion of the ritual, getting from the farmer the appropriate dakshina.

The Arya *bhat*s and brahmans do not admit shudra farmers' children[7] in their Sanskrit schools, but in their Prakrit Marathi schools they admit these children, and over and above their own monthly salaries, extract food on every full moon and moonless night, grain on many festival days, and even take a fourth from what the children bring everyday to eat in school; and teach them

6 The original has *navas*, a promise to the god concerned to do something in return for one's wish being fulfilled. [—*Ed.*]

7 Sir William Jones, Vol. IV, page 111. [—*J.P.*] [Original in English. [—*Ed.*]]

only the basic letters, arithmetic, modi,[8] some shloka in Prakrit relating to pretentious and false puranas, and a few songs, or teach them lavanis,[9] making them educated enough to write such things. Never giving them sufficient knowledge even to keep accounts of expenses at home. So how would they enter into the mamledar's offices and become even clerks?

At the time of fixing the marriage of the farmer's son, the brahman astrologer goes to the prospective groom's house, and arranging all kinds of diagrams of constellations, asks what the names of the children are, and proposing his own advantage to himself, his thumb dances on the digits of his fingers, and makes sure that an ill-fortuned planet is found in the signs, and in order to pacify that planet, they take money from the farmer for the beginning and for the completion of rituals. Then at the time of fixing the date of marriage, at the bride's house they take a folded piece of cloth and make various squares on it with rice, make the two fathers sit on them and arrange coconut pieces, turmeric, kumkum and other things; and without in the least thinking of the age of the bride and the groom or their varna, or their qualities, arrange a minimal Ganapati with betel nut and with a general bustle of *samarpayami*[10] they elicit money from the farmer, and then note the date on a piece of paper, cover it with kumkum and turmeric and put it into the hands of the parents; and then gathering everything, including money and things, take also the betel-nut Ganapati to crack him and chew him at home. Before the marriage in the Maruti temple, when the groom is given a dress from the bride's side, the *bhat*s and brahmans take an anna or two[11] and pocket it. When the groom enters the pandal, they put some mounds of wheat for the pair to stand facing each other and make both maternal uncles stand behind them, with naked swords, as supporters. Taking pieces of cloth from whoever is around, they

8 See note 2 on p. 140 of the present volume. [—*Ed.*]

9 Song, often erotic, mostly accompanied by dance in the popular theatre of Maharashtra called tamasha. [—*Ed.*]

10 Samarpayami (Sanskrit) literally means 'I offer'. One offers milk, ghee, etc. in a ritual and says samarpayami. [—*Ed.*]

11 An anna was the sixteenth part of a rupee in old pre-metric currency system. [—*Ed.*]

stripe it with turmeric and kumkum, and holding it between the pair, turn by turn sing shlokas, some in Raga Kalyan, some in Raga Bhairavi, finally saying '*shubhmangal*', they marry off the ignorant farmer's children. In the marriages of many rich malis and kunbis, without bothering about the hosts or their relations or guests, many uninvited brahmans sit down with panache and shawls, and create such confusion in the marriage-pandal for the dakshina, that the parents of the bride and the groom are not free properly to welcome the invited relations. Will such unscrupulous beggars ever be found in another country or caste? Then suddenly the *bhatji* actually performing the marriage makes the bride and the groom sit down beside each other, and performs all manner of ritual, saying '*dakshinam samarpayami*' intermittently, and then taking some sticks and things, lights a fire and puts ghee and other things in the fire, engulfs the couple thoroughly in smoke, in the name of the *lajja-homa*,[12] and goes home after taking lots of food and dakshina from the ignorant fathers. On the day of the completion, with the mediation of one or two cunning farmers, they extract money from the parents, and also take money for the removing the pandal. In the meanwhile, praising the rich farmer with similes of Karna[13] and other great donors, and with all kinds of tricks, they so excite the farmer that at the end of the marriage, a gathering of all kinds of brahmans is arranged, and, without distinctions, Vedic brahmans, shastris, Puranik story-tellers and *bhikshuks*,[14] all and sundry manage to get dakshina, and then go home. Some of the more epicurean brahmans having enquired if there is dance and other things at night, with tiny pagdis on their heads and minute shawls in their laps, sit right beside the invitees, reclining on bolsters, fill the two barrels of their noses with snuff, and filling the surroundings with snuff, listen to the singing of the *nayakins*.[15]

Now I will explain a little how the brahmans cheat in the name

[12] A marriage ritual. [—*Ed.*]

[13] A character in the Mahabharata, step-brother of the five Pandavas, famed for his generosity. [—*Ed.*]

[14] Different brahmanical professionals. [—*Ed.*]

[15] Women dancer–singers. [—*Ed.*]

of religion, and how they denude the farmer's children after the farmer dies of old age, until the children too die.

When the farmer's children build new houses, the shudra wage labourer works in the heat of the sun, carrying material. The mason and carpenter build towers with bamboo and climbing up like monkeys build the house with various joints of wooden beams. The owner, pitying them, promises a good meal to them at the time of entering the house, but before he can do that, the *bhat*s and brahmans frequent the farmer's house day in and day out, promising and cheating him with religion and getting silly recommendations from some administrator, perform rituals in his new house, sticking rag-flags in various corners, first making sure that they and their wives and children get a proper and sumptuous meal, leaving only stale and leftover food for the ignorant and guileless farmer and the workers which they eat with jaggery, while they themselves eat *pan*, and blessing the farmer, extract a dakshina from him and go home with their hands caressing their bellies. A few selfish sadhu *bhat* brahmans make friends with young farmers, and enticing them with promise of prestige and fame, arrange gatherings of brahmans in which some *bhat* brahmans are felicitated with shawls and things where everyone gets a dakshina. When the farmer builds new farm-houses or new temples or some such building, in the name of *udyapan*[16] the brahmans for sure take a meal and dakshina.

On every *chaitra varsha pratipada*[17] the brahmans read the predictions for the year at every farmer's house and take dakshina from them. Similarly, on Ramnavami and Hanuman Jayanti, if the brahmans can find a rich farmer in their lane, they get him to arrange a meal for brahmans and if they can find only a poor one, they alternately collect contributions from him and make sure of such a meal.

In the Jejuri yatra,[18] when the farmer along with his family

[16] A ritual to mark the conclusion of the building activity. [—*Ed.*]

[17] New-year's day according to the Maharashtrian lunar calendar. Beginning with this paragraph, Phule is discussing the holy days of the Hindu lunar calendar demonstrating how the brahmans loot on each. [—*Ed.*]

[18] Jejuri is a famous pilgrim-centre dedicated to the Lord Khandoba, about 50

goes to the lake etc. for bathing, the brahmans take one shivarai[19] as dakshina from all of them. This yatra has at least seventy-five thousand people, and if a murali sits on the lap of some innocent wealthy farmer, the dev-brahmans take money from him in the name of the *suvasini*.[20] Moreover, when the farmer buys the offerings for the gods from the grocer, the brahmans are in cahoots with the grocer, and thus exploit the farmer.

On every Ashadhi Ekadashi[21] the brahmans take at least one paisa dakshina even from the poor farmer who can give them grains for meals.

In Pandharpur, when farmers with their women and children go to the Chandrabhaga[22] for bathing, the *bhat*s and brahmans stand on the bank and take one shivarai from all of them as covenant.[23] This yatra does not have less than a lakh people; and from amongst the farmers some are made to give money for ten *suvasinis* and brahmans, or at least one, and the farmers are taken to their own houses, displaying the women of their home eating, taking each farmer separately, and saying, 'See these are your ten, if you feel like, give them some dakshina, or just pay your respects from a distance, so that they can send your dedications to God, and then eat.' Hundreds of brahman priests (especially those at Pandharpur) have become wealthy through such honest business.

In every Shravan,[24] instead of suing the vaidus and garudis for taking away their business of carrying cobras in baskets and visiting farmers' houses saying 'Feed some milk to the cobras' or '*naga dakshinam samarpayami*', the brahmans make cobras of clay or stone, and worshipping them, extract money from the farmer.

....

km. to the south south-east of Pune. [—*Ed.*]

19 A copper coin, a paisa, the 64th part of a rupee. [—*Ed.*]

20 A married woman. [—*Ed.*]

21 The eleventh day of the bright fortnight in the fourth month of the lunar calendar. In this calendar the month has two fortnights, one beginning with the new moon to the full moon (bright or Shukla fortnight) and the other from the full moon to the new moon (dark or Vadya or Krishna fortnight). [—*Ed.*]

22 The river at Pandharpur. [—*Ed.*]

23 The original has *sankalp*. [—*Ed.*]

24 The fifth month of the lunar calendar. [—*Ed.*]

On the Shravani Poornima,[25] without paying attention to the black thread in the mahar's neck, they tie Gagabhatta-like[26] sacred threads made of white thread on the bodies of pretentious kunbis, and jump on the food and the dakshina. They tie rakhees[27] on the wrists of all the farmers and take one paisa dakshina from them.

On Vadya Pratipada,[28] brahmans lure most rich farmers into observing 'devotional week', put veenas round their necks, and one by one, make them dance through the night and sing like parrots, while the brahmans themselves sit in style, reclining on bolsters, and every day take money from the farmers for this or that. On the night of the Gokulashtami, they read the third book of *Harivijay*, and take dakshina for Yashoda's delivery.[29] In the morning, for the completion, it is they who eat ghee and chapati first, and then, leaving the leftovers for the farmers and the drummers and others, go home.

Finally, on the last Monday of Shravan, the *bhat* brahmans cheat the ignorant and unsuspecting farmers and persuade them to make a gift of unlimited amount of grain. The excuse usually is that they must feed a brahman couple themselves. Thus having fed the women and children in their family to their heart's content, they condescend to give the peasant a couple of *puran-polis*[30] and a little rice and persuade them to believe that they have got their due.

On each Bhadrapada,[31] *bhat* brahmans take at least a paisa each from farmer women, young and old, in the name of Hartalika.[32]

[25] Full-moon of the month of Shravan. [—*Ed.*]

[26] Initially there was no custom of the sacred thread amongst the shudras. It started when in return of a gold balance, Gagabhatta [the Banaras brahman who anointed Shivaji. [—*Ed.*]] put a sacred thread around the kunbi king Shivaji. [—*J.P.*]

[27] These rakhees are made of cotton threads, and one gets about 25 for one paisa. [—*J.P.*]

[28] The first day of the dark fortnight. [—*Ed.*]

[29] Gokulashtami: the eighth day of the dark fortnight of the month of Shravan. The day of Lord Krishna's birthday. *Harivijay*: a hagiographical poetic narrative in Marathi on Krishna's life by Mahipati written in 1702. [—*Ed.*]

[30] Sweet roti stuffed with jaggery and ground Bengal gram. [—*Ed.*]

[31] Sixth month of the lunar calendar. [—*Ed.*]

[32] A ritual exclusive to women, involving the worship of Uma Mahadev. It is

On Ganesh Chaturthi,[33] after singing artis and clapping in front of the idol of Ganapati, they take some dakshina from the farmer. On Rishi Panchami, *bhat* brahmans make the farmer women dip into little puddles, and during the day, at the farmers expense, eat ghee and chapati; and in the night, pretending to listen to devotional songs, stare at the faces of renowned dancers, not even casting a glance at the masks of the clay Gauri in the farmer's house.

On Ananta Chaturdashi,[34] they take foodstuff from the farmer. In Pitr Paksha,[35] *bhat* brahmans create such chaos amongst the farmers and go after them, that let alone the Bhonsales, Shindes and Holkars, even the poor wage labourer women amongst them are not let off, and in the name of Ganapati, have to give foodstuff, dakshina, and slices of gourd, and touch their heads to the brahman's feet.

If, fortuitously, it's the Kapila Shashthi,[36] *bhat* brahmans take the rich farmer to holy places like Nasik, Vai and under the pretext of charity, take away lots of money, and from the poor farmers take at least a paisa each at the time of bathing.

Finally, on the amavasya, in their greed for foodstuff and dakshina, they make the farmer worship the feet of cattle.

On Vijaya Dashami, they take money from the farmer for worshipping horses and the apta tree, and on Kojagiri night, if it works, devour the farmer's milk.

On the amavasya, they take dakshina from the farmer for Lakshmi Pooja.

....

said to assure a happy married life, and a long life to the husband. [—*Ed.*]

[33] Fourth day of the bright fortnight of the sixth month Bhadrapada. [—*Ed.*]

[34] Fourteenth day of the bright fortnight of Bhadrapada, the day on which the Ganesh idols are immersed in water at the end of the ten-day festival of Ganesh. [—*Ed.*]

[35] The shraadhas to the manes of ancestors collectively performed during the dark fortnight of Bhadrapada. [—*Ed.*]

[36] A day on which six particulars synchronize: the day: Tuesday; the month: Bhadrapada; the date: the sixth of the dark fortnight; the nakshatra: Rohini; the yog: Wyatipat; and the mahanakshatra: Hasti. This synchronization is very rare, of course. Hence '*Kapilashashticha yog*' is any astonishing and unhoped for combination of favourable circumstances. [—*Ed.*]

On every Bali Pratipada in Kartik, while doing the farmer's arti, instead of blessing him with '*ida pida talo, baliche rajya yevo*',[37] they put shawls on their arms, and roam about the farmers' houses, asking for *mali*,[38] and force the farmers to be the hosts.

In the yatra at Alandi, when the farmer is bathing in the Indrayani with his family, they take a paisa each for covenant (*sankalp*); this yatra has about seventy-five thousand people. Later, on dvadashi, they give wordy blessings to the devout and for the meals of *dev-brahman suvasini*, take foodstuff from the well-off farmer and take simple things if the farmer is poor.

Also, in Bhonwar, they lure the ignorant farmers of villages into *vari*,[39] and turn by turn, for twelve months, on every dvadashi, they manage to extract brahman-bhojans. Not only that, they even flatter several rich farmers into giving a meal to a thousand brahmans. Finally, if a farmer in some other town has been punished by the council of farmers and sent there, they shave him, and in the name of restitution and penance, do they not altogether denude him?

On Vadya Dvadashi, *bhat* brahmans perform marriages for the Tulsi, holding partitions improvised from dhotis, sing a few shlokas and other verses instead of the *mangalashtaka* and collect money, and if possible other things from the farmer.

In every Paush month, on the Makar Samkranti, they read texts describing the fruit of the ritual and take dakshina from him, and promising him the accretion of immeasurable virtue, loot the ignorant farmer's sugarcane fields.

In every Magha month, on the Mahashivaratri, *bhat* brahmans read the text of the *Shivalilamrut* in temples in the farmers' lanes and take foodstuff for reading the complete text.

In every Falgun month, after worshipping the Holi, when the farmers scream and abuse because they have lost all money or rant

37 'Let all suffering be over. Let the Baliraja rule.'—*Ed.*

38 An adaptation of a Persian term originally equivalent to *zakat* (tax). In the 19th century, '*Mali magne*' meant extortion. [—*Ed.*]

39 Processional walk to Pandharpur in south-eastern Maharashtra. The town has the main temple for Vitthal, a local form of Vishnu. The *vari* takes place in Ashadh and Kartik, and thousands of devotees walk long distances to reach Pandharpur. [—*Ed.*]

against the Hindu dharma, even then these *bhatjis* do not allow them to put dust and soil on their heads without taking some dakshina.[40]

Over and above the annual festivals and rituals mentioned above, the occasional eclipses of the moon and the sun, the turnings of the planets are occasions for the *bhat* brahmans to take all manner of donations and feasts, walking the lanes of the farmers' houses turn by turn. Also, in order to make the weight of the Hindu dharma lie heavy on the farmers and so that they follow the brahmans unquestioningly, the *bhat* brahmans read and re-read hollow and ridiculous texts like the *Pandav-Pratap*[41] in the rich farmers' houses, and take money, along with dhotis and headgear. Some ungrateful brahmans lure the younger women of the hosts' family and teach them *kukuchaku*.[42] Meanwhile, if they can manage it, they make the farmer perform the Satyanarayana Pooja,[43] and pour ghee, milk, and all manner of oblations down their own throats, then feasting with their family, taking as much dakshina as they can, finally make the farmer carry the lantern as they go home.

If there are any who yet remain untouched by all this, the *bhat* Puranik collects all of them in the temple at night and makes them addicted to listening to stories of Radha and Krishna. At the time of completion, they induce jealousies amongst these, collect a lot of dakshina, then separately collecting money from all, sit in a palanquin, and go away, led and followed by their listeners.

Several illiterate brahmans, lacking the wits to earn their livelihood from the almanac, make one amongst them a white sadhu, put a veena around his neck, hard footwear on his feet, and making a shudra hold a large umbrella over him, sing 'jai jai Ram, jai jai Ram', and thus beg respectably in the lanes of the farmers' houses.

[40] The account of the holy days' loot ends here. He now moves on to the more infrequent and irregular occasions like eclipses etc. [—*Ed.*]

[41] A narrative in verse about the Pandavas of Maharashtra. [—*Ed.*]

[42] Lead them on to the wrong path. [—*Ed.*]

[43] One of the many rituals that Phule attacks mercilessly. See note 113 on p. 207 of the present volume. [—*Ed.*]

Several *bhat* brahmans make a young and handsome fellow amongst them into a yellow sadhu, and giving castanets in his hands, they dance round him as he too dances, and with great love sing 'Radha Krishna Radha' and gesturing like dancing boys, lure rich women into becoming their followers. And thus fill their own bellies, and have fun.

Because several witless brahmans do not have the cunning to do all this and enjoy themselves, they take a credulous clerk, turn him into a *devmahalkari*,[44] and the rest of them travel from village to village, making the farmer submit covenants and thus trouble him a lot.

Because several brahmans to not have the strength to study the Vedas and make a living respectably, they take a half-mad brahman from amongst themselves and make him a Swami,[45] and travel from village to village, telling all manner of lies like 'The swami recognizes what your wishes are and tells obliquely of some of them being fulfilled', take the farmer to see the Swami, and steal his money.

If the farmer is not completely humbled on this rack of dharma, then they get him to make pilgrimages to Badri, Kedar or other holy places, finally taking him to Kashi, Prayag; denude him of thousands of rupees, moustaches and beard as well, bring him home and finally, arrange large feasts for the completion.

In the end, when the farmer dies, the brahmans, presenting themselves as the (authorized and trained) brahmans who perform the rituals of death, make the family perform all manner of ritual, read the *Garudapurana*[46] everyday at the house and then on the tenth day, bring some respectable crow of a *bhatji*[47] from Dhankavadi or some such place, make the son pay him for crowing over the ritual, and along with the money for reading

[44] A messenger of God. [—*Ed.*]

[45] A Sanyasi or a Guru. [—*Ed.*]

[46] One of the puranas which lists and discusses the post-death rituals. [—*Ed.*]

[47] One of the many superstitions associated with the post-death ceremonies relates to offering lumps of rice to crows at the funeral-place. The superstition has it that if the dead man's soul has no unfulfilled wishes the crows will throng in large numbers and polish the rice-lumps away. Here Phule likens the greedy brahmans to crows!—*Ed.*

the *Garudapurana*, take at least metal jugs, or brass, umbrellas, walking sticks, mattresses, and pairs of dhotis as donation. They have also established the custom of the annual *shraadha* for the dead farmer, which is performed until all the children of the farmer are dead. There are also annual customs of various donations and things, which yield them things from the farmers' children according to their abilities, in the following manner: they flatter the farmer, giving him wordy titles such as Patil or Deshmukh, freely loot him of his produce at the time of the marriages of their own sons and daughters, and to put upon the farmer the stamp of their importance, they invite all the farmers for the occasion and after first feasting along with people of their own caste, they grade the leftovers precisely and then with great cunning serve the farmer along with their shudra servants, that too from a distance; but while enjoying themselves in all manner in the palaces of prostitutes, without prohibiting themselves the sucking of juices from the prostitutes' lips,[48] they think the farmer so low that they do not allow the farmer to touch their well or their water tank. How would they ever allow inter-dining or inter-marriage?

Hearing this narrative, someone might enquire, how is it that the farmers continue to be ignorant and are looted till today? My reply to this is that in the ancient times, the moment Arya *bhat* brahmans began to rule this country, they totally prohibited education for their subject shudra farmers and for thousands of years, they looted them as they willed. There is written material to this effect in their selfish texts like the *Manusamhita*. Later when a few objective and pure scholars were disturbed by this brahman cunning, they established the Bauddha religion and were increasingly liberating the abject farmer from the artificial religion of the Arya brahmans. Suddenly, the crown-jewel of the Aryas, the cunning Shankaracharya argued, with every means available, with the good Bauddhas, and tried to put an end to them in Hindustan. But the Bauddha religion was not even shaken and when it started growing day by day, Shankaracharya joined the Turki people and the Marathas and defeated the Bauddhas through the swords of

[48] A Sepoy Revolt by Henry Mead, pages 12 and 23. [—*J.P.*] [Original in English. [—*Ed.*]]

these. Later he planted a certain fear in the mind of the ignorant farmer along with the magic of the Vedic mantras, and forbade the Arya *bhatji* to eat the flesh of cows and drink alcohol.

After some time had passed, the bold followers of Hazrat Paigambar started to split the idols at Somnath, along with the artificial Hindu religion, with their swords and started to liberate the shudra farmer from the Brahma-cunning of the Aryas. From amongst the *bhat* brahmans, Mukundaraja and Dnyanoba lifted some imaginary parts from the *Bhagavat-bakhar*, and wrote tactical books in Prakrit called *Viveksindhu* and *Dnyaneshwari*[49] and crazed the ignorant farmer to such an extent that the farmers started to think of the Mohammadans as low, along with the Quran, and started hating them instead. After some time had passed, a saint called Tukaram was born amongst the farmers. Fearing that he would enlighten King Shivaji and remove the artificial religion of the *bhat* brahmans, one of them, a hardened Vedanti called Ramdas Swami, conspired with the wily Gagabhatta to poison the ears of the letterless King Shivaji,[50] and did not allow any friendship develop between the selfless Tukaram and Shivaji. Later, after Shivaji, his chief servant *bhats*, the Peshwas put his legitimate heir in prison in Satara.[51] In the final years of their rule, the Peshwas, instead of spending money from the taxes collected from the farmer, who was eating roots and *bhakri* and chutney, on dams so that his fields could have water, spent thousands on a flurry of gifts and donations to the *bhat* brahmans at the Parvati-*ramana*.[52] And spending not even a paisa on providing at least Prakrit education to the ignorant farmer, from the taxes collected from the farmers'

49 A commentary on the *Bhagavad Geeta* written in A.D. 1290. *Viveksindhu* was written earlier and is traditionally identified as the earliest work in Marathi. Phule does not make clear what was 'tactical' about these works or how these works can be taken to be attacks on 'Mohammadi' people. [—*Ed.*]

50 Later evidence, not available in Phule's time, suggests that Shivaji was in fact not illiterate. [—*Ed.*]

51 Phule was the first person who identified the Peshwas of Pune as the usurpers of political power which legitimately belonged to the ruler in Satara. [—*Ed.*]

52 An annual gathering of brahmans at the foot of the Parvati hill in Pune. At this gathering, the Peshwas doled out patronage to brahmans in proportion to their learning. See also note 51, p. 106 of the present volume. [—*Ed.*]

storehouses, which was already looted by the Pendharis,[53] in the Parvati-*ramana*, Bajirao Saheb (the last Peshwa) organized whole festivals of donations for the *bhat* brahmans, where a kedgeree of all kinds of sweets and coins, gold and silver, were poured out in ladlefuls, and we are not much surprised by this. In point then, that partial donor did not make any arrangement in his Parvati jurisdiction for the abandoned widows or orphaned children of the farmers, but has arranged only for people of his own caste,[54] *bhat* brahmans, pujaris, and a few uninvited brahmans, to have hot water for their baths in the morning, two first-class meals every day and at every fasting day, has arranged for pedhas and milk and other food, and on all festivals all the delicacies that they wished and has arranged for them to listen to singing and music throughout the day.

Our cowardly English government has allowed these customs to continue and spends thousands of rupees on this, which are collected from the taxes on the honest sweat and labour of the farmer.

At present, seeing that several shudras and atishudras are attaining humanity by converting to the Christian religion, the importance of *bhat* brahmans is decreasing and they are being forced to take up labouring occupations themselves. Several wily *bhat* brahmans are protecting the silly Hindu dharma, generating all manner of opinions, implicitly criticizing the Mohammadan and Christian religions, corrupting the minds of the farmers. But if from amongst the supporters of the ancient idol-worshipping religious people, Kaka and the leader of the Sarvajanik Sabha, Joshibuva, removed the scales of pride in caste in the Hindu dharma and looked at the condition of the farmers, they would not have been able to call this poor farmer, exploited by the prohibition on *ekpakshiya dharma*[55] ignorant, and if they had truthfully informed

[53] Marauders. [—*Ed.*]

[54] A Sepoy Revolt by Henry Mead, page 133.

> Having received an English education, he (the adopted son of the late Bajee Rao, the ex-Peishwa of the Maharattas) was a frequent visitor at the tables of Europeans of rank and was in the habit of entertaining them in turn at Bhitoor, etc. [—*J.P.*] [Original in English. [—*Ed.*]]

[55] Partisan religion; obviously partisan in favour of the brahmans. [—*Ed.*]

our English government of the atrocities on the farmers caused by religion, then perhaps the milk of kindness might have flowed from the government and it would not have consulted the lordly *bhat* brahman in the matter of education of the shudra farmer and might have found other solutions.

In sum, the ignorant farmer is so harmed by the *bhat* brahmans in terms of time and money, that he is left without the strength to send his little children to school and for generations the fear of the custom of 'do not impart education to the shudra farmer' implanted by the *bhat* brahmans is so strong, that he does not have the courage to send his children to school. The kind Governor, following the great George Washington of the democratic country of America, has allowed the ignorant shudras, who think that religion is what the *bhat* brahmans say and laws are what the English government makes, to elect their representatives to the municipality. But if the *bhat* brahmans, in the pride of their knowledge and the hypocritical status in purity–pollution, begin to cheat the ignorant shudras and atishudras, then our only prayer is the Governor not be held responsible for that, even though the *bhat* brahmans have got their desire.

Chapter Second

Because the white government officers are mostly engrossed with luxury, they do not have time enough to enquire into the real conditions of the farmers and because of this negligence most government departments are dominated by brahman employees. Both these causes have the effect that the farmers are looted and are without enough to fill their bellies or cover their bodies.

In general in the past, in the whole of Hindustan the foreign rulers, Yavani[56] kings, and some indigenous kings had lakhs of shudra farmers employed as sardars, mankaris, shiledars, bargirs,[57] foot-soldiers, artillery, camel and elephant riders and atishudras employed in the stables. Lakhs of shudra and atishudra farmers did not find it difficult to pay taxes because from each farmer's family at least one person was employed by the government. But now because these kings and sardars and badshahs are lost and have disappeared, more than twenty-five lakh shudras and atishudras have been rendered jobless and their burden has to be borne by those who cultivate the fields.

While it is true that because of the various actions of our brave English government the incidence of men being killed in all-too frequent battles has ceased altogether and there is peace everywhere, it is because hunting and war-expeditions have ceased that the virtue and courage of all people has ceased to be, and kings and sardars, like frightened women, engage in religious worship during the day and meaningless production of progeny during the night. As a result the population has increased too much as well. Because of this, the division of property amongst farmers has increased, so much so that some are reduced to surviving on the

[56] The word comes from Ionian (Greeks). In medieval Maharashtra it came to be associated with the Muslims. [—*Ed.*]

[57] Positions in the army. [—*Ed.*]

produce of what they sow in maybe eight or ten *pabhari*.[58] And because they do not have the wherewithal to maintain a head or two of cattle for cultivating these eight or ten *pabhari*, they entrust their land to their neighbours and suchlike, for half the produce or maybe in parts, and travel with their children and family to other towns to fill their bellies as labourers.

In the past, those farmers who had very little land and could not survive on its produce, would go into the nearby forest and would gather wood, fruits and leaves from trees like palash and mahua. By selling these things they managed to collect enough money for their basic needs, and depending on the town pasture for cattle-feed, could maintain a cow or two and a few sheep, manage on their produce and live happily in their own town. But now the cunning employees of our honourable government have spent all their foreign and multi-faceted intelligence to establish a massive Forest Department, including all mountains and hills and valleys. This culminates in the inclusion of unused lands and the town pastures as well. Now our poor and handicapped farmers' sheep and goats have no place to feed even on air in the forest. Now if they want to fill their bellies they have to work in the factories of weavers, iron-smiths or carpenters or as casual labourers; artisans in England are selling things here – tasteful bottles of alcohol, breads, biscuits, sweets, pickles, needles big and small, knives, scissors, sewing machines, heaters, colourful mirror and glass-ware, and thread, cloth, shawls, hand-gloves, stockings, caps, sticks, umbrellas, brass, copper, iron sheets, locks and keys, coal, various vehicles and carriages, harnesses, etc. and, finally, carpets – all made with machines, and selling them cheaper here. The goods produced here have lost their market, and many weavers and julahas and momins[59] are so poor that they are forced to near starvation and have to manage, in secret, on coarse wheat or rice powder, and many on the piths of mango. Several weavers, unable to bear the starving condition of their family, in

[58] *Pabhari* literally means ploughshare. Here, however, he is perhaps talking of the disintegration of land holdings and the consequent shortage of instruments of agricultural production generally. [—*Ed.*]

[59] Caste groups connected with textiles. [—*Ed.*]

the evening, buy a few paise worth arrack on credit and at home lie down as if dead. Several weavers bring silk and silver threads from the gujar or the Marwadi, to weave cloth and make dresses, but sell them off instead to feed their children and cheating the gujar or the Marwadi, run away from the town at night. How would these artisans, starving as they are, help the poor farmer?

Secondly, in order to maintain and prolong the dominance acquired by their ancestors through great effort and deception, and so that the shudras and atishudras serve them like cattle or horses or, like inanimate fields, produce things necessary and luxurious for their consumption, the *bhat* brahmans have inserted the notion that if any of the Hindus travel beyond Attuck their religion is polluted. In this the intentions of brahmans were realized, but others suffered a great deal. Because they have no experience of the culture and customs of other people, they really think of themselves as animals, instead of realizing that they are human beings. Because trade with other countries disappeared completely, they were rendered penniless and moreover, it is indubitable that the general slogans that reformed brahmans are repeating, 'improve our country, improve our country', at least on the face of it, must have been caused by the realization about religion mentioned above. All these artificial things have greatly harmed the *salis*, carpenters and other artisans and where these things will lead them to in the future is something that no one but a true well-wisher of the country can guess.

Some will object that the poor farmer should work as a labourer for the rich farmer who has enough land and manage to survive, but because the population has increased everywhere in general, farmers no longer have enough land to cultivate turn by turn, letting some of it lie fallow and because of this most of the land has become unproductive. They themselves have difficulty in feeding their own families so how would they be able to employ the poor farmers as labourers and help them survive? That this farmer, surrounded by difficulties, is not free to send his naked children to school is well known to our far-sighted government employees, and they collect, all in all, local funds of several lakh rupees, in the name of imparting education to the poor ignorant farmer, and a third of it is spent on education for appearances' sake, establishing a few schools here and there. Only a few farmers send their children to these schools. But the teachers themselves are not farmers and so do they have any commitment in this? It is not at all surprising that the people who, for their selfish religion maintain procedures of purity and pollution and bathe and perform rituals throughout the day, do not give proper education to the farmers' children and that their children remain dumb. From the local funds collected from the farmer, how many have educated themselves and become government employees? If this has happened, then the skilful Director of Education should prepare a list of all such employees, with designations and names, and publish it in the gazetteer so that the farmers will joyfully thank the honourable government, and the government gazetteers will have their eyes opened. The few teachers that are there in the villages are all brahmans. Their salary is not more than maybe eight to twelve rupees and their worth in a city like Pune is not more than four to six rupees. Such selfish, unscholarly brahmans, who are interested only in doing their job and filling their bellies, holding fast to their unnatural pride in caste and religion, openly preach to the farmers' children 'If you do not get government jobs after educating yourselves, do you want beg like us, house to house, with the almanac in your hands?'

While re-assessing the ignorant farmers' lands every thirty years, the European workers, blindly worshipping our virtuous government, do not say 'amen' until they have raised the taxes at least a little. But while everyday work is going on, are the lazy European workers, overly fond of hunting, spending most of their time in luxury and comfort, able to see how the brahman employees denude the ignorant farmer? Do they keep a watch over them?

When there are quarrels between the ignorant and dumb farmers over boundaries of their lands or over their turns at getting water from the common well, the cunning *bhat* and brahmans, visiting both sides, advise the two sides in a variety of manners and then on the next day favouring one of them, prepare an application, and send them to the mamledar. When the peon brings them the summons, they go to the kulkarni to accept the summons, who, after sending the peon away talks to the two parties separately, saying, 'You meet me at this time, and you at this time, alone, so that we can find a fine solution to the problem.' When the appellant and other people on his side visit his house at the appointed time, they are told, 'You should extend your kindness upto this amount then I will be able to visit the chief clerk in the mamledar's office so that he punishes the other side because all that is controlled by the chief clerk. And if what I say does not happen, then I will take your amount from him and return it to you, and you may give me whatever you think, by the grace of Bahiroba, and even if you do not give me anything, I will have no complaints. Your victory is my success.' Then taking double the amount from the opponents' side and some for their own efforts, they make an agreement, saying, 'Write the complaint the way I tell you to and give two or three false witnesses, then I will tell the chief clerk and not allow even a hair on your head to be harmed because you know how influential he is and how he decides for the mamledar. And now, if things do not happen according to this agreement, I will get the amount back from him and return it to you, but I will not return what I take for my efforts, I tell of that clearly right now. It's not as if my kitchen-fires cannot be lighted without your help.' Later, in the mamledar's office, at the time of taking statements, the brahman employees ask suggestive questions and take down favourable statements from the party that has warmed their pockets, but for the party which has not done that, they change the sequence of points, and prepare such statements that those who listen to them, or read them, will instantly form a negative opinion, instead of getting the factual picture of the case. Many brahman clerks completely omit some items while taking down the statements of ignorant farmers. Many brahman clerks take the farmers' statements home and prepare different ones and in the morning put them back in the files in the office. If this is the case, then even if the magistrate happens to be impartial, he might end up being unjust. After this, because the advocates have instigated the farmer to appeal to the European Collector, the shirastedar puts up before the Collector only those statements that support the party which has warmed his pockets, and at that time, if they cannot manage to get what they want, which is the golden words from the Collector's mouth '*tumchi takraar tarkati ahe!*',[60] while omitting to read the most important points made in the statements, then the shirastedar writes in an illegible hand whatever he feels like, and when the brave lord is about to go out for a walk with his lady, or if there is a harsh boss who does not understand Marathi, then because he is sleepy from the last nights' party or because he is about to go hunting, the shirastedar reads out exactly whatever the lord had said, and quite easily obtains his signature on the case.

If the cunning shirastedar cannot get done whatever he wants because the Collector is stern, then instead of being taken up in the main office, the cases of letterless obdurate farmers are taken wherever the Collector travels and the farmers are made to travel wherever the Collector goes, eating whatever they can get, walking with leaves tied to their feet which thus humble and soften up the farmer. The applications and papers of several totally illiterate farmers are completely omitted from the record, without even being filed for a day or two. Finally, when the side which has spent the more money wins, the town is divided into two. Then on the day of Pola,[61] and on the day of Holi, there are arguments as to who should be on the right side or who should give the chapati. After there are fights between the two sides and few heads are broken (there would be very few cases, criminal or civil, involving farmers, which do not have these 'key-holder' *bhat*s at their root), the *bhat* clerks, praising the farmers in appearance, in reality conspiring with the police patil, wake up the devilish group of police in the central taluk office. Then from there, behind the hungry police, carrying colourful things, dressed up in uniforms and head-gear, tying up their bellies with improvised corsets, a few drunk constables carrying blunt swords pant upto the village and round up the people from both sides with the help of the mahar and the police patil, arrest them, bring them to the police station and barring the guard, all the policemen and the magistrate, with the

[60] An Englishman's pronunciation of the Marathi sentence for dismissing the complaint. [—*Ed.*]

[61] The festival of the bullock. [—*Ed.*]

help of the ignorant police patil, visit the local Marwadi's shop, buy foodstuffs at what price they will, if someone offers them drink in the local bar, cooled with food and drink, returning to the police station half asleep, start the inquiry for appearances' sake. Having done that, they bring all the arrested people to the main station and present them to the inspector and on his orders, put them in cells, under remand, until the inquiry is complete. Next I will give examples of how the family of the imprisoned farmer sell off ornaments and trinkets, and that money is given to the employees in the police office. If one of the parties is more seriously injured, then the cunning employee takes money from the other party through the clerk and delays the presentation of the case to the magistrate until the wounds are healed and there is no evidence. Sometimes if their pockets have been warmed, the clerks speak to the moneylenders and make sure that the other party does not make their statements, or sometimes through the clerk in the village, threaten the chief witnesses and make sure that they run away to another village. If through all this a few obdurate illiterate farmers ignore the brahman employee's instructions, delivered through the clerk, and present themselves in the magistrate's office for presenting their own cases and making statements, since these farmers are illiterate, their memory is not in order and they do not have enough sense to see the pattern in the sequence of questions and reply appropriately, the employees frighten them to death at the time of statements. In some cases, at this time, they perform all kinds of tricks and frighten the farmers; so much so that the farmers do not dare make exhaustive statements about what they have seen with their eyes and heard with their ears. Moreover, several bold employees, the moment money is finally placed on their palms, fabricate evidence and turn witnesses, and with an eye to the law, arrange that the ignorant farmer is fined or sentenced as they will. Mostly, because the farmers do not have enough money to pay the fine, they borrow from friends, well-wishers and relations, and having paid the fine, the moment they come home, visit the moneylender for money to return the loans thus taken earlier and to secure the release of others and for appealing, but no self-respecting moneylender lets them stand at his door. When the moneylender seeks recovery convincing the bailiffs, and seeks to summon the farmer, because the Farmers' Law is partial (against his interests that is), he has to face ridicule in full court. Because several young men mug up various law-books and recite them like parrots, the moment they pass their examinations, our credulous government appoints them in high judiciary positions. But these young people, forgetting their social and fraternal relations, thinking themselves the legitimate heirs of the lords of the land, generally ill-treat old, senior and weak people from all other castes. First these people summon the witnesses and others, according to the custom of the government, at ten in the morning, but themselves turn up at twelve, then napping for half an hour, emerge wiping their eyes and instal themselves on the seat, and immediately put their hands in their pockets and fish out *pans*, chew on it, displaying their teeth like monkeys, then load the barrels of their noses with snuff, and squint at the people in court, when suddenly, the pleader, finely dressed up in red head-gear, black coats and suited-booted, twirling his moustache calls out, 'Your Honour!' Then this lord of the land, this honourable judge, caressing his belly, asks the lawyer, 'What do you have to say?' The lawyer, hands in his pockets, says, 'We are required to be present in the Sessions Court in relation to a murder case. Therefore, if you postpone the case it would be kind.' The moment he says this, the judge nods and the lawyer goes away in a horse-driven carriage, and it is then that the judge begins his work. I will give a small example. Many of these lords-of-the-land justices, in the vanity of their high caste or in the panache of yesterday's 'influence' do not speak to people of other castes except in the singular second person. If some self-respecting people do not bend down and salute them when these justices enter the court, these people are harassed unreasonably at the time of their statements. Especially if a society is formed against the brahman religion, then if a respected member of that society is delayed in presenting himself to the court, without any respect for his wealth or his elderliness, these justices revenge themselves (now why should the reformists rail against the government here?) by smashing them to smithereens while their statements are being made. It is well known indeed how these lords of the land ridicule and humiliate Buddhist Marwadis. Sometimes, if these hypocritical justices fail to understand the meaning of the arguments between the plaintiff and the defendant, then these pious people begin barking like dogs and bite them with their sharp words, in this manner – 'You are mannerless, we should whip you twenty times and count them as one, you are very cunning', and if someone makes even a minimal response, the cases themselves are cancelled. As if this were not enough, if these murderous justices are displeased with something, is it not possible that they take all the statements home, omit crucial items, make fresh statements and deliver such judgments as they feel like? Because the custom of authenticating statements with signatures or thumb impressions has been abolished. In sum, most lords-of-the-land justices have started to deliver judgments like Ghashiram Kotwal.[62] Several respected moneylenders have closed their businesses of giving and taking, but several brahman and Marwadi moneylenders, unmindful of these humiliations, give and take from the letterless farmer, in this manner. First without giving even a *pai* to the farmer in difficulty, they take IOUs from him and then, from the tribunal court, which is decorated by pensioners thrown out from government departments, take orders from it and then cutting the interest already, put the remaining in the farmers' hands. Nowadays, many brahman and Marwadi moneylenders are telling the *napati*[63] letterless farmer, 'We cannot give you money against land because of the government's laws, but if you sell your lands to us, we will give you money and when you repay the money, we will again sell the lands back to you,' and then they make vows etc., but it is very rare that the credulous and ignorant farmer gets his lands back from these pious and non-violent moneylenders. Apart from this, these deeply religious moneylenders harm the farmer in many other ways when they loan him money. When these moneylenders bring the ignorant farmer to the court (which has brahman munsifs) with all manner

[62] Commissioner of police of the city of Pune, appointed to the position by the powerful minister of the Peshwas, Nana Phadnavis. He was notorious for his arbitrary and cruel punishments. [—*Ed.*]

[63] Someone who is not credit worthy. [—*Ed.*]

of false records of accounts with their own books as evidence, the ignorant farmer, in the hope of real justice, sells off ornaments and things and spends whatever money he has for the case. But because there are no lawyers from his caste who would give him discerning advice, the judgments are against him and then the thoughtless farmer, on the advice a few scheming lawyers, appeals to the higher court. But because the Europeans in the higher court are engrossed in a luxurious and a peaceful life, the brahman employees in the government exploit the ignorant farmers. I will take only a few representative examples, thus: first the scheming lawyers take cash advances for incidental expenses for stamps, etc., the moment the contract is signed on stamp-papers. Then many scheming lawyers arrange for music and dance by the kept-women of the shirastedars, and make the farmer pay for them.

The government employee who exploits the ignorant farmer and takes bribes, and the desperate letterless farmer who gives the bribe, both are punished by law. Just as the poor farmer, who driven to desperation, gives a few stale tidbits to the robber *bhat* Phadke,[64] who is robbing people in daylight and thumbing his nose at the armed police, and his desperate brother, is made to pay for the police expenses by law, and just as the thieves of all castes who steal things from the farmers' houses are punished by law, why should there not be a law which punishes the farmer as well, who is robbed by thieves when he is asleep? If our councils of law make such a law and save the cowardly police's neck, then there will be great celebrations by our just government in Simla, near the heavens.

Several ritualistic brahman employees make the naïve ignorant farmer give donations to storytellers and devotional singers of their own caste. Several strategic cunning people corner the naïve rich farmers and make them construct temples for Radha–Krishna, or make them restore old temples in villages and arrange large ceremonies in the name of the completion. Several scheming employees trouble the farmer behind the backs of the European employees, and the farmers curse them, but they flatter the European workers day and night, who recommend them for

[64] A typical Maharashtrian surname. [—*Ed.*]

the promotions that they get. Also, most European employees find it extremely difficult to make speeches in Marathi for more than a few minutes, and God alone knows how His Highness the King at Satara, the General, the Lords, Nimbalkar, Ghatge, Mohite, Dabhade, Ghorpade,[65] farmers one and all, understand the speeches of these European employees who speak in '*tumi ami*',[66] and how they remedy the various complaints reported![67] Some scheming brahman employees, in the hope of behaving as they will, bring together verbose good-for-nothings and establish large associations in places and by other means, like pressurizing through their status, make several shudra farmers, grass-sellers, wood-sellers, contractors, pensioners or wealthy people become members of such associations as they wish. If the brahman shirastedar proves useful in some delicate matter in the European employee's house, the European employee recommends them to the government, gives them hollow designations of Raosaheb and suchlike and when this European employee is transferred to another district, these worthy Raosaheb prepare all manner of citations and get illegible signatures of some apparently important people in town and wealthy ignorant farmers, arrange a ceremony in the palatial house of some shudra contractor and honour the European workers with these citations. In sum, the losses caused by famine caused by God can be made up, but because the European employees are engrossed in luxury and laziness in all government departments large and small, and the departments are filled with *bhat*s, the losses they cause to the farmer, like the khot in Konkan cannot ever be made up. If one wants to write stories of these exploits, they would make up a book like *Mysteries of the Court of London*. And when the Christians could no longer tolerate

[65] The generals and sardars of the Maratha kingdom. [—*Ed.*]

[66] Imitation of Europeans speaking Marathi. [—*Ed.*]

[67] A Sepoy Revolt by Henry Mead, page 217. [Original in English. The comment which follows is originally in Marathi. [—*Ed.*]]

It would be more appropriate if the government honoured people who do not depend on the government for their income and run their businesses independently, and, at times, spend their valuable time in works of public good. Otherwise, as the popular saying goes amongst us, 'The honest worker will be apologetic, and the thieves shall have fun'. [—*J.P.*]

this condition of the ignorant farmer, they started protesting against the Education Department in Great Britain. So just as the gentlemen and some lords started looking into the matter of the Education Department in Hindustan, our loving Governor General established a committee for the inquiry into the Education Department, consisting of four or five scholars, and appointed Mr Hunter as the chairman, and he, along with his companions, trod through all the three Presidencies like the hunter Nimrod. But instead of visiting the poor farmers' huts themselves, with their handkerchiefs to their noses and for a while filling their eyes with the poverty; instead of taking statements from a letterless, half-clad farmer in order to subtly inquire into the tribulations of the shudra and atishudra caused by the farmers' ignorance; they have taken statements mostly from pious brahmans, from Hindu, Parsi and Christian communities and have collected all manner of citations in all manner of places, have turned their feet towards Calcutta. But we cannot infer what benefit the ignorant farmer will have from their report. In sum, Mr Hunter has not bothered to sit beside the pitiable and weak and ignorant farmer in order to collide with the selfless Mr Tucker (of the Salvation Army) in order to bring them out of the darkness of ignorance, so that the drum of Mr Hunter's nobility will resound and the sound will be heard on the other side of the world by the representatives of the democratic nation and their eyes will open and in their minds will be generated compassion for our black 'Red Indians'.

If evidence is needed regarding the matter on brahman government employees, it can be found easily by looking at the various cases filed and the various convictions for writing false statements, etc.

Chapter Third

How the Arya brahmans came from Iran, the origins of the shudra farmer, how our current government is forever introducing new taxes on the farmer and schemingly collecting money to increase the salaries and pensions of its own employees and how the farmer is now totally debt-ridden.

In all this incomprehensible, unthinkable, ether-like space, countless solar systems come into existence and pass away through the joining and separating of elements. In the same way, when every planet is following its own sun, on this planet earth, through the uniting of the same father and mother, different children are born; one intelligent, the other stupid. So on this evidence we cannot infer that intelligence and stupidity are hereditary. Also, at the time of the union of man and woman, depending on the balance of humours and on the qualities dominant in their minds, the embryo is formed accordingly. That is why the same parents give birth to children who are different in tendencies and nature. If we cannot say this, how could have Thomas Paine in England and George Washington from America, shamed various lords and kings who boasted of their hereditary bravery and wisdom? Moreover, many ignorant black soldiers perform acts of great bravery while fighting with the brave soldiers in Kabul or Egypt, only because they need the money or because they are threatened with court martials, and similarly, we have several examples from amongst the wise scholars in America, people like Parker and Merriam who have courageously and obdurately fought against the enemies of their nation even though they were farmers. Therefore, it is only proved that bravery or cowardice are not hereditary, but depend on the qualities of each individual's nature and context. If one thinks that this thesis is false, then one should look at all the kings and lords on this earth, some of whose ancestors were hunters or goatherds or farmers or servants or clerks or robbers or rebels and some whose ancestors were even exiled persons like Romulus and Remus. None of the progenitors are found to be kings. Now if we say that according to Darwin's notion, following the movement of planets in the whole solar system, the monkeys transformed into the different species of the new human beings, then this harms the notion that humans were created from the limbs of Brahma. Therefore, while negotiating with all these notions if we now say according to the Buddhist or Jain notion that human beings were created from duals, or according to Darwin we say that men and women were created from monkeys, or according to the Christian notion that God created men and women from clay,[68] or according to the brahman notion that the four castes of human beings were created from the brahman's body,[69] and move ahead, then we will have to say that when men and women were created, they must have had to live under trees or in tree-hollows or in caves,[70] and must have had to eat roots and fruit from the surrounding forest; and then in the afternoon they might have rested under the shade of a tree, away from the bright sun. They must have seen really high mountains with broken ridges and cliffs, and rows of peaks as if wearing white caps of mist, and below them in the valleys, huge trees, like banyan, peepal, and trees of jackfruit, mango and coconut, fig and pistachio and almond, all humbly bowing with the weight of fruit, covered with nets of creepers and grapevines, and in many places laden with bananas and multifarious flowers like lotuses and all around them the ground covered with leaves and flowers and an immense varicoloured carpet formed, and on it, trees laden with leaves and flowers, as if newly planted. Also, cucumber, and melons of all kinds recumbent in all the streams and rivulets and riverbeds, and everywhere the clear water flowing with wondrous and interminable melody. Nearby, on the faces of lakes, swarms of bees humming over the colourful lotuses and in places, on the shores,

[68] The Bible, Gen. 1:20, 2:7. [—*J.P.*] [Original in Marathi. [—*Ed.*]]

[69] Manusamhita, 1:31. [—*J.P.*]

[70] Captain James Cook's Voyages Round the World, Chapter V, page 262. [—*J.P.*] [Original in English. [—*Ed.*]]

herons, as if meditating on one leg, waiting for insects to come within reach. In the forest close by, herds of poor deer and sheep struggling for breath as they run hither and thither to save themselves from beasts like foxes and tigers, and in the trees a variety of birds singing melodiously enough to put Tansen to shame, and when they are so engrossed, high above in the sky, birds of prey like hawks and falcons circling and waiting to swoop down and take their lives. And then, the soft and cool breeze from the west bringing the scent of myriad flowers and rendering everything redolent. Seeing all this, how joyful must the original ancestors of humans have been, those who now call themselves Buddhists, Christians, Muslims, mahars, and brahmans! So be it. But must not they have had to live naked, with long nails and longer hair because they did not possess the knowledge to make tools or clothes?[71] Not knowing how to make pots from clay or metal, they must have had to drink water from the river, bending low like animals, or with cupped hands! How would they taste chapatis, if they did not know how to make pans or grinders? Must not they have had to walk barefoot, not knowing how to skin sheep or cattle? How would those who would have difficulty in counting upto hundred under the influence of somarasa,[72] know how to roast and eat cattle?[73] In sum, they must have been so ignorant that if some charlatan or cunning person had put before them the book of the Vedas,[74] cut on parchment, they would have taken it into

[71] The Bible, Gen. 2:25. Captain James Cook's Voyages Round the World, Chapter V, pages 257, 278 and 279. [—*J.P.*] [Original in English. [—*Ed.*]]

[72] By F. Max Müller, M.A. Lecture III, page 137. [—*J.P.*] [Original in English. *Somarasa* refers to a Vedic drink, presumably alcoholic. [—*Ed.*]]

[73] John Wilson's India Three Thousand Years Ago, pages 62 and 63. [—*J.P.*] [Original in English. [—*Ed.*]]

[74] Works by the late Horace Hayman Wilson, M.A. Professor of Sanskrit, page 6. Vrihaspati has the following texts to this effect. (Quoted in the Sarva Darsana, Calcutta edition, pages 3 and 6, and with a V.I. Prabodach, ed. Brockhaus, page 30):

अग्निहोत्रं त्रयोवेदास्त्रिदंडं भस्मगुंठनम् ॥ बुद्धिपोरुणहीतानां जीविकेति बृहस्पतिः ॥

'The Agnihotra, the Three Vedas, the Tridanda, the smearing of Ashes, are only the livelihood of those who have neither intellect nor spirit.' After ridiculing, he says,

ततश्श्च जीवनोपायो ब्राह्मणौर्विदितस्त्विह ॥ मृतानां प्रेतकार्याणि न त्वन्यद्विद्दते क्वचित् ॥

their hands and seeing that it did not have any smell or taste, it is unthinkable what they would have done to it. Because their ideas of food hadn't gone beyond fruit, they could not, as recommended by the Vedas composed these by barbarians, have stolen other people's cows or for that matter eaten them either under the influence of somarasa or on the occasion of *shraadha*. Because they would have been so pure, would they have liked to call these selfish writers their inheritors? Would these writers have had the gumption to stand before them and say, 'You are a Buddhist', 'You are Christian', 'You are Mussalman', and 'You are low because you're a mahar', and 'We are superior because we are brahmans'? So be it. After some time had passed and as the numbers increased, they must have made separate little huts of branches for their grandchildren and around them they must have put a fence of thorny bushes and branches and on the path leading inside, they must have, from clay or from dry stone, fashioned a gateway, and to prevent entry of cruel beasts at night, kept a guard there at night, so all the other people would have been able to sleep peacefully along with their little ones. Is that not why we village people give food to the guard for his labour to this day; and do we not in our times, instead of giving food, donate to the police fund, for all the policemen in the police department and other workers as well? What is the difference between these two? A stick in the mahar's hand and *vadyaanchi tikori*[75] in the hands of the policeman. So be it. Meanwhile, in this village, out of the negligible quarrels of children, serious quarrels must have developed, and the people of the village, young and old, would have sat under a tree and after inquiry, punished the offender. Because, they would not have known how to construct police stations or town halls like there are today. But, with the passage of time, as all the families would have increased in number, there would have been frequent arguments

....

Hence it is evident that it was a mere contrivance of Brahmans to gain a livelihood, to ordain such ceremonies for the dead and no other reason can be given for them. Of the Vedas, he says, त्रयो वेदस्य कर्तारो भंड धूर्त निशाचराः ॥ The three authors of the Vedas were Buffoons, Rogues and Fiends and cites texts in proof of this assertion. [—*J.P.*] [Original in English. [—*Ed.*]]

[75] Drumstick. [—*Ed.*]

and quarrels among them over the enjoyment of beautiful women and the nearby forest, and when these could not be settled amicably, most of the wise men of the village would have collected all their belongings and carried babies, and in general with all the men and women in their clan, would have gone away, and settled in other towns at a distance, and these wise men would have come to be called patils and deshmukhs and most of the people in the towns would begin to conduct themselves with their advice. Even today most people do the same, though the ignorant patils and deshmukhs have started fighting cases amongst the townspeople on the advice of the *bhat*s and kulkarnis. The second is that, when we have to arrange marriages we find ourselves asking questions to each others in this manner: 'Question: What is your name and the name of your town? Answer: Pune, and our surname is Jagtap. Question: Then are you related to the Jagtaps of Saswad? Answer: We are the same. Several generations have passed since our branch came to Pune from Saswad and nowadays we take our children to Saswad for rituals as our gods and goddesses are the same. Question: Then we should have no difficulty in arranging a relation, the Jagtaps of Saswad are our kin, so just ascertain the relation, and then we can negotiate and fix the marriage quickly.' Though this is the true story, someone might ask, 'Where is the evidence for what you say?' Then my reply is that the Aryans came from Iran and annihilated all the native astik and rakshasa peoples and repeatedly invaded and attacked all the surviving dasyus,[76] finally enslaved

[76] John Wilson's India Three Thousand Years Ago, page 196. They appear also to have been a fair complexioned people, at least comparatively, and foreign invaders of India, as it is said that Indra (the God of Ether or Firmament) divided the fields among his white complexioned friends after destroying the indigenous Barbarian races, for such there can be little doubt. We are to understand by the expression, Dasyu, which so often occurs and which is often defined to signify one who not only does not perform religious rites but attempts to harass their performers. The Dasyus, here mentioned, are doubtless the Dagyas of the Parsi sacred writings, and the Dakyas of the Behistian tables, rendered by 'countries' or 'provinces' probably of an exterior position to be the Goim and Gentiles of the Hebrews. They were not altogether Barbarians; for they had distinctive cities and other establishments of at least a partial civilization, though the Aryans lately from more bracing climes than those which they inhabited, proved too strong for them. [—*J.P.*]

them[77] and harassed them no end. How would the victorious Aryans be able to write the true history of the vanquished shudras in their books? After a long time had passed, when they could no longer survive on the fruit of the forest near the town, they started hunting, and fishing, and when even that was not sufficient, they started cultivating the land and that must have been very useful. When after some time they began to be able to devise ploughs and other implements, they must have cultivated large areas, and since their numbers must have increased proportionately, there would have ensued battles over boundaries and pastures, and there would have been bloodshed. It would have been very difficult for all the people to come together at one place and settle these matters and so a consensus developed that people from all the villages should choose a wise and knowledgeable person as their representative and all these representatives should meet in one place and settle matters by majority opinion; and so the custom was established. Thus till this day, we find the custom of settling all major disputes through elected juries. Later, when some clans went beyond the Attuck river and sowed the lands and established themselves and the population there increased immeasurably, for lack of rains the yield was totally damaged, the rivers and lakes and streams dried up and all the creatures of the forests went away to where water was available. Seeing the hordes and hordes of hunger-ridden people, some of the stronger people employed the weaker and taking them along, began to raid the more prosperous establishments and when they had established their domination,

....

[Original in English. [—*Ed.*]]

[77] John Wilson's India Three Thousand Years Ago, page 29. Of the Dasyas mentioned often in the Vedas in contrast with the Aryans, no such traces can be found, though they are once or twice mentioned by Manu. The word Das, derived from dasyu, ultimately came to signify a bondman. In this sense, it has its analogue in our word slave, derived from the Slavi People, so many of whom have become serfs in the modern regions of their abode. Some of the names of the Dasyas and other enemies of the Aryan race mentioned in the Vedas seem to have been of the Aryan origin; but we see from the non-Sanskrit elements in the Indian languages, that they must have belonged principally to various immigrations of the Scythian or Turanian family of the human race. [—*J.P.*] [Original in English. [—*Ed.*]]

decided to be kings. (Now if we research this, we will find that most hereditary kings had such pearls as their originators.) In order to settle these, people of most towns elected representatives from amongst the more intelligent and established a force to defend their countries,[78] and collected taxes to maintain that force, and appointed tehsildars, peons etc. Most people would have been comforted by this. Later, as all the areas became prosperous, the over-important representatives in the land of Bali, that is Baluchistan, saw the wealth of these robber kings mentioned above and became kings themselves and because the earlier republics had lost their glory and were diminished, the representatives of the ninety-six clans established their dominion over fifty-six countries this side of Iran and ruled without any obstructions with each others' help. Therefore their glory was not harmed for hundreds of years and in the kingdoms of the dasyu, astik, aheer, asur, ugra, pishach and matanga[79] people, all the citizens were happy and prosperous and there was found smoke of gold everywhere. Not only this, but also because amongst all these the dasyus were the most powerful, they must have dominated the Yavanas so much that most Yavanas must have been honest and friendly with the dasyus and because of that, the dasyus used to help them in every possible way, and deal with them fairly. The custom of calling the dasyus *dost* must have started from here, and the dasyus would put them in their place if they behaved cunningly and acted up when the opportunity arose, and from there, the Yavanas and Aryans must have started calling them by antagonistic terms like *dushman* and *dushta*; because the words *dost*, *dushman* and *dushta* are related in their roots to the word *dost*. Finally, when all Yavanas, like the Iranians (Aryan), Turkish etc., could no longer bear the fame of the dasyus, 'the eighteen castes' among them (indicated by eighteen types of turban) began attacking the dasyu areas again and again, to loot their gold. But the lieutenants in King Bali's service, the great warrior heroes Kalbhairava and Khanderao did not fail in defending the kingdom. Meanwhile, after the Aryan

[78] The original term used is desh. [—*Ed.*]

[79] Professor Bhandarkar's suggestion in Godbole's History of Maharashtra, p. 1. Item 2. John Wilson's India Three Thousand Years Ago, page 28. [—*J.P.*]

people in Iran[80] invented the bow and the arrow, and from amongst the Iranian kshatriyas, adventurous robbers like Varaha destroyed fifty-six kingdoms on this side;[81] and the Arya kshatriya Narasimha poisoned the tender mind of the young prince Prahlad and killed his father with his help. Later when the Arya Vamana felled the heroic dasyu king Bali, he looted all the gold from the bodies of women; so the dasyus fought many battles to drive away the Aryans from their countries; however, the Arya kshatriyas[82] invaded the dasyus twenty-one times and scattered them to all places, so much so, that some of them had to go away to the other side of the world, to the forests of America, by a pathway[83] near what is now called China (where later a sea was formed, and which is now called Bering Strait), because many of the ancient dasyu (shudra) people there had customs and simple faiths which matched those of the dasyus. The chief name there, *Kashik* matches with *Kashika*; the word *korikancha* matches with *kanchan*. They believe in the same auspicious and inauspicious signs as here. Among them, there is a custom similar to one that the shudras have here, of burying the dead after covering them with cloth and burying some gold along with them. Though the shudras are now

[80] John Wilson's India Three Thousand Years Ago, pages 17 and 18. [—*J.P.*] [Original in English. [—*Ed.*]]

[81] John Wilson's India Three Thousand Years Ago, pages 20 and 21.

Among peoples hostile to the Aryas, we also find noticed the Ajasas, Yakshas, Shigravas, Kikatas and others. The enemies of the Aryas are sometimes expressly mentioned as having a black skin; 'He (Indra) punished for men those wanting religious rites tore off their skin. The Pishachas are said to have been tawny coloured.' [—*J.P.*] [Original in English. [—*Ed.*]]

[82] John Wilson's India Three Thousand Years Ago, page 49. Dr John Muir, in his 'Original Sanskrit Texts', pages 44–56, has given a series of passages sufficient to prove that according to the traditions received by the compilers of the ancient legendary history of India (traditions so general and undisputed as to prevail over even their strong hierarchical pre-possessions), Brahmanas and Kshatriyas were at least in many cases, originally descended from one and the same stock. Some of the cases referred to by Dr Muir are the same as those of the parties mentioned in the first paragraph of this note. [—*J.P.*] [Original in English. [—*Ed.*]]

[83] W.H. Prescott's History of Peru and Brazil, Vol. I, page 66. [—*J.P.*] [Original in English. [—*Ed.*]]

penniless, instead of salt, they used to bury the dead with rich spices, like the American shudras. Amongst them[84] are found names like here, 'Topaji, Manku, Artil Yallappa and Artil Balappa'. An area called 'Kanada' is also found there. But these must have been invaded by the Chinese or the Aryans later, because they too have forbidden education and knowledge to the ancient American people, and thinking them low, have become lords of the land and are worshipping the five elements along with the stars in the sky. But here, the caste-relations of the Arya Nana[85] Peshwa, in the anarchy of Parashuram, killed all the progeny born of the widows of the six defeated *aris*, and he (Parashuram) dispersed the clans of the dasyus in general and of those that remained in the areas, formed two classes, shudra (*das*) and atishudra (*anudas*) and the Arya brahmans made many selfish and torturous 'laws'[86] to harass them. Some of the written-down items are found in the one-sided and heartless books like the one by Manu. These are like the following, 'Wherever there is a shudra ruler, the brahmans should not live there, the brahman should not teach the shudra and not only that, he should not allow the shudra to even overhear the chanting of the Vedas. The Aryans should not travel with the shudras at pre-dawn. The dead body of a shudra could be carried out only by the southern gateway. The shudra was not allowed to touch a brahman's dead body. Even if the king is starving, he should not take as taxes parts of the produce from a brahman, but the king should arrange for annual feasts for the brahman. If a scholarly brahman finds a treasure, he alone has the right to use them, but if a king finds a treasure, he should give half of the money to the brahman. Whatever the crime a brahman might perform, he should not be harmed, but merely exiled. The brahmans should employ shudras for labour, because God himself created the shudras for the service of the brahman. If a brahman

[84] W.H. Prescott's History of Peru and Brazil, Vol. III, Appendix No. 1, pages 156, 157, and 159. [—*J.P.*] [Original in English. [—*Ed.*]]

[85] A Sepoy Revolt by Henry Mead, pages 135, 136 and 137. [—*J.P.*] [Original in English. [—*Ed.*]]

[86] The Laws of Manu, Son of Brahma, by Sir William Jones, Volume VII, pages, 211, 214, 217, 224, 260, 335, 392, 397. [—*J.P.*] [Original in English. [—*Ed.*]]

frees a shudra for having been of use in some delicate matter, whichever other brahman wishes should enslave the shudra, because that is why God created him. If a brahman is dying of starvation, he may use whatever the shudra possesses. There is an original law, which states that if a brahman dies without inheritors, the king should not take his property into possession, but if anyone from the other castes dies thus, the king could do so if he so wishes. If a brahman man knowingly commits a crime, he would only be exiled, without taking away his possessions, but if the same crimes are committed by a man of the other castes, his punishment would be strictly according to the legal provisions for that crime, even if that means execution. If a shudra cannot find employment with a brahman, they should earn their livelihood with their own skills. Even the intelligent shudra should not amass too much wealth, because if he does so, he would become proud and start abusing the brahmans. A brahman should never beg from a shudra because if he uses that money for the rituals, he will become a chandal in the next birth. If a brahman kills a dog, cat, crow or owl, he should perform the Chandrayana ritual of expiation, as if he had killed a shudra. If brahmans kill several invertebrate creatures or a thousand vertebrate creatures, all they have to do is perform the Chandrayana ritual. If a shudra beats a brahman with a grass-stick or smothers him with a dhoti or silences him while speaking or abuses him, he should prostrate himself fully at the brahman's feet and beg forgiveness.'[87] Several such atrocious writings are found in the books of the Arya brahmans, many of which we are ashamed to write down. Let that be. After this the Aryans were appointed as kulkarnis in various villages and included in their own religion some of the cowardly dasyus like Prahlad, who, while holding an enmity with the Arya brahmans did nothing about it from beginning to end. That is why there is a custom of calling them deshastha brahmans.[88] Because the original shudras of the area

[87] The Laws of Manu, Son of Brahma, by Sir William Jones, Vol. VII, pages 398 and Vol. VIII, pages 33, 42, 73, 79, 85, 105, 106 and 118. [—*J.P.*] [Original in English. [—*Ed.*]]

[88] Deshastha and konkanastha are sub-castes of Maharashtrian brahmans. Deshastha: from the *desh*, plateau. Konkanastha: from the Konkan, the

and the deshastha brahmans are related to each other in terms of their customs, colour and their clan gods, and secondly, till recent times, there was no inter-marriage or even inter-dining between the deshastha and the konkanastha brahmans. But the Peshwas started the custom of inter-marriage and inter-dining with the deshastha brahmans. Having established such a system and having become the lords of the land then, they became dominant amongst the eighteen clans of brahmans and were called 'great',[89] and they themselves, having conquered hell and heaven, thinking that there was nothing more left to be achieved, instead of rubbing red soil on their chests and flexing their muscles, started performing rituals day and night, applying sandalwood on their bodies and saffron on their foreheads, started enjoying themselves at their own leisure. Some of them, under the influence of bhang[90] started to construct all manner of terribly selfish books, some started looking for the path of yoga, the rest of them started calling each other 'superior amongst the eighteen varnas'. Around the same time, the Arya brahmans started persecuting some of the nomadic dispossessed (Jew) people to force them to accept their religion. These people were infuriated and constructed several books against the Aryan religion and started worshipping the *lingas* that they possessed. This is how the religion of the lingayats must have come about. After this, all the shudra and minor farmer slaves who were under their dominion were fully denounced by the Arya brahmans. They completely prohibited the imparting of knowledge to these people and their condition was gradually reduced to worse than that of beasts, and because they became enemies of letters and were therefore without knowledge, till today the Arya brahmans denude them in matters of government and religion, so much so, that it can be easily proved that the condition of even the Africans who were forced into slavery in America was better. But recently, a few hundred years ago, the Mohammadan rule felt pity for them, which forced these people to convert to Islam in order to free them from the traps of the Aryan religion and made them

....

coastal belt of western Maharashtra. [—*Ed.*]

89 'Heavy' or 'superior'. [—*J.P.*]

90 An intoxicant. [—*Ed.*]

equal Mussalmans and happy. Because we find the custom amongst many of the ignorant Mussalman mullahs and *bagwans* who perform rituals in marriages that are similar to shudra or atishudra rituals. Similarly the Portuguese rulers forcibly converted thousands of shudras, atishudras and brahmans to Roman Catholicism, and freeing them from the artificial Aryan religion, made them happy. Because we find amongst them clans like that of the shudra brahmans, who have surnames like Gokhale, Bhonsale, Pawar. But nowadays, it is for everyone to see that thousands of suffering shudras and atishudras have chosen to deny the religion of the brahmans and willingly convert to Christianity, and we can see this clearly. Perchance if you are not sure of the suffering of the shudras and atishudras, you should observe and think about the various enslaved farmers like Shivaji Maharaj of Satara, Damajirao Gaikwad of Baroda, Patil of Gwalior, Lakhya Bargir of Indore, and Yashwantrao and Vithojirao Holkar, great warrior kings all, and you will realize how several misfortunes came upon them and their clans because they were illiterate; so I will write no more about that. Let that be. That the fifty-six kingdoms here neglected the republican state, and therefore the dasyus were defeated by the Arya brahmans and are being exploited till date is indubitable, as is the fact that this was appropriate justice for their actions, but the Grecians beyond Iran from the beginning valued the republic and it was close to their heart. When the boastful Iranian Xerxes undertook an expedition to destroy Greece and travelled there with his large army and stationed himself on its borders, a few nationalist soldiers from the city of Sparta raided the camp, coming from the pass at Thermopylae, scattered the Iranian forces, and sent them back to Iran. When this example was followed by the Roman people of Italy, because of the republican state they became superior in knowledge, wealth, and skills, in the continents of Europe, Asia and Africa, and there came about great and famous rhetoricians amongst them and nationalist warriors like Scipio. They defeated, and punished great generals like the African Hannibal. Then they went west to the island of Great Britain in the ocean, where the people were painting their bodies with red or yellow clay and wearing animal-skins; and taught them the use of clothes and vessels, and were ruling over them, teaching them the lessons of a republic with a stick in hand; when suddenly there came about Julius Caesar, who was deluded by his achievements, having established his dominion over hereditary kings in several kingdoms, sacrificing six lakh Roman soldiers, he turned away from the mother, the republic, and intended to enslave her children, become emperor himself. But there were pure-minded people there who thought that they would not be able to bear the humiliation resulting from the establishment of an empire and one amongst them, Brutus, stood in the path with a naked dagger, as Julius Caesar walked to the senate[91] to assume the throne. And Julius Caesar looked into his eyes, Brutus, deeply ashamed in his heart, covering his face with an end of the toga, felled Julius Caesar, stabbing him with the dagger, without caring for their mutual friendship, so that his citizen-brothers could be freed of the impending chains of an empire. But because earlier Julius Caesar had entertained various officers, spending vast amounts from the coffers of the state, most of the other leaders were indebted to him, so there ensued a general battle and the republican state and senate collapsed, and thus, after the rule of twelve Caesars, when the Roman glory was about to turn to ashes, the Romans left the English and other people to their own devices and came back to their own country, Italy. But at the same time, because the people near the English, Scots and Saxons, were great contrivers, they contrived a wondrous threesome pancake, like mixing brass and copper with gold, mixing republicanism with hereditary lords and kings, and satisfied all. Because most of the land there is hilly and not sufficient to support cultivation for all, while they pursued all manner of skill and business, and were becoming leaders in skills, knowledge and wealth, the followers of Muhammad Paigambar in Arabstan obliterated the original Aryan people and their kingdom and invading several times, took over the whole of Hindustan, which had been chewed dry by the brahmans. Later, as the Mussalman emperors were busy listening to Tansen-like music during the day, and in the *zenan-khana*[92] at night, the skilful British

[91] The original term used is *prajasattatmak rajya-mandir*. [—*Ed.*]

[92] Harem. [—*Ed.*]

hit them on their heads and acquired this country; but I am not saying that this was a great achievement. Because one-tenth of the total population, the brahmans, had deprived the nine-tenths of people of strength, intelligence, knowledge, skill and courage in matters of religion and state, hiding behind their scheming religion and on the strength of their pens. But later when the British realized that the nature of the shudras and atishudras is not naturally obdurate but that they conduct themselves on the brahmans' strategies, they enticed the brahmans in various ways, handed over most matters to them and spent all their time in the pursuit of various pleasures – expensive clothes, objects, horses, carriages and food – spending money as they wished and then in order to have enough money to give extraordinary salaries and pensions to European and brahman employees, they increased the taxes on the poor farmer, who was labouring day and night on his lands and eating his *bhakri*[93] with water and salt, and increased them every thirty years; and they gave vague indications that they would educate the farmers' children, and slapped another 'local fund' onto his head. They established excise posts every six miles on the road which the farmer took to sell the produce: grains, cotton, opium, *jowar*,[94] so that he could pay the instalments of the local fund and started collecting lakhs of rupees in these posts. The farmers who were hard-pressed were maintaining themselves on the wood of the forests and various edibles, but the government swallowed these forests and slapped a heavy excise duty on even the salt with which he was eating his *bhakri*. Also, while pretending that they wish to preserve the farmers' crops by giving plenty of water, they were in fact thinking of giving fat salaries to their countrymen, the European engineers and to give loans freely to European moneylenders. To place that loan on the shoulders of Hindustan, they have spent lakhs of rupees from that loan and constructed canals in many places. And though the price of water is whatever they wish, do they arrange it so that the farmers' lands get water when needed? The careless European engineers entrust everything to the brahmans, and spend time in leisure with their

[93] Bread made out of jowar, a kind of millet. [—*Ed.*]

[94] Barley. [—*Ed.*]

ladies behind curtains. And here the cunning brahman workers flatter the engineer and make sure that all manner of resolutions are passed. I will give only one as an example, which is – if the farmers' crops are burnt after the timely water dries up, the responsibility does not lie on the head of the Irrigation Department. Do not the European and black employees, who swallow thousands of rupees as salary, have enough sense to calculate how many gallons of water are available in the reservoir and give orders for water-supply only to those land-owners whose lands can be supplied water till the end? The farmers' noses begin to flow while begging the employees to release water. And when water is not available from them, if they go to their superior officers for justice, instead of water a stream of rude language ensues.[95] What shall we say to this behaviour of the servants of the government, who, instead of supplying water equal to the high prices charged from the farmer, speak rudely to him, in the pride of their high castes? In sum, because our just government entrusts matters to their lazy and scheming inferiors and does not reduce the rate of water, at present the farmer becomes bankrupt and auctions his house and land and has to give the money to these heartless servants. Therefore our compassionate government should give a tap each to all farmers according to their lands, from which the farmer will not be able to draw more water than needed for his lands. If this is done, then the government will not have to spend money on its servants who release the water. The money thus saved can be used to reduce the water rates and the Irrigation Department will not have to set aside the proposal of the government to reduce the water rates. Also, a new and tremendous expense, similar to the local fund, has been imposed on the ignorant farmer, and this is municipal. This is the excise that the municipality imposes on the farmer when he brings his vegetables and produce into the city to sell it there. Sometimes when the farmer brings a cartload of produce, he has to sell it to the treacherous middlemen, who buy it at arbitrary prices, then he has to pay the excise and, bearing the

[95] This charge would not hold for people like Vishwanath Dajee. Very few men so free of prejudice can be found among the brahman government servants. [—*J.P.*]

costs of the transport from his own pocket, he has to return home to his children empty-handed. Listen to this – in the city of Pune alone, the income of the municipality is now trying to equal that of the Sangali *samsthan*.[96] Similarly, even ten or twelve *samsthans* will not be comparable to the tall municipality of Mumbai. The situation is like the famous saying, 'The appearance is very nice, but God knows what is inside'. Wherever you look, there are broad roads with stone gutters, all around there are lamps on foreign lamp posts, in many places there are foreign-made water taps and there are toilets and garbage carts. But even though the earlier kings were idolators and were not scholarly like the English, they had, for the sake of their subjects, planted trees on both sides of major roads, built small bridges, little strongholds and castles and in many places they built dams, canals, wells, reservoirs; and in cities like Ahmednagar, Aurangabad, Bijapur, Delhi, and Pune, they had built strong water pipes, tanks, temples, masjids and rest houses, toilets, baths, and supplies of drinking water, spending money from the government coffers. But since our great philosophic and monotheistic ruler has started to spend money collected from the citizenry, through the municipality, on completing such public works, the subjects' inner strength of honestly earning a livelihood is weakening and thus the government is, in a way educating them in dishonest ways. Moreover, it has come to the notice that in these prosperous times, the four crore[97] population does not have enough to eat and not a day passes when they do not feel the pangs of hunger. Therefore if our just government fixes a reasonable tax on the letterless farmers' lands and educates them in agricultural matters, they would not cleave to ungrateful brahmans like the Peshwas,[98] Tope, Khasgiwale, Patwardhan and Phadke and lose their lives. Moreover, from the day the English started ruling this country, the educated and skilled craftsmen in England have started producing goods with

96 Samsthan: princely states in colonial India. [—*Ed.*]

97 Journal of the East India Association, No. 3, Vol. VII, page 124. [—*J.P.*] [Original in English. [—*Ed.*]]

98 A Sepoy Revolt by Henry Mead, pages 133 and 134. [—*J.P.*] [Original in English. [—*Ed.*]]

machines made with their own intelligence and are selling these goods here at cheaper rates than those of goods produced by all the letterless mangs and ironsmiths and weavers here, thus forcing them into starvation. Because the goods produced here – rice, cotton, leather, etc. – have no market here, these are bought by English businessmen at such rates as they wish, and by selling them to English craftsmen, several people have become millionaires. In sum, because of all this, the farmer cannot even recover the costs of planting, and he borrows money from the Marwadi to pay the governments' tax. But do the *bhat* brahman employees find time for carefully enquiring into this, busy as they are in luxury and ritual bathing? Moreover, some over-enthusiastic native servants, who are members of associations with very prestigious names, have spread the rumour, of their own devising, that 'the farmers are debt-ridden because they spend uncontrollably on marriage ceremonies', and because of this, our knowledgeable and shepherd-like State Secretary, who travels in a four-horse drawn chariot, could not bear the hollow glory of the farmers, and has altogether removed the excise on English goods! Unmindful of the interest given to the big moneylenders there, about five crore per annum, he, through the Law Council, which does not know the trauma of poverty, and through the white and the native 'pure' employees, has contrived to stop the interest paid to the poor moneylender. If the government really feels compassion for us poor farmers, why does it not stop paying about a hundred crore rupees interest to the foreign moneylenders? Then we shall see how the farmer's feet do not firmly find the ground. But our government should suddenly devise a new expedition in some foreign land and spend the saved money on it, so that its fame as a just government will spread all around, and kind and generous people like Mr Wedderburn should, instead of scolding the government for not stopping the payment of interest to foreign moneylenders, and instead of starting new banks, not blame the poor farmer for failures. Also, unless our Governor General recommends a reduction in the salaries and pensions of people on salaries above a hundred rupees, in all departments in general, big and small, like the Army, Justice, Forest, Police, Education, etc., and takes care of that matter, the farmer will not be able to get enough cloth to wear, enough food to eat and be able to get rid of his debts. Even if the farmer works day and night on his land, with his wife and children, he is not left with even three rupees per person per month, after paying taxes and the local fund; whereas the average European and native servant does not find fifteen rupees enough for miscellaneous expenses and drinks and food. So who will listen to us when we enquire about how much money is spent as the lordly Collector's unrestricted miscellaneous expenses?

Therefore if we compare the condition of the shudra farmer, with eight heads of cattle, who has four or five working sons and the daughters and daughters-in-law, in whose family they strive all the time to labour more in other farms and at home and who does not owe a *pai* to the brahman, gujar or Marwadi moneylender, to that of the white soldier, the difference is more than that between Kashi and Rameshwar. Here is the farmer, ploughing his land, controlling eight bullocks and pushing the plough in a land strewn with sharp and dry grass, unclad, barefoot, with a strip of cloth to cover his head and a small pouch of tobacco at his waist; and here is the white soldier, pantalooned, a red coat over a shirt, with a silver embroidered rakish cap on his head and on his feet boots of soft foreign leather over cotton stockings, a leather corset on his waist and a triggered gun on his shoulder, parading on the breezy ground for an hour in the morning or in the evening. Here is the farmer's best dress – a coarse *mand-cholna*, a *bandi*, a *pasodi*, a *kharvi pagote*[99] and country boots strung with thread, whose breakfast and lunch is of *bhakri* made from coarse grain like millets[100] with salads of carrot or sweet radish, or dried fish, and if these are not available, nothing more than a chutney to eat with his *bhakri*. Is even this chutney-*bhakri* available on time and enough to fill his belly? The house he lives in is beside the cattle-shed, with a

[99] *Mand-cholna*: double pajama; *bandi*: half-shirt; *pasodi*: jacket; *kharvi pagote*: headgear. [—*Ed.*]

[100] The original has *jondhale, nachani, konda-bhonda*. [—*Ed.*]

few calves tied near his head or feet, so that it stinks of piss all over, a torn mattress and a torn strip of cloth for his bed, his drinking water is the ditch dug beside the local pond dirtied by the buffalo sitting in it, and he falls ill and gets high fever, there is only a big zero in the name of good medicine and knowledgeable doctors, and over and above all this, there is the sword of the tax and the local fund hanging over his neck. Will any skilled doctor, native or white, say that this unfortunate farmer will not lose his wits? There, the government imports rich clothes, handkerchiefs, stockings and boots for the white soldier, buys good wheat, rice, grains, healthy young cows, the meat of lambs and goats, and foreign liquors like port, clear oil, ghee, milk, sugar, tea, salt, chillies, spices, forks and knives, and get fresh food cooked for him by a Christian cook and feeds him. For him to live in, the government has spent lakhs of rupees and build tall, two-storeyed barracks, which have iron cots, pillows, bed covers and thick covers and there is a lamp hanging in the middle to light them up. In the courtyard of the barracks, bathrooms have been constructed, which have taps of 'filtered' water, and also clean and convenient toilets have been arranged for. If because of indigestion he catches a fever or begins to cough, a hospital has been constructed for his health, which have in them instruments and medicines worth hundreds of rupees and doctors have been appointed at salaries of thousands of rupees per month and they have been given porters along with *palanquins*. Moreover, he does not have to think of giving or taking, for he does not have any taxes on his house, does not have to pay for sweepers, water, roads, land or the local fund and does not have to worry about natural calamities.[101] And on this evidence we point to the native 'pure' employee and say, look at this native servant, lying there flushed red like a drunken white soldier, taking bribes from the ignorant farmer, and kow-towing to the white employees. What uncontrolled expense is this! How shall we speak of it? It is important to say to this extravagant government that there will be terrible consequences of this exploitation unless our foreign government, which worships the formless transcendent God, stops trusting the rosy writings of newspapers or of the associations

[101] The original has *asmani va tolanchya sultani*. [—*Ed.*]

formed by cunning brahmans and reduces for sure the salaries of all its white and black employees, educates the ignorant and suffering and weak shudra farmer[102] and reduces all the tolls and taxes which have been slapped on him. We stop for the moment.

[102] A Sepoy Revolt by Henry Mead, page 280, 81, 82, 83, 85 and 86. [—*J.P.*] [Original in English. [—*Ed.*]]

Chapter Fourth

The condition of agriculture, with that of the farmer.

In the beginning of this chapter, instead of negotiating the penurious and pitiable condition of the farmer labouring on the land day and night, I will inform you of the real condition of the debt-ridden and ignorant farmer from amongst the mali, kunbi or dhangars, who calls himself Maratha because his father's grandfather's daughter, or his mother's grandfather's aunt was married off to a chief or secondary son in the Shinde or Gaikwad clan. One day a farmer was walking towards his village from the Collector's tent in the breezy mangrove beside the river, striding in anger and grinding his teeth. He seemed about forty and a little demoralized. He had a white twisted turban on his head, which was tied down with a cloth, he was wearing a double half-shirt made of khadi and old curled Satara boots. A *jot*[103] on his shoulders, and on it a *kharvi*[104] purse, and the clothes had yellow and red stains from Holi. The heels were strong and thick, but he was walking a little oddly because they had developed cracks in a few places. He had a beard and moustache, which were hiding his front teeth. His forehead and eyes were large and the pupils were grey. He was fair and reasonably pleasant to look at. The face was a little rounded though. After reaching home around two in the afternoon, he went to the kitchen and taking a sheet off the peg, he spread it on the ground and with a rolled up blanket under his head, lay down to sleep, covering his face with a handkerchief. But he could not sleep, thinking of his meeting with the Collector – 'He was still busy with his breakfast and tea, and he did not listen to the truth that I was telling him, and did not allow me to pay my instalment later.' He could not sleep, and putting his hands on his chest, as if a

[103] A kind of shawl made of coarse khadi. [—*Ed.*]

[104] A dark maroon cloth. [—*Ed.*]

little crazed, he started talking to himself thus:

'Unlike other villagers, I have not warmed the hands of the *bhat* servants and so they have spoken to the white officer and doubled my tax, and in the same year the rain was indifferent and my fields and gardens were burnt out, and then suddenly Father died. There were a lot of expenses for the rituals. So in the first year, I assured the garden-plot to the brahman moneylender, registered it in his name as well, for the money to pay the taxes with. Later he calculated the interest, doubling and tripling it, and took over my garden-plot. The moneylender's uncle is a clerk in the revenue office, his cousin is the Collector's secretary, his brother-in-law is the munsif and his father-in-law the taluk's police officer, and moreover, most of the people in the government offices are his caste relations, so if I had argued with him, they would have troubled me no end and reduced me to a dry summer,[105] on the smallest excuses. Thus in the second year, I sold off the few ornaments the women of my house had on their bodies and put all that money into paying the taxes and later borrowed money every year from gujar and Marwadi moneylenders to pay for that. Now they have filed suits against me, which have been lying in the court for so many years. I have paid so much in bribes to the court officers, peons, scribes, lawyers and all, that I am at the end of my tether. Now sometimes one finds government servants who do not take bribes, but they are even more useless than those who do, because they are nonchalant and do not care about the poor farmer at all, and the clever lawyers take money from us, in the name of these servants and put the bite on us regularly. And if we do not do that then we have to accept the orders secured by the moneylenders. Now no moneylender lets me stand at his door! I paid off the tax instalments last year with my newly-married elder daughter's ornaments and now her father-in-law does not let her live in his house. Oh, how unfortunate I am that I sold off her ornaments to avoid a calamity and ruined her marriage in the process! And now, how do I pay this year's tax? There is no money to buy new *mot*,[106]

[105] A graphic phrase meaning total deprivation. It is not much in use in contemporary speech. [—*Ed.*]

[106] For drawing water from the well. [—*Ed.*]

the old ones are torn and the sugarcane is drying up. The corn has also gone to waste. The cattle-feed is about to finish, as is all the dried grass and fodder. The bullocks are weak because they do not get enough to eat. The women's clothes are in tatters and they are forced to wear ancient bedsheets bought for marriage. The children have to go about half-naked and feel ashamed of meeting people. Because the grain in the house is nearly over, we are surviving on sweet radishes. I do not have enough money to feed our mother with good food as she prepares to die. What shall I do? How will I be able to till the land if I sell the bullock? I cannot think of starting a business because I cannot read or write at all. If I leave my province and go to alien places, I have no skill which will help me fill my belly. If I swallow a potion made of roots, the able children might be able to survive somehow, but who will look after the old woman and, along with my little ones, look after my wife? At whose doors can they knock if they need help? Where will they beg?' Thus finally sighing, he fell asleep weeping. Later when I come out, wiping my tears and look around, I see that his house is single storied and tile-roofed. Beside the house, there is a covered shed for cattle. There are two or three bullocks, old and ruminating and a few large empty containers are pushed into a corner and outside, in the courtyard, there stands an old cart for eight bullocks. On it, there is a broken basket.[107] On the left, a square platform is made, on that there is the tulsi plant, and beside it, there is place for storing water and on that there are a few clay pots filled with water and beside it, there is a crudely tiled bathing place, with a half-wall on three sides. Outside it, water has collected in a small ditch and it is filled with insects and worms. Beyond, under the white chafa tree,[108] there are a few children dancing, half-naked, with all manner of stains on their bodies, noses running, sweating and stinking, playing with lumps of mud. One of them is playing at being a shopkeeper, with anklets of seeds on her feet, pretending to sell arrack. Many of the children giving her pebbles and seeds as coins and drinking water, are shuffling about, falling on each other, pretending to be drunk. Behind the house stands a cattle shed

[107] The original has *turathyacha kurkul*. [—*Ed.*]

[108] A variety of fragrant flowers. [—*Ed.*]

made with wooden beams and pillars. In it lies a buffalo who has just calved and a wretched mare. There are all manner of insects sticking to the walls. In the cracks of the roof knots of hair are stuck all over, collected from the head while combing. Beside this, there is a chicken run. A few bamboos and *zaap*[109] are lying about and on the other side a corner for washing hands and feet is constructed and a stone slab for washing vessels. The open drains have collected all the leftovers and flies drone over it. There is a waste-heap beyond and large green flies are buzzing over it because little children have been shitting there. Beside that, because the heaps of grass and fodder are finished, lie small heaps of leaves. In the other corner cowpats are stacked, beside it, under the tree, there are broken implements lying about and a *vilayati dhattura*[110] grows under them, and a mangy bitch who's just littered lies there, growling at passers-by. Beside it lies a heap of waste fodder, and in the remaining area sits a youngish woman, with her back to the house, arranging cowpats. She is upto her knees in the dung, pounding it with her feet. In the kitchen itself, there is uneven flooring and one sees the waste from grinding and cleaning and cleaned vegetables lying about here and there. Here is heap of pith thrown about, and there a heap of rotting onions. A stale stink rises from them. In the middle, an ancient woman is lying on a sheet, groaning. Beside her head lies a plate of food – a bowl of crushed *bhakri* softened in the liquid of the dal, and a jug of water. In the cradle a little baby is weeping loudly. Besides all this, in places one finds a line of a child's piss, at some other place a patch of white ash where a child's turd has been cleaned up. Several corners of the house are red and dark from tobacco spit. In one corner sits a large grinder, to be drawn by three or four women, in another there is a large mortar and pestle and in the corner near the door under the broom, all the dirt pushed there after sweeping the floor, and on top, a rag which was used to clean a baby's arse. There beside the cooking fire stands a dirty frying pan and the milk pot. Beside it, the cat has covered up its shit with ash. The walls are covered with stains left from squishing bugs and insects

[109] Broken off leaves or matted branches of the coconut tree. [—*Ed.*]

[110] A kind of thorn apple, presumably of foreign origin. [—*Ed.*]

on them, and fingers wiping off snot. In a small cabinet is the oil pot, tooth powder, a horn comb, a rickety mirror, and on a ledge three or four stone lamps are stacked for the night. An oil stain spreads from them onto the ground. Maybe once in a year all the grease is scraped away. In another cabinet beside the flour basket are placed pieces of stale *bhakri*, in the third cabinet there are green chillies, garlic, coriander, and baskets of mangoes, on which flies eat from one side and excrete from the other. And in the fourth stands a heap of old and torn footwear. A flintstone lies beside them. Old and worn bedsheets hang from one peg, and on another, bedcovers. On a third peg, torn clothes. As I go into the kitchen against the wall, in the middle stand containers big and small. One of them however is secured with a country lock. Here too, clothes of the daughters-in-law and daughters and other women hang on a series of pegs. On one such peg hang the reins and saddle and an empty bottle of oil. On another hangs an oil can. At the end of the room, in a corner, clay pots are stacked over each other. There are five such stacks. Two baskets hang from the beam and they contain pots of yoghurt and ghee. On this side a place for the idols of gods is constructed of untreated bricks. In the lower shelf lie iron implements, axes, scythes and such. On top a cloth is spread and on that silver icons are placed in a row. Beside them stands a small lamp and oil can,[111] a small bag of incense hangs nearby. And down there, on a gunny-bag made of *burnus*[112] the farmer is deep asleep and snoring. In one corner stands an old barrel of a gun, and a roll of mattress. In the other corner stands the blade of a plough, other implements, and a stick. Moving upwards; a mini-floor is constructed with wooden beams and a hard and firm flooring made from mud and clay and other things. All over that are set little pots in which all manner of beans and vegetables are planted. A garland of corncobs strung together is drying, hung in a corner and beside that some vegetables are being dried. In another place there are gourds and things put to dry. Parts of farming implements are lying about, and all kinds of pieces or bundles of cloth have been put into nooks and crannies. If you

[111] The original has *dom dom shadavalachi zholi*. [—*Ed.*]

[112] A kind of felt. [—*Ed.*]

look up you can see that the tiles of the roof have not been changed for three or four years, and wherever the rotting undergird of grass has been stuck together again with grass ropes rats have made holes in it. There are no windows or ventilators of any kind anywhere in the whole house to let in fresh air. The beams and corners and supports and pillars are tarred with black smoke, and in most empty spaces spiders have weaved most artistic and delicate webs, like mosquito nets, on which a thousand baby spiders are playing. On the undergird of the roof, on the beams, on pillars the poisonous shells of insects and spiders are sticking, and especially on wooden spaces there are heaps of dust mixed with rat shit and cockroach shit and for years a broom has not touched them for lack of time. Suddenly, the kind of dust storm which rises because of the heat before summer rains, swept through the house, and as the dust rose and filled the house with the wind streaming in through the gaps in the roof tiles, and the poisonous dust filled the snoring farmer's open mouth, and he woke up coughing. The poisonous cough so troubled him that he nearly fainted and he started moaning and thrashing about. His sick old mother somehow managed to stumble upto him, and putting a blanket roll under his head, and cupping his chin, staring into his eyes, said, 'Oh lord! Please open your eyes. So many times have I given money to Rambhat so that Shani should not harm you, and that too sometimes without your knowledge, selling off grain, and have made the brahman sit with his rosary in front of Maruti, and fed so many brahman women!! Dear child, so many times have I spent money without telling you so that the gods will be pleased with you. Why did not that god speak through the Collector's mouth today, and allow you to pay the taxes in instalments? O you damned *bhat*s, you lied to me about Shani and Satyanarayana,[113] and extracted meals and money from me! O you cunning brahmans, from the very birth of my dear child you have threatened me with ill-favoured stars and taken money from me, where is all the virtue that you collected? O, you have cheated me so much in the name of dharma that with that money I could have saved my child's

[113] A ritual which is supposed to grant wishes. It is also performed at the end of memorials, etc., to thank the Lord for His kindness. [—*Ed.*]

neck! He could have been happy! O it was Raghu Bharari,[114] one of yours, who brought the white man first to Talegaon. It was you who lied to these ill-informed white officers and beggared us, and it is you who now pretend to be united and rail against them. Not only that, as the malis and kunbis got beggared, and you couldn't any longer make money out of them, you brahmans, converting to the white man's religion, wearing pantaloons and shoes, with white cloth on your heads as if for mourning, marry fair looking devout converted Christian girls, and standing right at the office, say to the malis and kunbis that 'All the ancient scriptures of our brahman ancestors are false and selfish. The idols of gods that they constructed in these are meaningless. All this is falsity, used to fill their own bellies. Now they have even started Satyanarayanas in the white platoons, and are making all you malis and kunbis dance to their tunes. Therefore you should not be taken in by their cunning words and worship gods of stone or metal. Do not get into debt for the sake of Satyanarayana ceremonies. You should look for the formless God, that is what will save you.' Let that be. But instead of advising the malis and kunbis, you should walk the lanes of your relations, and tell them – 'Burn all your false scriptures. Don't mislead malis and kunbis and dhangars!' Telling them to do this, again and again, and making them behave accordingly will surely reassure the farmer. Also, if we behave according to the advice of you brahman padres, then your caste-relations in the offices will, lying to the white officers, ruin our children. Suddenly, the farmer came to his senses, and putting his arms around his mother, started weeping.

Now I will briefly describe the condition of all those people who are paupers, weak, constantly labouring on their farms, completely ignorant, malis, kunbis and dhangars, and if you pay attention to their condition, it will be a kindness to them. Brothers, if you yourself investigate, you will easily ascertain that in all the villages big and small, the farmers' houses used to be large and the roofs tiled. In every house, in the kitchen there would be an iron blower, iron utensils, on the stone stove there would be an iron pan, and a pot of milk and clay vessels for cooking down there, and

[114] A cousin of the last Peshwa. [—*Ed.*]

maybe copper pots, pans and so on. Besides these there would be a variety of grains stored in a stack of vessels, and green vegetables as well. On the floor there would be grain bought last evening from the moneylender. In a nook there would be sheets, and clothes made from old saris, nets for carrying cowpats and things, a lamp with an oil-can, combs and the kumkum box. Upstairs there would be firewood, usually the three-sided cactus, stored. On the floor, there would be all manner of implements. Beside the door, outside, there would be the stored water and the open place for bathing. On the right, there would be the stable for cattle, with a roof over it. The women of the house, who labour all day on the farm along with the farmer, having finished the daily chores at home, would be wearing a length of cotton and a choli, with hollow bangles,[115] a small gold mangalasutra round their neck, and copper toe-rings, the only make-up she has is *kohl* in her eyes and the big kumkum on her forehead. The children of the house, minding the cattle through the day, are naked, and instead of silver bracelets, wear little earrings with copper wires. They have no other ornaments. The farmer himself wears a waist-thread made from old saris, a langoti[116] made of khadi, and a small torn turban on his head, and if he can't find simple dhotis, then he wears coarse cloth round his waist, for the rest, he is naked and wears old patched up shoes, or shoes held together with string; and therefore he is unable to work in the farm in the cold and rain. Illiterate as he is, he does not have the rational power to think, and so he trusts the old tales in *Harivijay*[117] and suchlike because the brahman tells him to, and does he not then waste his time and money on pilgrimages to Pandharpur and the various Krishnajanma and Ramjanma and Satyanarayana ceremonies, and at Holi, spend time watching lewd plays? Because he has no love of knowledge, and because he is ignorant and, instead of telling him the benefits of knowledge,[118]

[115] Of silver or some low quality alloy (*katheel*). [—*Ed.*]

[116] Loin-cloth. [—*Ed.*]

[117] A hagiographic account of Lord Krishna's exploits, full of fanciful stories. [—*Ed.*]

[118] A Sepoy Revolt by Henry Mead, page 293. [—*J.P.*] [Original in English. [—*Ed.*]]

there was the tight system of ensuring that he would never get knowledge so that he would continue to be a slave. Even if our present government does not seem to have such evil intentions, on the evidence of their outward behaviour it can be proved that employees of the Education Department do not have any true sympathy for the cause of the farmers' education. Because till date the government has swallowed up many lakhs of rupees in the name of local fund, meant for the farmer's education, weighed against that, they have not been able to educate even a single farmer enough to enable him to function as a collector. Because the schools in villages are filled with *bhat* brahman teachers,[119] whose worth is less than that of the potter working with mud and clay, who have no knowledge on which side to grip the farmer's plough, wordy administrators merely, dependant entirely on the farmer, how will these teachers, whose ancestors demeaned the farmer to the lowest of states, proud that they are the best of human beings, be able to teach the farmers' children any useful knowledge and discipline? When they do not get any job in the cities despite several attempts, they apply for jobs in the Education Department, move to villages and somehow survive as teachers. But because many of the farmers who could not survive on farming in their villages, migrated to bigger cities, and laboured in whatever employment they got and survived, only a few children of these farmers have become scholars. But these seven-and-a-half children seal their own mouths about how the brahman employees of the government destroy their ignorant caste-relations because most government offices are dominated by brahmans, and become close friends of brahmans and begin to rail against the government in associations and meetings established by the brahmans. They begin to drop turds with fear for if they do not rail along with the brahmans, the brahmans will publish in newspapers and books all kinds of matter about them, and moreover, say all kinds of things against them to the mamledar, shirastedar, magistrate, engineer, doctor, judge, who are all brahmans, and might even, at the slightest opportunity, endanger their jobs. As if this is not enough,

[119] A Sepoy Revolt by Henry Mead, page 288. [—*J.P.*] [Original in English. [—*Ed.*]]

several brahmans have, ignoring the prohibition on travel across the sea, travelled abroad and on return, joined their caste-relations again. But these seven-and-a-half troublesome nincompoops, unashamed of their ignorant relations, invite these brahmans home, and perform rituals, and honour the brahmans. What can one say to such ungratefulness? One might want to say that they cannot fill their bellies without depending on brahmans, but then do not several XX[120] manage to fill their bellies in town? Let that be. Nowadays the farmer's meals consist of stale pieces of *bhakri*, on which is put a lump of red chutney, at noon he eats some form of dal with *bhakri*, and at night ground grains in the water of the dal. Sometimes he has to survive on carrots and sweet radishes, and he never gets enough *bhakris* on time. Therefore if he suddenly feels hungry while working on the farm, he puts aside his plough, and eats whatever is edible around him - green mangoes, tamarinds, whatever he can get, then he gulps down a lot of water and again takes up the plough; and whenever he does get enough *bhakris* to eat, he eats them up greedily, without even drinking water while eating, so he burps through the day and then he gets indigestion and he has no money for any herbs and medicines! So finally he catches typhoid and has to die. In the houses of many farmers, festive meals consist of sweet chapatis, fried stuffs and in the end, rice with dal. As for the pauper farmers, if the gujars or Marwadis do not lend them money, they somehow manage with jowar *bhakris* and things. Thus most farmers cannot pay the taxes unless they borrow money, and such humbled farmers cannot even marry their daughters without having to give some 20–25 rupees for that. Moreover, some totally debt-ridden farmers' sons, if the gujars and Marwadis do not lend money for their marriages, begin to quench the fire of desire by other means, and they eventually waste away with tuberculosis because of that. Some other time, I will publish an essay called 'The Cultivator's Thrashing'[121] with evidence from renowned doctors and scholars regarding this. Many a youth surreptitiously begin to visit brothels,

[120] The two crosses are as in the Marathi text in the *Collected Works*. Clearly an obscenity is indicated. [—*Ed.*]

[121] Obviously, like *The Cultivator's Whipcord*. [—*Ed.*]

and eventually die, and the rest that remain are lured by the life of crime and robbery, and eventually get killed.[122] Those young kunbi, dhangar or mali farmers who somehow or the other manage to borrow money for the marriage have to, after a day's labour on the land, labour on the grinding stone and sing women's songs[123] like a eunuch, and do all other manner of errands in the evening. Similarly, the young women of the town, along with the groom's mother, sit cutting onion, grind turmeric, and roasted bajra.[124] So the stench and grime of all these items sticks to the groom's mother's clothes as she works through the night, and anybody who stands near her has to suffer. In the courtyard a small pandal is created with branches of *shevri*, mango, and little shade is thus made available. The wonder of the ill-tuned drums of the mahar or the mang is different still. Once the groom is called Gadanganer,[125] some rice and a bit of jaggery put on the plate with a nailful of ghee, then all the children walking around with the bride and the groom go at it like wolves and polish it off in minutes. The marriage feast would start on the street, without any sheet spread to sit on. On the day of the ritual, people would bring their own plates from home, and if along with jowar *bhakri*, or ground jowar, a few pieces of intestine or rib fall into the plate, they would indeed be fortunate, because the legs of the mutton would be hung up at home to feed the guests and children for two or three days. In the meal for the town, crushing fried things into the rice, with carrot or potato preparations on the side, the farmer finishes his meal with a lot of water, and burps. In this meal, there would not be ghee worth even a little per thousand people. When the farmers' meals are conducted with such pomp, all the misinformed brahmans spread rumours in their associations, and suggest to the executive that the farmers are debt-ridden because they spend inordinate amounts

[122] Several ignorant farmers, shudra and ramoshis followed Vasudev Phadke, and were sent to prison, and many were hanged. [—*J.P.*] [Original in Marathi. [—*Ed.*]]

[123] O son of brahman, why are you out with a pen and an inkpot –
I am sure, to harass the peasant and the low-caste.' [—*J.P.*]

[124] Millet. [—*Ed.*]

[125] Calling the groom or bride a Gadanganer refers to one of the ceremonies which precede the wedding. [—*Ed.*]

of money on their children's weddings! Had these people ever,[126] in their grandiose and vacuous 'public' association, admitted a mang or mahar farmer, and sat beside him? Or have at least one of these people, who preach the knowledge in the Vedas all over the towns, said that farmers spend too much while sitting in a farmers house and eating the food that they got there? There people have fun playing the role of coquettes in farces, singing songs sung by the farmers while grinding grains, but has any one of them been seen grinding huge amounts of grain in their own children's weddings? If someone has and informs me thus, I will be grateful to him. Do these people ever do any farming things with their own hands? What do they know of the sting of farming? So be it. But do the women in their houses ever work like the women in the farmers' houses? Walking behind the plough, sowing grain and things, weeding the farm along with the husband, lifting up heavy loads of ash, cow dung, waste matter, or, when in summer there is not much work, labouring as stone-breakers on roads? Instead of helping their *bhat-bhikshuk* husbands, the moment they wake up, they make themselves up, finish the daily chores, and sit listening to scriptures or mythological stories; at the time of marriages, they do not even touch the grinder, and wearing expensive clothes, generally parade around, making shudra women carry things, and shudra men carry umbrellas over their heads. Farmers do not, like these hypocrites, arrange sumptuous meals for their own relations, and careless of women in the house, listen to all manner of lewd songs and dances, and pay large amounts for that. Have these *bhat*s and white officers left any strength in the farmer to arrange for a good meal at least once his life? How can we ever argue with these voluble people? Their ancestors have, in ugly books like the *Manusamhita*, posited caste distinctions, and made moves against the shudras. Had they not done this, they would have been able to perform a miracle. Which is that, without bothering the ladies of the governor's family since they are like delicate velvet flowers, had they invited the wives of a few European collectors along with their children to a marriage in a farmer's house, and made them

[126] A Sepoy Revolt by Henry Mead, pages 234, 270 and 271. [—*J.P.*] [Original in English. [—*Ed.*]]

share in the work, and made them chief invitees, I will bet my name on this, that seeing the dirt, the confusion, the conditions and the food,[127] they would have run away with their children, and I swear to this in public, in the presence of the nosy court attendant who moves around with yellow bamboo sticks, and a round turban. Both these white and black employees have so completely denuded the farmer, behind the government's back, in order to enjoy themselves day and night, that the governor feels ashamed to invite him to his court. O, cannot the farmer be invited to the governor's court, the farmer, on whose labours[128] the government depends for its army, its ammunition, and the inordinate salaries of its black employees, and the lassitudinous luxury of the white ones, and their pensions? O, should such be the condition of one who is the foundation of all nation? He does not get enough food to feed his belly, not enough cloth to cover himself, and the sword of the taxes to be paid is constantly hanging on his head, and the hunting dogs of the lords do not even sniff at him? What should we say to this? He cannot even read things written in his own script, how can we expect him to read up books on farming techniques in other languages and improve his farming? How could he who is always starving,[129] send his children to larger towns, to study in agricultural schools?

Now let us turn to the present condition of the farmer. Since our generous and kind government began to rule in this brahmanic[130] nation, they have started killing bullocks and cows and calves, without any proper ritual, and have started eating them, along with Mussalmans, mangs and mahars, one of the important resources of the farmer is diminishing. On top of that, because of the lack of rain there was a drought, and the cattle were destroyed by lack of fodder. Secondly, because of the rules of the Forest Department and the inadequacy of pastures, the cattle could not

[127] A Sepoy Revolt by Henry Mead, page 44. [—*J.P.*] [Original in English. [—*Ed.*]]

[128] A Sepoy Revolt by Henry Mead, page 198. [—*J.P.*] [Original in English. [—*Ed.*]]

[129] A Sepoy Revolt by Henry Mead, pages 334 and 358. [—*J.P.*] [Original in English. [—*Ed.*]]

[130] The word Phule uses is *sowala*. See note on p. 88. [—*Ed.*]

be fed, their offspring became weak and cattle was seized by diseases, and thousands died, and the farmers had to uproot their pegs. Next, because there was not enough cattle to labour on their farms, the farmer could not take proper care of his fields, and the yield has decreased. Moreover, our cunning government, through its brahman employees, has carried out surveys every thirty years and have established levies and taxes as they willed, and the farmer, losing his courage, has not properly tilled his lands, and therefore millions of farmers have not been able to feed themselves or cover themselves. As the farmers weakened further because of this, they started dying by the thousands in epidemics. There was drought to add to the misery, and thousands of farmers died of starvation, but in spite of all this, their numbers did increase, and that led to the tilling of the same lands in increasing proportion, and the lands could not be rested. So the yield of the lands decreased. Moreover, every year vast amounts of grain, cotton, leather, wool were being exported to alien countries, and because of inadequate information or because of their own rough nature itself, the white engineers and doctors and employees wasted large amounts of manure into the sea, and now most of the lands are close to being fallow. O, these foreign white engineers, in cahoots with white doctors devise schemes[131] to make money, and sell the goods manufactured by craftsmen from their own countries, waste unlimited amounts of local people's money, and then make sure that there are buildings named after them. Later if the all the local citizens are ruined along with these buildings, why should they care? Having made money and acquired fame, they are done. Sometimes it does not rain one year and there is not enough crop. Sometimes because there are not enough bullocks, the crop suffers. Sometimes because the moneylender does not lend money in time to buy fresh seeds or sometimes because the farmer uses seeds bought last year, the crop suffers. If for these heavenly or earthly reasons, the farmer does not get a sufficient yield, and goes alone to the brahman employee's house to tell him of his condition and of his crops, he finds the brahman, newly bathed, sitting with stripes of holy ash on his

[131] Phule uses the word schemes here as if it were a Marathi word. He talks of 'skima', which would be the plural form if 'skim' were a Marathi word!—*Ed.*

body, enveloped in incense-smoke, engrossed in worship, some other sitting with an old and dirty book, reading it, and someone else counting the beads, while thinking of women. Hearing his footsteps, without opening his eyes the brahman asks, 'Who is it?' Farmer: 'My lord it's me, a farmer.' Brahman: 'Why have you come at this holy hour? If you have brought vegetables and stuff, hand it in inside, without touching the children. Come to the office in the afternoon and make an application in your name, then I will talk to the officer myself. Now go.' Then the farmer turns and walks straight to the Collector's tent in the mangrove, and saluting the butlers, the jamadar and the sepoy, and standing at a distance from the tent-door, what he sees is that some white officer dressed in a Mughal manner, with a velvet carpet under his feet, bathed in lavender perfume, is busy eating, some other is lying face down on a couch and is busy reading rosy descriptions in a book and is therefore disinterested, so the sepoys rudely turn the farmer back and he cannot even tell his woes and plaints to the white officers. Therefore there is not any manner in which the farmer can convey his condition to the white officers, who are inured in their customary luxury, status, attendants; or to black officers who are engrossed in their wealth, their higher caste and colour, and their rituals of purity (neither is there any interaction between the women and children of white and black officers and the ignorant women and children of the farmers' houses to establish a communication). Both these officers are so completely different from the farmer,[132] and such alien people will survey the farmer's lands, and give him relief? During the survey sometimes the white officers go on a hunt, and having tired themselves fully, sleep for long hours in the tent, and the 'pure' employees conduct the survey with the assistance of the cruel kulkarni clerk, the letterless cowardly patil and a few drunk hoodlums of the village, and if relief is to be given in the tax, then those who would give it are the alien white officers from across the sea! And if after all this, the farmer does not get any relief, should he pay the tax with money

[132] Why doesn't that upstart from the red or the green garden know this? Why does he pretend to be innocent? [—*J.P.*]

borrowed from the Marwadi moneylender,[133] or should he avoid it, and become a robber? Or how else? Let that be. But when the ignorant farmer borrows money to pay the taxes, these brahmans dress up as *bhats* and blocking his path, give him all manner of blessings and surely extract some money from him. If there is timely rainfall, and the farmer gets a reasonable crop, since the cowardly employees of our brave government have disallowed use of firearms and other weapons to the farmer, he cannot protect his crop from wild boars and pigs. Of the remaining crop, the brahman, the Marwadi moneylenders, Gujarati traders and brokers from other castes keep an eye on the crop and grab whatever they can of it. Not only this, but even the Gujarati brahman cooks in traders' households have started claiming some amount of jaggery. Let that be. Eventually when the farmer returns from the market and enters the town gate, a few hoodlums and the patil demand to be given drink, and if he does not, then we can be sure that after a few days, he will receive a summons of some kind or other. What a just kingdom this is, wealthy in knowledge! But in this just kingdom, there was a time when it was possible to travel from the southernmost point to the northernmost, carrying gold, without being challenged. But at present, the goddess of wealth cannot find food and clothes in the houses of the farmer, deprived of education and clothes, and has therefore gone away to her father, the ocean, and beyond the seas, the English people have shed laziness, following her wishes, and have become industrious and hard working, and have started treating all women young and old with equality, so she has not become a domestic servant in their houses. And now even though they speak sweetly to all the farmers, and collect money as they will, they avoid educating the farmer. The main reason behind this must be that they realize that the moment the farmer educates himself and acquires knowledge, he will carry his whip on his shoulder, and he will bring the goddess of wealth back to his own home, and make her stay there happily. Because if this ever happens, the English will have to scream and yell, and travel to America, and somehow manage to fill their bellies by

[133] A Sepoy Revolt by Henry Mead, page 29. [—*J.P.*] [Original in English. [—*Ed.*]]

working hard day and night. And if the goddess of wealth had not gone to her parents' place and stayed there quietly, these *bhat* brahmans would have made much of their norms of purity that they would not have stopped even at telling their own parents to keep off because they were dressed in ritual clothes. They would have said, 'Do not touch us, do not let your shadow fall on us.' So it is difficult to infer what these lords of the land would have reduced the farmers to. But I can tell with full certainty that they would surely have buried mangs and mahars in the stones of these new buildings. Now if the mangs and mahars seek to improve their lot and humanize themselves, then there too black *bhat* Christians are constantly at the white missionaries' ears, and ensure the farmers' failure. There too, those who became Christians from amongst the higher castes manage to maintain a series of differences and inequalities, that is what we have seen. Moreover, nowadays several educated *bhat*s and brahmans are going to England,[134] taking with them their ritual pots and pans, and what stories these victorious people, in the pride of wealth, will tell of the poor farmer and shudras and atishudras to the English people, and what difference these stories will make is something that even our poor Governor General will not be able to guess. Because in the time of our industrious ex-Governor Temple, these *bhat*s and brahmans who were supervising over the poor farmers who were labouring for food on various canals and lakes had wreaked havoc, so much so that the condition of the defeated Africans whose children were stolen and sold in America was better. If we tried to write this down to convince you, then even a better book than *The Cultivator's Whipcord* will be written. We could look into this if I find the time. But at present, if instead of talking about Hindustan in London, if these people bring Mr Fawcett and Mr Gladstone, wise men both, to India and stay with them in the farmers' houses for a week or two, then instead of returning to England to blabber about Hindustan, they would directly escape to America, and if this does not happen, these children of *bhats* and brahmans may write what they will in newspapers about this book, and fill their bellies. In

[134] A Sepoy Revolt by Henry Mead, page 286. [—*J.P.*] [Original in English. [—*Ed.*]]

sum, since there is no book amongst the malis, kunbis and dhangars which could be said to have come from God, like the Bible, brave and great kings among them, like the Shindes and Holkars, and the lords of the farmer's children, and cows, cannot even read even basic books of Sanskrit conjugations because of the obstacle of the Arya *bhats*, they do not know that they are human, and what their real rights are. If we say this is not so, then why would the farmers have maintained the tradition of washing the brahman's feet, and drinking that water? Why would they have worshipped stone and metal idols, cows, and snakes, and plants, and treated them as gods? Because the Arya brahmans have kept them ignorant for their own selfish purposes, the farmers do not have the power of balanced thought, and believe in all manner of ghosts and creatures and practise all manner of mumbo-jumbo and magic and waste their own money. They lose their lives too, because they do not believe in medicine but in shamans and magicians. Let that be. We could take this up some other time. Thus because they are tethered from all sides and have lost their essence, and because they marry off their children when very young, the tender semen of the farmer is decaying, and his children are born weaker and weaker, and powerless. In the older days, nobody could withstand the farmers' slingshots, but now in the present British rule, his grandchildren and great-grandchildren are so weak, even street walkers can humiliate him. Secondly, because they are married at an early age, when the children come of age, they sometimes do not like each other's looks, behaviour, nature, and then there is rift between them, and thus several rakish young men have abandoned their young wives,[135] some of whom now have to live out their life in their parents' home, the remaining, shelterless, are tossed about in life, and eventually die. The parents marry off children without the children's consent at a young age,

[135] I read this fourth part in Mumbai city last year, in April 1883. From that day, those learned people from amongst the shudras who have abandoned their wives because they were not fair of colour or good looking are very angry with me, and instead of being ashamed, or repentant, and bringing them back home, these people have been privately, or secretly, or through published pieces, have been [sic] maligning me. Who can possibly shut them up? [—*J.P.*]

and then if the farmer does not like his wife by marriage and he marries another or keeps another, then I would find it difficult to say that they are unjust, but what can one say to them marrying yet another, and yet another, four or five such wives? In my opinion they should marry a fifth woman, so that when such a person dies, his children will be free of performing rituals of the dead body. Also, from amongst the kunbis, there are some farmers who somehow manage to read texts like *Vyankateshstotra*, or *Tulshiakhyan*, or *Rukmini Swayamwar*,[136] and after they have married twice or thrice, they become self-important personages in the village, and in company of the cunning brahmans, give false evidence here, sign false receipts there, and harass the poor of the village no end. Amongst the malis, there is not even this much reading skill. But while listening to all manner of folk tales and folk performances, and religious tales, once they manage to memorize a few devotional songs, a few anecdotes and a few verses, they become the very cornerstones of such activities, and after that, they think of all the scholars and learned men as nothing. Once they manage to turn the tables on some scholars, they become proud and soon marry for the second and the third time, in spite of their first wife. They now have silver rings on their fingers, pearls in their ears, beautiful caps on their heads and carpets to sit on, beside which lie dirty tobacco cloth-bags, and filthy spittoons. If one chews a *pan* with them because they insist, one almost throws up while spitting in them. Then they sit beside some hangers-on, who are preparing ganja,[137] and tell stories of their own little victories, and call themselves descendants of this or that personage, and thus become important people. The wives of those whose turn it is to feed these people, do so on time, from their own earnings of their own occasional labour. Having slept soundly in the afternoon, these executives come out of the house, and striding along with legs spread wide, rocking on their feet, twirling pale moustaches on the holes of their mouths, these executives collect some good-for-nothing followers, and as they move through the lanes, teasing a few innocent young women here and there, create factions in the

[136] Names of some of the innumerable mythological texts. [—*Ed.*]

[137] A strong preparation of marijuana, used chiefly for smoking. [—*Ed.*]

caste, and when these matters are settled in the panchayat, rifts are created even amongst relations, and then these people poison the ears of everybody around, in the end making it difficult for some women to live at their parents' homes or at their husbands' homes. Finally, these active personages threaten the poor in a variety of ways and extract money for the day's drinking and go home, where they eat whatever is kept in the women's baskets, fruit and suchlike, and while the women cook, they sit there and talk sweetly to them. In marriages in the town, these good-for-nothings make sure that they get a feast. If such devilish, letterless people are the leaders of the ignorant farmer, how will their condition, or the condition of their farmlands ever improve? Let that be. From the information I have collected, I have presented here a sample. If you yourselves collect information, you will realize that at present, the farmer is in a perilous condition, as if by the wrath of God, and that the information given here is very little. But I cannot bring myself to state that this will match with the information that our industrious government has collected through the white gazetteers and black *bhat* mamledars. Because it is difficult to find a government department in which the *bhats* have not entered. At the base of all this misery lies the ancient injunction of the brahmans that the shudra farmers should not be educated. The various storytellers and mythopoets, *bhat*s, have impressed this idea on the farmers' minds so deeply that the farmer thinks it sinful to educate his children. Also, we have already experienced that because of his penury, the farmer cannot educate his children. Therefore our multi-faceted government should in proportion to the taxes that it collects, the various local funds and other collections, close down all the Marathi and English schools in villages, and, looking upon the farmer with kindness, start a school for making teachers from amongst the farmers themselves, and spend money in each taluk, from the local fund to provide food and clothes and books to farmers' children, and start boarding schools for them. Once such teachers are ready, it should make a law that the farmers' children should study only in schools run by these teachers, until they come of a certain age, so that at least a little education is imparted to the farmers; but until real education and knowledge is available to them, the strong imprint of the scheming brahmans will not be erased from their minds. And until this is done, the farmer will not come to his senses. But even if our dilly-dallying government, which switches things from this hand to that hand, spends the total local fund on recruiting brahman professors and directors into the Education Department, the farmer's children will never receive an education from them. Because the fence that the mahar builds for the farmer's land is blown away in the wind. These are, after all, hired mules, by evening they will collect silently at the public charity house. This I will whisper in the ear of our government, and finish today's subject.

Chapter Fifth

Suggestions for the Arya *bhat* brahmans regarding us shudra farmers, and the measures that the government should take.

Before beginning this fifth and last chapter, I will make some suggestions to the cunning Arya *bhat* brahmans, so that they do not meddle in the issue. I pray to God that the eyes of the native, ignorant dasyu[138] shudra brothers will be opened, along with those of the foreign and learned[139] government. Because now they are wrapping up and hiding their swords of religion and rapiers of the shastras in ritual cloths, and ignoring totally the mangs and mahars. They are exhorting and advising all the factions who are complaining in their own ways about the hierarchies in this country, shudras, Parsis and Mussalmans, especially the youngsters, that unless they all concentrate and unite, there will no progress possible in this country. I am attempting here that the letterless farmer should not undertake any rash action hearing this. The rest is in the hands of their destiny.

Because in the past the ancestors of these cunning Arya *bhats* and brahmans established, through the strength of their archery, their complete dominance over the dasyu shudras, from that day onwards till today, for thousands of years, the defeated shudras were kept ignorant of their own human rights, and these shudras came to believe in this selfish religion, rather than the public and human religions as found in the books of the Bauddhas, Mussalmans and the Christians. They became completely dependent on the brahmans, and began to think it great a virtue to despise other human beings and criticize the true, rights-based

[138] Slave. [*—Ed.*]

[139] *Vidwan.* Although one cannot be certain, this usage is probably ironic, as he seems to talk in a number of places of brahmans' dominance in the administrative structure. [*—Ed.*]

religions. Thus the brahmans came to do what they will with the shudras, and the shudras themselves came to believe that it was the right of the brahmans to do so. Later it became habitual to think that the shudras should not be suspicious about anything that the brahmans did, and that was their duty, and this continues upto the present. And because the government in England, and its white employees are thoroughly ill-informed of this condition, they fail to take appropriate action. Thus the overall condition of all the shudra farmers is now so abject, and these brahmans, with the cunning intention of becoming blameless, and making the farmers do things for them, are advising the shudras, through their newspapers, meetings, associations and through their books that 'these shudra farmers should remain loyal to the brahmans and unite with them, otherwise this unfortunate country will see no progress.' Now it is clear from this hollow advice that their intention is merely to cheat the farmer with false promises of progress and upliftment because the custom of treating shudras like slaves was started by the ancestors of the brahmans, and that custom still continues. How will the farmers and the alien brahmans unite? With their skills and education, tremendously successful people like Dr Franklin and Thomas Paine have laboured day and night, and the American people have pushed down all the artisans of all the nations of Europe, and brought in money from there to the tune of crores every year. This knowledge and education the ancestors of the brahmans shut tight by prohibiting it in their selfish books. Therefore the progress of true soldiery and archery was completely stifled. One might want to say that we can see with our own eyes how the young members of great families like Shinde and Holkar ride horses and make a bombastic display of spears and other weapons, but these unfortunate souls cannot even take positions and with the help of binoculars, fire cannon balls. All they do is twirl their moustaches, and exploit the farmer, ruining the reputation of their great families. Thus it was that greedy conquistadors from the French, the Portuguese and the Mussalman rulers invaded this country and took away inordinate amounts of wealth with them. Many of them defaced the selfish religion of the brahmans. And finally, several Mussalman warriors carried thousands of brahmans by their ears, and converted them to their own human religion, and performed circumcisions. But the right upto this time, the prohibition on teaching the shudra farmers' children in the Sanskrit schools continues. Therefore, how will there be unity between the farmer and such brahmans? Now looking at the order of nature, it can be seen that everything except knowledge is common to men and all other creatures. For example, the beast knows nothing more than eating, sleeping, copulating, protecting its offspring, defending itself from enemies, and to burp and growl after eating, and therefore the beasts cannot improve upon this and therefore their original condition does change even a little, whereas man has a natural and peculiar intelligence. It is through intelligence that he has reached high up, above all the creatures of water, beasts, birds and insects, and it is with this intelligence that he invented the wonderful skill of putting down his thoughts on paper. This enabled people of all the four continents to note the errors they had made and their experiences, and now there is an immense storehouse of such experiential knowledge in the world, and using this experiential knowledge in combination with their intelligence, European people are communicating their knowledge through the wireless machine, thousands of miles away, helping each other in times of famine, sending lakhs of tonnes of food through ships and trains and helping each other survive. From amongst this species of intelligent human beings, the shudra king Shivaji troubled the monotheist Mussalman badshah no end, and protected cows and brahmans along with their selfish religion. In memory of this, the treacherous servants of this letterless shudra king, the Peshwas kept his ignorant descendent under arrest in the fort at Satara, and assigned the investigation to the inordinately cruel Trimbakji Dengle, while they themselves distributed coins and rupees to people of their own caste in Pune, and while doing sacred things like the Krishna Leela, began to punish people of the tailor's caste, along with the shudra farmer, for wearing the dhoti like a brahman. Not only this, contemporary brahmans think of cow-piss as sacred and purifying, the cow which has been eating the farmers' turds, and drink cow-piss and purify themselves. And the same *bhats* and brahmans, through the trick of their selfish religion,[140] think of the shudra farmer as low. Thus, how will the farmers and brahmans unite?

Several of the Arya brahmans serve sentences of rigorous imprisonment for forging documents, printing currency, or bribery. Several of them, for being *shaktas*, eat meat and do other unholy things with impure mang women, but think lowly of shudra kings like Bhonsale, Shinde, Holkar and do not inter-marry with them. Most *bhat* brahmans enact all manner of impure things with the dancing girls or harlots in town, but the same Arya *bhats* think it sinful to inter-marry with the simple and innocent farmers' daughters. So how will the farmers and brahmans unite?

Most of the *bhats* and brahmans do not allow the shudra farmer to touch the stone or metal idols in their temples, and do not eat with them, even at a distance, but put leftovers in his plate, and are done with it, so how will the farmers and brahmans unite?

When the unselfish followers of Hazrat Muhammad Paigambar stepped into this country, on the strength of their holy monotheist religion, they began to decimate the selfish religion of the Aryas and *bhats*. So some shudras very enthusiastically started embracing the Muhammadan religion. Then the scheming Mukundaraj took some Sanskrit passages and polished them up with a little atheist opinion and wrote this Prakrit book called the *Viveksindhu*,[141] in order to entice the rest of the shudras, and then until the British started ruling, the Arya *bhats* told the shudra farmers ridiculous stories from the *Mahabharata* and *Ramayana*, and lured them into fighting with the Mussalmans and did not allow the farmer to educate his children in the company of the Mussalmans. The moment British rule was established, the Arya *bhat* brahmans secured all the important positions very easily, and now they are

[140] Sir William Jones, Vol. II, page 224.

> It is, indeed, a system of despotism and priestcraft, both limited by law, but artfully conspiring to give mutual support, though with mutual checks; it is filled with strange conceits in metaphysics and natural philosophy, with idle superstitions and with a scheme of theology most obscurely figurative and consequently liable to dangerous misconception; it abounds with minute and childish formalities with ceremonies generally absurd and often ridiculous. [—*J.P.*] [Original in English. [—*Ed.*]]

[141] Ocean of reason. [—*Ed.*]

eating up the farmer.[142] And though they think of the British and other Europeans of being as lowly as the mangs and mahars, they do not allow the shudra farmer even a glimpse of the texts of the Vedas, which their ancestors thought the holiest of all. But now several of their scholars put all these texts under their arms and run door to door to teach them to the white foreigners. But these *bhat* brahmans, are they not more or less selective when teaching the farmers' children in village schools, run by the government? So how will the farmers and brahmans unite?

If through the general agency of Europeans like the religious missionaries, the children of the displaced farmer educate themselves a little, and if through the kindness of white employees, they secure employment, the *bhat* employees in many offices tell all kinds of tales about them to the white employers and finally get them driven away, and several *bhat* employees in order to please the white employees misreport the farmer's crop and yield and later, blockade the farmer's pleas and representations in a variety of ways and frighten him to death. So how will the farmers and the brahmans unite?

Most of the Vedic scholars, storytellers, mythologists, etc. are extracting all manner of meals and annual gifts, using all manner of tricks, from the ignorant shudra farmer kingly clans like Bhonsale, Shinde and Holkar and are getting thousands of feasts and daily gifts of cows and other donations. In contrast, none of the brahman rulers of princely states like Aundh, Bhor and Sanghi feed anyone. Even in the times of drought they would not condescend to distribute food. Neither has a single brahman *samsthanik*[143] remembered those annual covenants of thousands of rupees, and the frequent feasts gotten out of the shudra farmer, and in return educated even a single child of a farmer, providing books, and food etc. So how will the farmers and the brahmans unite?

In most rich brahman households, when the daily alms are given, there is a process of selection, in which the brahman beggar

142 A Sepoy Revolt by Henry Mead, page 225. [—*J.P.*] [Original in English. [—*Ed.*]]

143 Rulers of princely states in colonial India. [—*Ed.*]

is given rice, and the shudra and Mussalman beggars are given some millet or just told to move to the next house. Therefore, would it not be quite right to say that people like Judge Tucker, European, of another religion, are far more kind than the Arya *bhat* brahmans? Because he spent money from his own earnings to educate brahman and shudra children and taught them English, and these children are now employed right beside the white employees and are doing roaringly well. This is called understanding! This is called kindness! This is called charity! This is called progress! Otherwise, the Arya *bhat* brahmans will unite when needed and after the need is over, one looks this way and the other that way. Because it is the *bhat* brahmans who are going to benefit. But if the learned Arya *bhat* brahmans really wish to unite the people of this country and take the nation ahead, then first they must drown their cruel religion,[144] which is customary amongst both the victors and the vanquished, and they, publicly and clearly, must cease using any artifice in their relationship with the shudras, who have been demeaned by that religion, and trample on inequality and the Vedanta opinion; and till a true unity is established, there will be no progress in this country. If by chance, in their inherited and customary cunning the Arya *bhat* brahmans join hands with a few half-baked shudra scholars and manage some progress, that improvement will not last for too long. If a few belly-filling clerks from amongst the shudras unite with the *bhat* brahmans, and they in turn attempt to take raw mangoes from the green garden and arrange them for ripening, then they will ruin not only the mangoes, which will be valuable in the future, but also the dried grass on which they are set and all the skilled farmers will have to hang their heads in shame. This, my prophecy they should store in the holiest of holy places in their homes, is what I am asserting here.

Now I will go to the cool mountains of Simla, and resting there for some time, I will call upon our government beyond the seas, and in the presence of our supremely kind Governor, suggest measures for improving the farmers' condition:

[144] A Sepoy Revolt by Henry Mead, page 227. [—*J.P.*] [Original in English. [—*Ed.*]]

Now our good and law-abiding[145] government should keep aside the greed of money and appoint detective doctors to keep an eye on the farmers' behaviour, and if the farmer misbehaves and loses his health, or begins to steal and do other sinful things, then arrangements must be made for proper punishment; without that they will not become moral. Unless laws are passed forbidding the farmer from marrying more than one woman and forbidding him from marrying his children at an early age, their offspring will not turn out strong. Because the white employees are ill-informed there is a disproportionate number of *bhat* brahmans appointed, and therefore they do not have to slave in the farms, and their women do not have to fill their bellies by frequenting the market with produce. Moreover, because the farmer is ignorant, the *bhat* brahmans benefit immensely from caste distinctions and hierarchies. Thus the brahmans, employed in government jobs, and the mythologists, storytellers, teachers in schools strive day and night, using all their cunning, to prevent the breakdown of these distinctions and hierarchies. Therefore until the farmers' children become able enough to manage positions in government, not more than the proportionate number of brahmans should be employed in government jobs, and the remaining posts should be given to Mussalmans or Hindus or Britons. It is only then that they (the brahmans) will stop obstructing the education of the farmer. This, their artifice, has become invisible to white eyes because in most government departments, it is the brahmans who are employed. Thus the brahman caste becomes more and more educated, and wealthy, whereas the farmer becomes poorer and eventually pauperized, and sometimes take part in the brahman's rebellions and loses his life. Moreover, the brahmans have so impressed their cunning religion on the minds of the farmers that they think it virtuous to plead guilty for murders that they have committed on the say of the brahmans. This wastes the energies and labour of the police and the Justice Department. Therefore in order to educate the farmers' children, there should be teachers

145 Phule uses the word *dharmik*, which can be translated both as religious and as law-abiding or following a rational code. He probably has the latter meaning in mind here. [—*Ed.*]

from their own castes, who can hold the plough properly, weed the farm and do other things as well. A law should be made which will ensure that children are sent to the schools run by such teachers, and for the first few years, some lower and easier divisions should be created, enticing them with degrees equal to those of brahmans, and unless other castes are prevented from forcing the farmer to perform rituals in their marriages, the farmers' children will not be interested in education. Then, later, those children who will pass the Marathi VI division, along with a test in farm labour, and who will be well behaved, they should surely be made patils of the village – if the benevolent government makes such a law, thousands of farmers will compete to educate their children in the hope of their becoming patils. And when there are such educated and qualified patils in all villages, the cunning *bhat* kulkarnis will not be able to make the farmers fight amongst themselves and file cases against each other, and that will benefit our government immensely, since in a short time the farmer will be able to pay more tax than now, and the unjustifiable swellings in the police and justice departments can then be reduced. Also, the government should for a time believe that there are no *bhat* brahmans to be employed, and as capable people come up from amongst the farmers, they should be employed as mamledars and in other government offices in big and small positions, and trained to do these jobs. Until this happens, the farmers' feet will not find the ground, and the government's revenue will never increase. At present the government is keeping a sharp eye on the deception and treachery in the exchanges of the Gujarati and the Marwadi, but instead of keeping an eye on the false measures and rotten things in their shops, the government should keep an eye on the drink-loving patil.

Let that be. Now I will suggest measures for improving the lands of the farmer, which are increasingly become fallow –

The benevolent government should educate all the farmers, and until they become mature enough to use machines to do the usual things on the farms like European farmers, all the white people and the Mussalmans should slaughter goats and sheep instead of slaughtering cows and oxen; or they should import cattle and slaughter and eat them here, because otherwise there will not be sufficient supply of cattle for the farms, and there will not be enough compost and other fertilizer as well, and so neither the farmer, nor the government will benefit. The essences of leaf, grass, flower, dead insects and animals, is washed away by summer rain, therefore our industrious government should, as and when convenient, use the white and black soldiers and the extra manpower in the police department to construct small dams and bunds in such a way that this water would seep into the ground, and only later go and meet streams and rivers. This would make the land very fertile, and the soldiers in general, having got used to working in open air, will also improve their health and become strong. Even if they labour to the value of one anna every day, this will mean an increase in the government's earnings to the tune of twenty-five lakh per year, because our careful government has, including the police department, at least two lakh sepoys. Similarly the government should, in all the hills and valleys, build lakes wherever possible, so that the small dams in the lower areas will fill with water, and the wells too will have a supply of water and the land for fruit and flower and vegetables will be used, and the government too will benefit along with the farmer. Therefore the government should maintain these bunds in good condition, especially in the backwaters. The government should conduct surveys of all the lands in its territory, employing water specialists, and wherever it is found that there is enough water to be drawn from more than one source, these places should be clearly marked in the maps of the towns, and the government should give some awards to farmers who dig wells without its assistance. Also, the government should allow the farmer to collect all the silt and other things extracted from rivers and lakes, as in the olden times, and it should also return all the cow pastures to the villages, which it has included in its 'forest'; it should, however, make sure that no firewood is collected, or land tilled in the areas that belong to it, and it should also forbid the cutting of wood for selling as wood for construction and destroy the oppressive the Forest Department. Our own government should, spending money from its own coffers, purchase breeds of good sheep from several countries, bring them here, and when they are bred here, their droppings will make for a good supply of fertilizer and their wool will benefit the shudra farmer. If the government does not have the courage to allow the farmer to possess old guns in order to protect his farms from wild beasts, then the government should assign that job to our clean black police department, and if a farmer's crop is devastated by wild boar, then the loss should be made up from the salaries of the senior officers or from the government's coffers – and until such a law is passed, the farmer will not be able to sleep peacefully at night and he will not be able to labour fully on his farm during the day. If the government sincerely wishes to improve the condition of the ignorant shudra farmer, and increase its own yield, it should hold annual tests and competitions of greatest yield and greatest skill, and give awards to the best farmers. Calculating the yield average every three years, the best farmers should be given titles, and if the educated children of the farmer, along with good maintenance of their own farms, also learn some iron-work and carpentry and take exams in those subjects, the government should take them abroad for them to see the agricultural schools there, so that the farmer will immediately improve his farming and be happy. Our moral government should keep a sharp eye on the various professional women and organize hospitals for them in each taluk, and the government should make sure that no immoral songs are sung by the various performing artists, and punish them if they do, because unless this is done, the ignorant farmers' morals and natural tendencies are not going to improve. In general, in all the territories, the number of shudra and atishudra soldiers and policemen is very high, and they fight against the greenish people of 'Egypt' and 'Kabul', shoulder to shoulder with the white soldier. In general, the shudra and atishudra farmer is slaving on his farms, along with women and children, day and night, until he is exhausted, and paying the various taxes, funds, etc., but our charitable government does not even think of educating the farmers' children enough to enable them to read a book on farming or relevant notices in newspapers, and while lakhs of farmers do not have enough cloth and enough food, our government spends inordinate amounts of money on the salaries and pensions of people in the army, the police, the justice departments, who are employed to protect and ensure the farmer's happiness and security. What should we say to this!!! Our government gives pensions worth hundreds of rupees per month to many of these apples of their eyes, white and black employees having worked on a fat per month salary of thirty or thirty-five. Many of the black and white employees become too weak and blind to work for the government, and cheating even some very good European doctors, manage to get pensions, the white employees escape to England, and from amongst the black employees, many become suddenly young, as if Jesus Christ himself has roused them from the dead, and polishing their moustaches with wax and blacking, find employment in municipalities or in offices of big traders and earn thousands of rupees. Our watchful government should, without changing the salaries of any of the army carriage bearers, or construction workers, iron-workers, carpenters, the casual employee, etc., slowly reduce all the inordinately increased salaries of all the black and white employees and slowly reduce the pensions as well. Unless the things written above are thought of, the foundations of the government will not be strengthened, and the farmers' fated penury will not change, and the days of his starvation will never end.

In sum, then, in all the chapters of the *Whipcord*, we have not described at all the condition of the eminent kings and lords amongst the shudras. The reasons are, first, because of their hollow wealth, and second, because of misfortune, they are alienated from the farmer. Therefore I have in bold strokes described here only the pitiable condition of the middle and lower level of shudra farmers, in the city of our Governor, under the rule of the Governor General, and our particular government beyond the seas has been informed. After this, if the government wishes that the brahman's children should perform its last rites, then it should continue the custom of extracting the Royal Fund from the crushed bones of the shudra farmer, and annually spend enormous amounts to educate the brahman's children. I have nothing to say against this as of now.[146] But it should at the least spend the money collected under

[146] A Sepoy Revolt by Henry Mead, pages 69 and 235. [—*J.P.*] [Original in English. [—*Ed.*]]

the false promise of educating the farmer's children honestly on educating these children,[147] so that I would be able to claim to be happy at the fruit of my labour of all these days. But if it does not do so, it will be responsible to God.

Now I first remember with gratitude all my childhood Mussalman neighbours and playmates, in whose company I began to have true thoughts about the falsities of the selfish Hindu religion and its false ideas of caste distinctions, etc. Second, I express my gratitude to the Scottish Mission in Pune and the government institution – through whom I acquired some education and understanding of what a human being's rights are, and the devout European gentlefolk who have assisted these with donations. Then I thank the independent rule of the British government, because of which I could express my views without fear, and pray to the kind Force which runs the world, that their children and grandchildren flourish, and I also pray that this Force will help my ignorant, ill-fated shudra farmers to open their eyes and come to their senses. I take courage from this hope, and now I sit in peace, watching for those who turn back, because my *Whipcord* has hurt them.

Date 18
Wednesday
Month July
Year A.D. 1883
Pune, Peth Junaganj

Jotirao Govindrao Phule
Member of the Satyashodhak Samaj

[147] Pages 301, 308, 313. [—*J.P.*] [Original in English. [—*Ed.*]]

Appendices

Translated by G.P. Deshpande

While I was working on this *Whipcord* many people spoke to me on the proposed book. I present here two typical examples.

I. The one who calls himself a pure maratha

Just as I completed the second part of *Whipcord* a gentleman wearing a brahman-like headgear visited me. It appeared that he was looking rather closely at the things in the room. I tried to place him. He could not have come from Marwad[148] because the headgear did not show the usual three extensions of a big headgear hanging at the back. He could not have been a tailor either as his headgear did not have any needles stuck into it as is customary with professional tailors. One could not place him among the goldsmiths, as he did not have a protruding chest. One could not yet describe him as a brahman because one had not heard him speak. As I was thus trying to figure out who he could be, he turned to me and asked if I had not recognized him.

JOTIRAO: Yes, indeed, I have not. I apologize.

GENTLEMAN: I am a maratha from a maratha family.

JOTIRAO: You may be a maratha. But what is your caste?

GENTLEMAN: My caste is maratha.

JOTIRAO: Well, all Marathi-speaking people from mahars to brahmans are known as marathas. It is not possible to locate anybody's caste if only the term maratha is used.

GENTLEMAN: In that case my caste is kunbi.

JOTIRAO: And, pray, what do you do to earn your living?

148 In western Rajasthan. [—*Ed.*]

GENTLEMAN: Well, not so long ago we had earned a lot of money, almost to the tune two hundred thousand rupees when we served the Maharaja of Satara. We have been living off those earnings since. All you ordinary folk on one side and we on the other!

JOTIRAO: But then how is it that you have chosen to visit me?

GENTLEMAN: I have no favours to ask of you. But then I hear that it is your argument that the brahman government employees exploit the peasantry. If there are government employees of peasant origin they would not indulge in such exploitation.

JOTIRAO: Yes, that indeed is my view. I argue that in all government departments there should be representation of the peasants in proportion to their numbers. If that is the case there will be no exploitation of hapless peasants.

GENTLEMAN: How can that be? Will you please explain? Let me be certain.

JOTIRAO: Imagine for a moment that you are appointed to investigate criminal affairs. Now your caste fellows, kith and kin often fight among themselves. The matter comes to you for investigation and justice. Would you use impolite language with them?

GENTLEMAN: No, never.

JOTIRAO: Why?

GENTLEMAN: Simple. An appointment of that kind is ephemeral. I could be dismissed from the job at any time. If some fellow reports against me to the Collector, my 'officership' will disappear. I cannot afford to make my kith and kin my enemies by using insolent language. I eat with them. I get my children married within the caste. If my caste fellows turn against me, my family will be destroyed. I will have to abandon my children in the name of God. Just see. My children have spent all their life with theirs'. Their houses are adjacent to mine. Our children play together at one place. Our source of water is the same. Our farmlands share common borders. Our animals share grazing lands. In times of need we share our agricultural instruments and we lend each other animals like buffaloes and oxen for agrarian operations. Womenfolk in our households lend each other whatever is needed for food. In short our customs and etiquettes are the same. Our funeral rites are the same.[149] In the event of death a in the house, or any other calamity, we feed each other. How can I use impolite language or take bribes from my own kith and kin? It can only turn my own people into sworn enemies. No, I can't do it!

JOTIRAO: Extend that logic. Since the brahman employees do not belong to their castes, they would not and do not mind harassing the illiterate and hapless peasants. What does your conscience tell you?

GENTLEMAN: I do not know what to say. But then there are some educated people among the peasant castes. They would not even get together and publicly discuss ways and means of helping the peasants. These cowards are interested in women and cursing the brahmans. Outwardly, however, they would be abject slaves to brahman employees.

JOTIRAO: Even the employees of the education department would not discuss the problem of peasant education in their depositions to the Education Commission. Thus misleading the Commission, they cheat the generous Governor General. How can the cowardly shudra learned members beat them at the game? Is not that right? Let alone finding fault with the brahman employees, he cannot afford not to kowtow even to the pettiest of the brahman clerks. If he does that by mistake, he is so vehemently insulted that the poor man starts wondering if his account was at all truthful! Why are you silent sir? Anyway, the next time you wish to discuss the problem of brahman employees, please make detailed enquiries, collect as much information as you can and then come over here for a discussion.

GENTLEMAN: No, no. I am now convinced that because of the monopolization of jobs by brahman employees not only the ignorant peasants but also this benevolent government has everything to lose. But then how come the so-called 'Director' in a government office cannot see the damage?

JOTIRAO: Simple! If they spent their time in looking at the

[149] Earlier peasants carried out these rites themselves, but over the last 30–40 years, brahmans have started overseeing these. [—*J.P.*]

sufferings of the ordinary people, how and when can they have a good time themselves?

GENTLEMAN: Oh, my God! If this is the state today, it is frightening to imagine what the poor, illiterate peasants must have suffered under the Peshwas!

At this point the gentleman concluded his conversation and left.

2 November 1882, Pune J.G. Phule
Member of the Satyashodhak Samaj

II. A shudra sadhu[150]

As I concluded writing the third part of the *Whipcord*, a saffron-clad shudra sadhu, an enthusiastic, garrulous member of the Kabir sect parading a holy tulsi garland, a regular visitor to Pandharpur came to my house and sat on a bench in my courtyard. I asked the sadhu what it is that he desired. To which the sadhu replied:

SADHU: Are you Jotirao Phule?

JOTIRAO: Yes, indeed, I am the one.

SADHU: You are born a Hindu. Because of your English education you have been lately attacking Hinduism. So I thought I should discuss with you if the four principle Vedas, the main scriptures of Hinduism, are indeed divine in origin and satisfy myself. I have come here with that purpose.

JOTIRAO: Have you yourself actually seen the four Vedas with your own eyes?

SADHU: Well, yes. I have seen all of them in a brahman's house.

JOTIRAO: Can you offer any reliable evidence to prove that these books were written by God Himself?

SADHU: Nothing, apart from what the brahman told me during our chat.

JOTIRAO: OK. To begin with, do you think God has a definite shape?

[150] The original title is '*Kabirpanthi Shudra Sadhu*'. We have omitted 'Kabirpanthi' from the title since Phule's polemic is not against the Kabirpanthis alone; his polemic targets a larger ideological position among the shudras. This appendix has been abridged slightly. [—*Ed.*]

SADHU: How can he? God is supposed to be shapeless Paramatma.[151]

JOTIRAO: How is it then that this shapeless God authored the four Vedas?

SADHU: Only the brahmans can answer that question. You'd better ask them.

JOTIRAO: Secondly, is it the case that God authored the Vedas with a view to liberating mankind?

SADHU: Yes, indeed.

JOTIRAO: Thirdly, in which language did God compose the Vedic scriptures?

SADHU: In the Sanskrit language.

JOTIRAO: Fourthly, is Sanskrit understood and spoken all over the world?

SADHU: Very few people know this language.

JOTIRAO: This would prove that the Vedas were not written for upliftment of all mankind because most people of the world do not at all speak or know Sanskrit. How can a scripture, which people don't understand, liberate them?

SADHU: Maybe when they were written, people all over the world spoke Sanskrit. It is possible that later various kinds of languages developed.

JOTIRAO: This would mean that God did not know that there would be a multiplicity of languages in the future. Does not it go against the omniscience of God? Further, many German, Scottish, English scholars like Max Müller have studied the Vedas rather well. Is not it surprising that they did not disown Christianity[152] and adopt the Vedic religion?

SADHU: Maybe the thought of having to bathe thrice a day with a white thread around his neck like the brahmans in the climate of Europe scared Max Müller. In any case he alone can answer your question. How can I say anything on it?

JOTIRAO: If God had created the Vedic scriptures for the liberation of entire mankind, the *bhat* brahmans would not have prohibited

[151] Grand Being encompassing the cosmos. [—*Ed.*]

[152] Ever since Pandita Ramabai has shown the so-called religion of the Aryans its place, a nameless coward among the cunning (defender of the Aryans) has been awestruck and has shut up. [—*J.P.*]

the shudras and the atishudras from studying the Vedas. The *bhat* brahmans have thus violated God's commandment and are not the shudras and atishudras suffering for that? Why should they trust either the God who is supposed to have created the Vedic scriptures or the scriptures themselves? Or indeed why should they call themselves Hindus?

SADHU: The *bhat* brahmans have never prevented the shudras and the atishudras from studying the Vedas. Several *bhat* brahmans go to the missionaries and teach there the Vedas there. The shudras are much too poor and resourceless to the study Vedas. What can the brahmans do? At least that is what the brahmans argue.

JOTIRAO: This proves that you do not know anything of the brahmans' intrigue and conspiracies. Let that be. Are the missionaries who live off religion rich enough to pay for their Vedic studies? And then how about the Shindes and the Holkars, rulers of the princely states? These shudra rulers are surely not paupers. They could have studied the scriptures. Why did they not? I think you must understand that these *bhat* brahmans have been historically making tonnes and tonnes of money off these very rulers. Have they ever thought of running a school for the children of the shudra peasants? They could have educated at least some of them. But they did not, for that would have been the end of the brahmans' monopoly over learning. If they had educated some of the caste brethren of these rulers, there would have been some non-brahman equals of the brahmans. The present state when they are all falling flat before the brahman would have drastically changed. They did not want it.

SADHU: OK. If this is the case why can you not persuade these rulers to start schools for their shudra brethren?

JOTIRAO: Even in their courts the dominance of the brahman officer continues. They would not even let a small fellow like me reach the prince and be heard!

SADHU: Oh, my God. I never imagined that the brahmans would have had such cunning! I am now convinced that when the shudra princes come of age these cunning brahmans would not hesitate to write to the British authorities that, as these princes cannot manage their affairs, they should not be given the charge of their states just yet. Having thus improved the British authorities they must be turning these princes into performing monkeys!

JOTIRAO: I am sure that these brahmans will one day pay for their sins!

SADHU: Thanks. Time for me to take my leave of you!

JOTIRAO: OK! Bye-bye!

Pune, April 6, 1883

J.G. Phule
Member of the Satyashodhak Samaj

On Infant Marriage and Enforced Widowhood

4 December 1884

Written in English by the author

In June 1884 a Parsi social reformer, Beheramji Merwanje Malabari, submitted to the then viceroy, Lord Ripon, two notes on child-marriage and imposed widowhood for consideration and action by the British government. The government forwarded these notes to the Presidency governments. It had also sent them to leading personalities of the time. Phule was one of them.

Phule reacted to the notes in a positive way, with a great deal of sympathy for brahman child-widows. These brief notes are significant for two reasons. One is that while Phule is unforgiving in his attack on brahmanism, he is not against brahmans per se. There are many passages in Phule where he makes the distinction between brahmans and brahmanism. In fact, one could argue that Phule desired the smashing up of the brahmanical structure not simply because it would free the shudratishudras, but because it would free society as a whole. Secondly, these comments on the law-givers with their 'malice towards female sex' are among the first gender statements in India, and flow from Phule's recognition that all women, irrespective of caste status, are to be included among the shudratishudras.

We get some idea of Phule's English prose style through the submission to the Hunter Commission and these comments on Malabari's proposal. It is not as aggressive as his Marathi prose style. But the concerns that mark his Marathi writing are all present there. These notes are a good example of controlled, yet hard-hitting writing. The way he shifts from his otherwise polemical style in Marathi to a neat, brief, and to the point statement in English is admirable. Clearly, he understood the understated character of even the most assertive statement in English. A comparison between his Marathi and English writings is revealing: one is aggressive, polemical and unforgiving; the other is firm, clear, and relatively understated.

Opinion from Jotteerao Govindrao Phulay on Note No. I, by Mr. B.M. Malabari on Infant Marriage in India

I concur with Mr. B.M. Malabari's laudable undertaking, and hope that something may be done by our enlightened Government to alleviate the miserable state of the deluded people of this country. Although Mr. B.M. Malabari is not pressed under the immediate burden of our customs and manners, invented by Aryan Shastra makers, he treated the subject so remarkably well that the Shudrathi-Ati-shudras and Brahmin widows will thank him [in] future undoubtedly. I also now beg to add a few remarks on the middle and lower orders, the downtrodden aborigines of this country. In the course of marriage if any slight dispute takes place between the parties, the poor girl has to suffer all her life-time. After the marriage is over, should a defect in her family happen to come to the notice of the boy's father, the innocent girl is considered an outcaste. If the boy is younger than the girl, she is not well fed, clothed and cared for properly, nay, she is not allowed to remain with her rich parents. If her father-in-law be ignorant and poor, the girl, not being fed well, is stunted in her growth. In short she is more heavily loaded with work for days and nights than American slaves. Thus she is so unbearably tyrannized that she is obliged to put an end to her life by committing suicide; and the crime is very often hushed up by bribing the village Patel, Coolkerni (the quarrel-monger) and Policemen. Many poor parents on the bridegroom's side are thus, by incurring debts for marriages, ruined on accounts of the premature deaths of their daughters-in-law. Besides the husband boy, on coming to his proper senses, does not like his wife and marries one of his own liking. Being thus accustomed, he is induced to marry two, three, or four wives at a time in succession, and thus renders his whole family discontented, abusive and quarrelsome. These ignorant wives are not only obliged to poison each other, but sometimes their own husband. Now the enlightened Hindu of Bengal has made excellent suggestions to University graduates, and these, as they suppose would be a fair beginning for the educated class, but, I think, their suggestions are not *universal and applicable to all the classes of Shudras and Ati-Shudras*, because very few of the former attend the University and the latter are not at all admitted even into vernacular schools and allowed to sit and learn with the higher class boys. In conclusion, unless our wise Government use some compulsory measures, the ignorant, middle and lower classes will not come to their proper sense, because the so-called higher classes of Hindus, who hold responsible posts under Government, have by their cunning and shrewd ways, purposely misguided them in matters of *religion* and *politics*. I therefore suggest that Government should rule that boys under nineteen years of age, and girls under eleven, should not be allowed to marry. In case they do, some reasonable tax may be levied on the parents of the parties married, and the money thus obtained should be used in the education of the middle and lower classes of Hindus. But the education should not be transmitted through the medium of *Brahmin teachers*, for, while educating, they create in the minds of the pupils wrong religious ideas and lead them astray. Even the subsidiary kings, Sindia, Holkar, and others are, we find, cheated in the open daylight under the pretence of invented religion, and are induced to extract tax indiscriminately from the cultivators without giving them timely allowances. But there is strong hope that His Highness the present Ruler of Baroda will try his utmost to educate and better the condition of the ignorant cultivators as His Highness has received a good and sound English education.

Opinion from Jotteerao Govindrao Phulay on Note No. II, by Mr. B.M. Malabari on Enforced Widowhood

Now I touch upon the most delicate subject of enforced widowhood upon Brahmin women. The partial Aryan Institution inconsiderately allows polygamy to males, which causes them to fall into new habits of wickedness. When his lust is satisfied with his legal wives, he for novelty's sake haunts the houses of public women. He then contracts venereal diseases from them and is obliged to seek medical assistance at an exorbitant cost, for himself and his wives. When medical treatment ceases to cure him and his wives he loses all hopes of getting children. In this deplorable condition of his life if the lewd husband finds his own wife to go out during night he suspects her of leading a vicious course and so, punishing her severely, turns her out. In old age in order to obliterate the stigma upon his character, the shameless fellow becomes a religious man and hires public harlots to dance and sing in the temples with a view to venerate the stone idols, for his own satisfaction. After the death of this wicked man, his young and beautiful wife is not allowed by the same Aryan Institution to remarry. She is stripped of her ornaments; she is forcibly shaved by her near relatives; she is not well fed; she is not properly clothed; she is not allowed to join pleasure parties, marriages or religious ceremonies. In fact she is bereaved of all the worldly enjoyments, nay, she is considered lower than a culprit or a mean beast.

Moreover, the Aryan Institution enjoins Brahmin males to marry even the lower class girls during the life-time of his first wife: but his real own sister is prohibited to remarry, after the demise of her first husband. Such partial and unjust prohibitions necessarily lead the helpless Aryan widow to commit horrible and heart-rending acts of atrocity. To prove the above assertion I insert the following instance. One of my Brahmin friends named Rao Saheb Sudashive Bullal Gowndey, who was an officer in the Inam Commission, employed in his house a Brahmin widow as cook, whose name was Kashibai. The poor Kashibai was a well-behaved and beautiful young woman of a respectable family. She was a chaste woman. She served several months in his house. But in his neighbourhood there lived a shrewd and cunning Shashtriboova of a Brahmin caste, who tried his utmost to mislead this ignorant woman. Kashibai at first resisted his inducement but at last she fell victim to his desire and immediately became pregnant. Afterwards by the persuasion of her paramour, she tried several poisonous drugs to commit abortion, but all her attempts failed. After nine months were completed, Kashibai gave birth to a beautiful son and for the sake of her disgrace she murdered the innocent infant with a knife and the corpse was thrown into the well behind the house of her master. Two days after she was arrested by the police on suspicion, tried before the Session Court in Poona and was sentenced to transportation for life. This crime Kashibai committed, that her character may not be spoilt among the Brahmin community. Her case brought to the notice of the public the unjust and partial character of the Aryan Institution, and so the people were struck with horror. Although my means were not sufficient to defray my expense yet I was compelled to establish a foundling house, in my own compound in Poona, for the Brahmin community immediately after Kashibai's trial was over. The enclosed copy of printed notices were then pasted on the walls of the corners of street, where the Brahmins reside. From its commencement up to the present time, thirty-five pregnant widows came to his house and were delivered of children, of whom five are living and thirty died by the injuries done to them while in the womb by the poisonous drugs which the mothers must have taken with a view to conceal their pregnancy. Many of the beautiful and helpless ignorant young widows of the respectable Brahmin families have turned out [to be] private and public prostitutes on account of this wretched system. How abominable and degrading is the system of Aryan Institution, which compels Brahmin widows to drag their lives in so miserable and shameless ways, that even modesty shrinks back to enter into particular details. In conclusion, I most respectfully crave the favour of your enlightened English Government to remove the tyranny of enforced widowhood, exercised upon the helpless women, by the relentless system of Aryan religious institution. I therefore propose that no barbers should be allowed to shave the unfortunate Brahmin widows. It is quite evident from the partial Aryan religious institution that, when it prohibits the widows from remarrying, why the widowers should be allowed to remarry? If the favour be shown to the latter then the poor widows must of necessity be permitted to remarry. There is no doubt that the selfish and wicked law-givers must have added such unjust and nonsensical clauses into their shastras with malice towards female sex.

Letter to the Conference of Marathi Authors

11 June 1885

Translated by G.P. Deshpande

The Conference of Marathi Authors was founded in 1878. Its second plenary session was organized by Justice M.G. Ranade on 24 May 1885. Ranade wrote to Phule on May 13 requesting him to participate in the plenary session. Phule did not. But he sent a reply to Ranade, which was published in the 11 June issue of the journal *Dnyanodaya*. This is another example of how Phule always related to all problems keeping in mind what in his view was the main contradiction in contemporary society. His taking part in the Conference, he felt, would not benefit the shudratishudras. That is Phule's refrain.

An interesting thing about the letter is the last sentence, which is written in a dialect which the Muslims of western Maharashtra use in their speech: '*Sadhe hoke buddheka yeh pahla salaam lev*'. It sounds like Urdu or Hindustani but does not quite follow either the grammar or syntax of Urdu and Hindustani. It is Marathi for all practical purposes. His use of this kind of language would certainly have shocked the contemporary brahmans. But Phule clearly seems to emphasize that this 'Mussalmani' or 'Bagwani' speech is as much Marathi as brahmanical speech!

Dear Sir,

I acknowledge the receipt of your letter regarding the proposed conference of the (Marathi) authors and I was delighted to receive your request that I should participate in the conference. But then, esteemed sir, the conferences and the books of those who refuse to think of human rights generally, who do not concede them to others and going by their behaviour are unlikely to concede them in future, cannot make sense to us, they cannot concur with what we are trying to say in our books. The reason is that their ancestors, with a view to taking revenge on us, included in their pseudo-religious texts an account of how they turned us into slaves and thus gave our enslavement religious authority. Their dated and decadent texts are witness to this phenomenon. These upper-caste authors who are forever miles away from reality and who can only make ceremonial and meaningless speeches in big meetings can never understand what we the shudras and atishudras have to suffer and what calamities we have to undergo. All this is not entirely unknown to the high-caste founders of various conferences and organizations. They pretend to be modernists as long as they are in the service of the British government. The moment they retire and claim their pensions they get into their brahmanical touch-me-not attire, become caste chauvinists, incorrigible idol worshippers and, what is worse, treat the shudras and atishudras as lowly and contemptible. If they happen to be in their touch-me-not ritual dress they would not even touch paper notes as if that were a blasphemy! How can these Arya brahmans improve the lot of this unfortunate land? Be that as it may. We the shudras do not any longer wish to trust these people and their specious and dishonest stories, for they cheat us and eat off our labour. In a word, we the shudras have nothing to gain by mixing with such people. We must ourselves think about our situation and how we should relate to these upper-caste people. If these leaders of men are genuinely interested in unifying all people they must address themselves to the discovery of the root of eternal love of all human beings. Let them discover it and may be formulate and publish it as a text. Otherwise to turn a blind eye to the divisions among the human beings at this hour is simply futile. Of course, they are free to do what they like. I would nevertheless be thankful if my short letter is placed before your Conference for consideration. In any case, accept the salute of this old man.

Your friend,
Jotirao G. Phule

Satsar

June–October 1885

Translated by Urmila Bhirdikar

Satsar (The Essence of Truth) was a journal which Phule tried to publish in 1885. Two issues were published, and both state Phule's theological position. But *Satsar* also had another, more immediate purpose, which was perhaps more important. Pandita Ramabai, a learned Sanskrit scholar from Pune, embraced Christianity in 1883 while in the USA. There was a storm of protest and condemnation in the brahmanical press of Pune. Phule used the columns of *Satsar* to defend her right to convert and to attack the fierce criticism of Ramabai even by the so-called modernizing and reformist brahmans. Two issues of *Satsar* constitute the only non-Christian defence of Pandita Ramabai; a brave act by someone who did not convert to any religion himself.

The Essence of Truth
By
Jotirao Govindrao Phuley

Satsar
This booklet has been published by Jotirao Govindrao Phuley
In the public interest

Printed at Pune in Saujanyamitra Press
1885

Price one anna

Preface

Since a few shudras and atishudras are able to read and write because of the efficacy of the English rule, we have brought out this first issue of this small book called *Satsar* in order to prove to the world-hater Arya brahmans how the shudras and atishudras have been excessively cheated by the cunning Aryas for thousands of years. We shall not bind ourselves to the promise of publishing further issues of this book at any specific time. But if our impartial and thoughtful discerning Muslim, Christian and Hindu brothers extend their generous support to our humble efforts the further issues may indeed be presented every week.

The Author

Satsar Number 1

The shudra members of the Satyashodhak Samaj had a conversation with several gentlemen. Some of the important parts have been noted here. We present them before our discerning readers.

SHUDRA: When Pandita Ramabai came to Pune and delivered several lectures proving the importance of the Hindu religion I was not impressed. For how would a poor woman like Ramabai know the ways in which the creators of the Hindu religion have severely criticized women and shudras and atishudras through their tyrannical writing about them? Maybe her trip to England afforded her the opportunity of comparing Hinduism with Christianity. She thus came to know of the unreasonable stubbornness and the sheer partisanship of Hinduism and that prompted her to give up the Hindu religion and accept Christianity. If you could invite Ramabai back to India people can come to know about it and many of them will open their eyes. Moreover, many people are keen on seeing such a scholarly lady.

BRAHMAN: From her letters home it seems that she is at this time minutely studying the Brahma dharma. And I feel that she will come back to India quite soon.

SHUDRA: What is Brahma? Shall we say that Brahma is that which gives birth to brahman, kshatriya, vaishya and shudra from its mouth, arms, thighs and feet, respectively, or is it the one that gave birth to Manu who created extremely shameful and unjust scriptures or is it the name of the primary cause of the creation of nature as said by several of your logicians? Let us know for once what the Brahma of your Brahma Samaj is really like.

BRAHMAN: The Brahma of our Brahma Samaj is the one that does not recognize and goes beyond caste inequality. It is a formless Brahma.

SHUDRA: Since you Brahma Samajis do not believe in caste

inequality, why don't you convert all the mahars and mangs to Brahmaism and assimilate them in your Brahma Samaj?

BRAHMAN: Brahma Samaj wishes to convert the mahars and mangs to Brahmaism. And all of us Samajis are working towards it. But you shudras must help us in these efforts. When all of us came into this country from Iran we deprived the aboriginals here, the mahars and the mangs, of all their possessions, enslaved them and became their rulers.

SHUDRA: I see. Now pray tell me were the shudras already enslaved before arriving in India from Iran or did the Aryas enslave the shudras on their way to India and brought them along or your brahman ancestors enslaved the shudras after they came to India? Which one of these (three possibilities) is the truth? Give us a prompt answer. Why do you now take time to reply? Since you did enslave the shudras and atishudras and have tortured us through generations as if it were your inherited right, until today, you should first restore to the mahars and mangs their due human rights and apologize to them. Having accomplished that, if you would then come and consult the ignorant shudras like us we shall see what we can do. Frankly, we do not want anything to do with your Prarthana Samaj, Brahma Samaj and the like. Enough of your clever stratagems.

BRAHMAN: If you do not wish to help us then you yourself should tell the mangs and mahars their human rights and lead them on the right path.

SHUDRA: Your ancestors came from Iran and invaded all the original inhabitants of this country. They deprived them of everything and became their rulers. They enslaved the shudras and deprived them of their right to learning. Many of them were reduced to untouchability and in this way they were tortured in every manner. We find utterly cruel writings about this in the scriptures written by your ancestors like Manu. Don't we see for ourselves that you Aryans ruined the shudras completely? Therefore, in order to erase the trace of your ancestors' low deeds you now want to educate the mahars and mangs and incorporate them in the associations you have planned. Why should we shudras render help to you in this matter? You should yourselves pick up the thorns your ancestors had spread in the path of the mahars and mangs.

BRAHMAN: You seem to assert a separate identity, separate from us, for the shudras. How can this be? Don't we include Vyasa[1] who was born of a koli[2] woman and Vasishtha[3] born from a chandal[4] woman among us and respect their descendents like brahmans? How can you then think of yourselves as separate?

SHUDRA: Even if we accept the position as argued in your texts that the mothers of Vyasa and Vasishtha were from the shudra families, it cannot be denied that their fathers were not atishudras. In fact they were brahmans. Therefore is it a wonder that your ancestors incorporated Vyasa and Vasishtha among brahmans? Because the seed is brahman. But is there any proof in your books about the brahmans having incorporated into themselves the progeny of a brahman woman and an atishudra man?

BRAHMAN: What kind of clever formulations on this question are in the Hindu scriptures is more than I can say.

SHUDRA: Why does not the eternal Brahma that you pray to, closing your eyes firmly, in your Samajmandir, tell you about the real state of the past conditions of the mahars and mangs and open your eyes?

BRAHMAN: Let that be. But can't you see that when the number of Arya brahmans is so small then how could they have defeated and enslaved the shudras and atishudras, who outnumber the brahmans by nine times?

SHUDRA: Why should that be a surprise? Don't your scriptures carry the stories of your great war heroes who shoot their weapons uttering mystical words and thereby destroy thousands of the enemy? Further, does not recent history tell us that a handful of Muslims and Englishmen became your rulers, rulers of over twenty crore people?

BRAHMAN: We Brahmas do not believe in books full of such stories.

1 Vyasa is traditionally identified as the author of the *Mahabharata*. [—*Ed.*]

2 Fisherwoman. [—*Ed.*]

3 A sage in the *Ramayana*; a guru of Lord Ram. [—*Ed.*]

4 Person born of mixed varna. [—*Ed.*]

SHUDRA: Then where do you derive your Brahma from? From which book, unrelated to these fanciful stories?

BRAHMA: This is really the limit. If someone even utters the words Brahma or brahman you lose your temper.

SHUDRA: When your Arya ancestors became the rulers on earth and lords of the shudras and atishudras taking support from the word Dharma and ruined the lives of people like kunbi, mali, agari, koli, bhil, ramoshi, mang and mahar, why should we be angry with virtuous people like the Christians and Muslims even if they became the rulers of your Aryan ancestors?

BRAHMAN: That is not how it is. We Prarthana and Brahma Samajis have resolved to discard all the false principles in the Hindu, Christian, Islamic and other religions and conduct ourselves according to the remaining true principles in them.

SHUDRA: You can get away with whatever criticisms of Christian scriptures that you might make. It has been observed that anyone can catch hold of a preacher, beat him up, hit him and pound him and at the instigation of cunning impostors the children of ignorant shudras can follow them about screaming and shouting at them and throwing mud at them. But remember that the Muslims are not going to allow you to even touch their Quran. You cannot even think of dealing with them in this manner. Do not see such dreams. Anyway, let that be.[5] Have you Brahmas prepared a separate book which finally dismisses the falsehoods and pseudo-principles of Hinduism and incorporates only the true principles of the Hindu religion?

BRAHMAN: We have not yet compiled such a book but we are thinking about it.

SHUDRA: So on what basis do we shudras and atishudras and of course Pandita Ramabai trust your assurances? Where is the book? And, later, if a nasty conspirator like Parashuram or Nana Peshwa[6] is born among the brahmans and if a wily

5 Phule is quite critical of Muslim fundamentalism in his writing; although he does not use that term. Phule's criticism of fundamentalism is probably the earliest of its kind in India. [—*Ed.*]

6 Parashuram is supposed to have destroyed the kshatriyas twenty-one times. Nana Peshwa was one of the last brahman rulers of Pune. [—*Ed.*]

brahman like Shankaracharya taking support from them begins to proclaim that whatever has been written in the scriptures of the Arya brahmans is from God himself, do you think that the ignorant mahars and mangs will be able to confront such a braggart? How will the mahars and mangs stand up to you who have been double-crossing saintly scholars of Christianity and Islam?

BRAHMAN: (*jokingly and smiling*) Why do speak in this way Tatya?[7] Haven't we condemned the prohibitions about women's education following the Brahma Samaj? Haven't we been making special efforts towards spreading education for women?

SHUDRA: Do not say whatever comes to your mind. In fact the Hindu women are able to get education because of the efficacy of the English rule.[8] Because of that rule, general education and the like have become quite common. Not only this, but all the big and small associations established by all of you are the fruit of the education imparted by the English. Now you must stop boasting about your Brahma Samaj. Anyway if the shudras and atishudras ever get an opportunity like your women to get education then all of you Arya brahmans will have to leave your brahmanism.

BRAHMAN: If such a situation arises we will become sanyasis. But Tatya which religion do you belong to?

SHUDRA: Forget God and serve the brahmans! Do you think this ought to be our religion? We shall adopt Christianity or Islam whenever we feel like for our convenience. Or perhaps we shall ask for a religion for us from our Creator.[9] You do not have to worry about us. But you must take care not to become a sanyasi and waste your life by opening the path of Christianity for an educated woman like Pandita Ramabai.

7 See note 64 on p. 124 of the present volume. [—*Ed.*]

8 A Sepoy Revolt by Henry Mead, page 247. [—*J.P.*] [Original in English. [—*Ed.*]]

9 The term Phule uses here is *Nirman Karta*. Later he coined the term *nirmik* for Creator. [—*Ed.*]

Kondaji Patil of Malyache Kurul[10] had heard this conversation attentively. Later, after lunch, he had a conversation with his colleagues at the Satyashodhak Samaj.

KONDAJI PATIL: Tatyasaheb, after I listened to your subtle and wise conversation in the morning, I thought of a question. All the brahmans are always saying that one should not look for the origin of a river or a brahman. What is the great secret behind this saying?

TATYA: You will not immediately understand the conspiracy of the brahmans.

KONDAJI PATIL: But do let us know what you have to say on it. If we don't know it then what will you do?

TATYA: If the Arya brahmans used to assimilate their progeny in their caste even when it was born of a shudra or atishudra woman why do they not accept the precious offspring born of their Yavana[11] concubines and shudra prostitutes today?

KONDAJI PATIL: Their brahman forefathers educate them and give them their typical headgears. Then they put the sacred threads on and parade as special and important among the kunbis. This elaborate brahmanization must be avoided by the shudras.

TATYA: Let them wear whatever kind of headgears or threads around their necks. What is it to you? But it would be befitting indeed if they were to own up to the brahmanical frauds that they have spread among you *kulavadi*[12] folks.

KONDAJI PATIL: Brahmanical fraud has spread all over India. It's small wonder if the brahmans are critical of Pandita Ramabai, genuine brahman that she was, she had spent her life hitherto in the tyrannical Hindu religion and then was baptised by the Christians. This conversion angered the brahmans because she exposed the falsity of their religion. But then how was it that some shudras lamented her conversion?

TATYA: Even if many of the shudras have lamented over her it is not

[10] The village which Kondaji Patil belonged to. In the nineteenth century it was quite customary to refer to people in terms of their village as identification. [—*Ed.*]

[11] See note 56 on p. 170 of the present volume. [—*Ed.*]

[12] Sharecroppers. [—*Ed.*]

right to criticize their lamentations. These days, even when the great scholars and the lords of ignorance among the brahmans are rolling in the gutters along with their pure equipment of worship, nay, with all their useless articles, having drunk the alcohol which the mlechhas[13] brew out of rotten ingredients, our shudra and atishudra brothers still consider their drunken caste to be pious. What then is the greatness of such shudras when they call out to the brahmans saying Pandita Ramabai is unpurified when the priest sprinkled a little clean water over this chaste virtuous woman? Why, many brahmans drink the precious substance in the bottles and then turn a beggar's face to England, and still they say Ramabai is unpurified while they themselves are all the time craving for a bottle. Is this the great glory of the brahman braggers? But let that be. Now if you wish, raise such questions that will open the eyes of the shudra brothers. But meanwhile if the editor puts in this conversation in his newspaper without distorting it like the other editors, we can take it up later according to your wishes.

After some days had passed, one day, after lunch, there was the following conversation between Yashwant and Jotirao Phule.

YASHWANT: Tatyasaheb, what is your opinion about the writings in the Arya scriptures that the real dharma of the shudras is to serve their Arya brahman lords?

TATYA: Since the writers of those books were not your ancestors and since the term dharma has many meanings the cunning Aryas have interpreted it so skilfully that it has not been understood even by the great founders of religions. How did you think the ignorant shudras would understand it easily?

YASHWANT: In what ways did the Arya writers interpret the word dharma, because of its many meanings, according to their convenience?

TATYA: The Aryas have written about how they invaded India and enslaved the original inhabitants – dasyus. They say that the dasas should serve the Arya brahman. This is the dasyu's

[13] See note 8 on p. 67 of the present volume. [—*Ed.*]

dharma.[14] Later, even when first the Muslims and later the English seized the country and made the Aryas their servants, the Aryas continued to maintain their hold over the shudras because by then the shudras had become so powerless and reached such a state of ignorance that they began to consider the false scriptures written by the Aryas to be given by God. The word dharma has many meanings such as it is the dharma of the thief to steal, that of the cheater to cheat, that of the horse scratcher to scratch the horse and that of the cunning man to cheat the ignorant and make his living. Arya brahmans kept aside the original, true meaning of the word dharma and created their dharma (religion) by devising a scheme of mystery and magic around it thereby deceiving all the shudra and atishudra people.

YASHWANT: Do you mean to say that even though the Aryas have heaps and heaps of books none of them contains the true meaning of the word dharma?

TATYA: If the books of the brahmans had the true meaning of dharma and had they maintained their conduct according to it then Pandita Ramabai and many other learned brahmans would not have converted to Christianity.

YASHWANT: From what you say it is clear that nothing can prove that God created shudras and atishudras to serve the Arya brahmans. But since the day we were caught in the clutches of the Arya brahmans, they have made us, the shudras and atishudras, powerless, weak and ignorant and they are pursuing us, mischievously hiding behind the word dharma. But how is it that even the scholars among shudras do not utter a word against the deceitful mischief created by the brahmans in their big Samaj?

TATYA: My child, the founders of that Samaj were the cunning Aryas who were staunch idolators and such believers in the pride of their caste that they would not touch an English book when they had bathed and purified themselves. That is why, in order to preserve the menace of their dharma they have included a rule in their statutes that nobody should talk about dharma.

[14] Duty of the slaves. [—*Ed.*]

YASHWANT: Here the brahmans have really checkmated the shudras and atishudras. But we can talk about it later. But what is the intention behind this Samaj of the brahmans?

TATYA: It must be to bring the government to its senses by warning them against making the same kinds of mistakes in today's laws as Manu did in the past.

YASHWANT: It is a great surprise that the members of this Samaj only patter like a parrot in a cage and waste time in such a time of emergency, instead of taking some action for defending and protecting the precious members of society.[15]

TATYA: How can you say this, my child? Our wise rulers have until now spent crores of rupees from the royal and local fund on educating the brahmans. Then they appointed them on responsible posts and made them happy in every way. The reason must be that the scholar brahmans would come in aid of the government in times of crisis.

YASHWANT: That means that the pure and scholarly brahmans will confront the Russians without bothering about the impure and lowly shudras and atishudras.[16]

TATYA: Do you have any doubt about it? In matters of battles and wars these scholarly brahmans will not let themselves be impurified by you shudras and atishudras. Let the time come and we shall watch this fun as well.

YASHWANT: Let us see the greatness of repeating the names of gods a number of times and rituals like Satyanarayana. But Tatya, most of the Arya brahmans are always saying that if one converts to Christianity one loses ones patriotism. What do you have to say about it?

TATYA: All it means is that the ignorant shudras and atishudras should believe in the blessings of the brahmans and serve in wars risking their lives and starving or eating groundnuts while the cunning brahmans should eat their fill twice a day and sit in some airy and safe temple and count the rosary and have fun chatting in the nights. And when the shudras and atishudras

[15] Yashwant uses the word *hirat*. The use is ironical. [—*Ed.*]

[16] The reference here is to the great game in Asia being played by Britain and tsarist Russia. [—*Ed.*]

come back victorious, within no time will they call their children ignorant and blame them for not having the knowledge of ruling and then imprison them so that the brahmans can enjoy royal power. If the Hindus who have converted to Christianity did not have pride for their nation then all of them would not have asked for weapons from the English rulers for defending the nation.

YASHWANT: If the brahmans start fighting in the battles like the native Christians then I will go to some temple of Mariaai or Rokadoba[17] and make a little offering from the meat dish and eat the rest happily. Why do you smack your lips, Tatya?

TATYA: Do you think I am a brahman? I too will share some of your meal any time you say and worship the goddess of Power.

Unless our impartial, thoughtful and discerning Christian, Muslim and Hindu friends support our meagre efforts generously, I will not have the courage to publish further issues.

Dated 13 June 1885 — Jotirao Govindrao Phule
Pune, Peth Juna Ganj — Member, Satyashodhak Samaj

[17] Non-brahmanical godheads. [—*Ed.*]

Satsar II
The Essence of Truth

Series No 2

Jotirao Govindrao Phuley

This booklet was prepared in public interest by
Jotirao Govindrao Phuley

Printed at Jagadhitechhu Press, Pune

First Edition
Copies 2000
October 1885

Price 1 anna

I would like to thank Purushottam Maruti, Mr Jyaya Karadi Lingu, Mr Rajanna Balu Contractor, Dharmaji Baburao Dhayarkar and other friends.

Preface

These days, because of the efficacy of the English rule a few of the harassed women are able to read and write a little. We have tried in this issue to bring to their notice how the cunning Arya people have tortured women for thousands of years, and how they continue to do it even today. In one or two places we have admonished some of the unworthy quarrelsome sons rather harshly and we sincerely request our loving mothers and sisters to forgive us for this. Here is the second number.[18]

[18] The original has 'salaam', literally salute. [—*Ed.*]

Satsar Number 2

YASHWANT JOTIRAO PHULE: Tatyasaheb, in the first issue of *Satsar* you had asked a question to the brahmans regarding the Arya and brahman creators of the Hindu religion breathing fire on women and the shudras and atishudras and writing tyrannically about them. Which of these writings are about women? It would be very good if you explained them to me yourself.

TATYA: My child, your curiosity is somewhat genuine and commendable. Today, because of the efficacy of the English rule and due to the efforts of Pandita Ramabai many great scholars among the brahmans felt ashamed and began to make their ignorant and powerless women scholars like themselves in order to free their sage-like ancestors from blame. If, however, we were to discuss the tyrannical writings of the mercilessly cruel Arya brahman writers and write about them in our pamphlet right in the beginning, it might prove disadvantageous in many ways. For, the moment the daughters of the brahmans realize the artful duplicities the books of the Arya writers had imposed on them, they will expose all the storytellers in the temples and disgrace them. Moreover, fearing that there will be constant arguments between mothers-in-law and daughters-in-law in the brahman families and they will give rise to all kinds of fights many brahmans will not allow their daughters and daughters-in-law to go to school and be in the position to read our *Satsar*. In this way instead of improving the conditions of these poor women, we will cause them sorrow.

Secondly, it was about three thousand years ago that the Arya writers of this country wrote a number of tyrannical pieces in their books. How will today's orthodox brahmans understand the subtle manoeuvres in them? For, these days they have started to believe that all these books are eternal and have emanated straight from God. Moreover, many brahmans and some shudras too, the moment they can read and write a little English, start a newspaper for their livelihood. The others begin to compose odd books and set up a shop to sell them. How will the editors of such newspapers and writers of books, who are interested in only filling their bellies, understand the schemes in the books of the Aryas? These books are intended to confuse people so that they cannot discern true from false. We can also say that because of the misconceptions of those who work in the Education Department in this country the shudras and atishudras cannot even read. Very few of them can read a little. Therefore, excepting the few brahman scholars we do not know what the ignorant people will do by reading an imposter's thoughtless writings.

YASHWANT: What you say is right. From the example of Pandita Ramabai's scholarship in Sanskrit and because of her guidance, the Hindu Mahila Samaj has acquired the status of a women's society. Many scholars felt that they should teach women English so that they would acquire real knowledge. That is why with great effort they established a separate English school for women. The credit for all this activity should belong to Pandita Ramabai. Scholarly, thoughtful, kind and studious Ramabai went to England with a great deal of determination to pursue English studies. However, when she condemned the partisan Hindu religion and converted to Christianity many thoughtless editors of newspapers in Maharashtra abused the poor woman comparing her to the fox in Aesop's tales. One naughty editor was so inflamed that he attacked all European women and blamed them by wildly misinterpreting traditional customs. The English gentlemen were immensely ashamed of this and as they were about to pick him up and send him to gaol, he readily repented, feigning madness and escaped by expiating the sin. Did he do right?

TATYA: My child, even before Pandita Ramabai came to Pune, Tarabai Shinde of Buldhana wrote a book called *Stree Purush Tulana*.[19] In this book she has given excellent advice to men,

[19] See Rosalind O'Hanlon, *A Comparison Between Women and Men: Tarabai Shinde and the Critique of Gender Relations in Colonial India*, New Delhi:

for most of them behave as they will and sinfully in the presence of their women. Naturally their respectable women feel bad, but since they are powerless and ignorant they are infuriated and great storms of bad deeds arise in their imagination. She (Tarabai) therefore decided to advise the menfolk. Her advice is a little stern and pungent, and an adamant editor of a newspaper did not like it. And because of this, or because he was afraid that if he tried to oppose the contents of her book the tables of vices mentioned in the book might turn against himself, he rejected all the advice in the book and repaid Tarabai's debt by criticizing her. [. . .]

Since I felt that one should have nothing to do with so vainglorious a youth that he is unable to crush a laddoo like even we old people can,[20] I have stopped dealing with him. Had he educated his wife at home like the honourable Madhavrao Govindrao Ranade[21] and had he then criticized Tarabai or Pandita Ramabai, the trumpet of his fame would have been heard in America. This woman-chaser[22] does not even deserve to take Pandita Ramabai's name, for what is the extent of his understanding? Can he himself write as systematically and yet piercingly as Tarabai? If we weigh him against Pandita Ramabai he will come up short. He should at least have looked at his own face in the rickety mirror which he got as a gift from his father-in-law. Anyway, I have heard there was a rumour about him that he had abandoned his caste and forcibly sent his young wife all the way, beyond the black waters, into the isle of exile to study the emotion of sorrow. If this is true then he should bring his wife home and get her to refute Tarabai's book letter by letter. But before doing so he should not insist as a first condition that she go to a holy place like Vangani and purify herself with the

OUP, 1994. Buldhana is a small town in the Vidarbha district of Maharashtra. [—*Ed.*]

20 A graphic phrase meaning a thoroughly good-for-nothing youth. [—*Ed.*]

21 Justice Ranade, who died in the early years of the twentieth century. [—*Ed.*]

22 The reference is to either Bhalekar or Lokhande, his colleagues of the Satyashodhak Samaj, whom he accuses of womanizing. Phule makes the point that they are not as consistent and dedicated as the brahman Ranade was. [—*Ed.*]

footwash of a fisherwoman.[23] If the rumour I have reported here is utterly false then he should write to us so that we can mention it in our next issue of *Satsar*.

YASHWANT: Let it be, leave him alone now. Do you think he will get his wife back from the isle of forced exile? And if that pupil likes the English education and refuses to accept his invitation then the husband will face ridicule.

TATYA: In that case he should be straight and not bare his teeth and charge at other people's daughters. If he hears anything about anyone he should make sure that it is the truth and then he should, without worrying about anybody, publish the person's name and bring him back on the road. But who is the loser if he follows a selfish and opportunistic reformer and then lets his horse tread freely in farmers' lands and in the bargain brings upon himself this blemish?

YASHWANT: Who is this quarrelsome fellow? And why do you not reveal his name even when he bullies others in this way? It does not become you to spare such a woman-hater.

TATYA: My child, he is after all our biped brother. Let alone calling him by the name of the quadruped on the street,[24] we should not even stare at him, for, if we do so he might start barking according to his nature. Many wise people do not even touch his writings. What do we have to do with the inauspicious name of such a man? Let him take people's names and expose his wits. And it is not the virtue of a good man to behave like him. All of us human beings make mistakes. Therefore it becomes us to forgive such a quarrelsome man many times over. Moreover, many newspaper editors have to fill their bellies by lambasting a milder newspaper, or at least an old grandfather. Such meanness becomes them. But most of the scholarly and dignified editors do not suddenly name names and malign the whole of womankind.

YASHWANT: You say that most respectable, dignified and scholarly editors do not gossip about a woman and disgrace all women.

[23] The reference here is to a news item in *Dinabandhu*, the weekly of the Satyashodhak Samaj, which accused Phule of doing just that. [—*Ed.*]

[24] In many Indian languages the term is also used to indicate someone who is not distinguished for his reason. [—*Ed.*]

But many people along with some obstinate editors do say that women have all the vices like brazenness. If you tell us what you think about it will open people's eyes.

TATYA: Child, if you think about it fully you will see that it is men who are more partial, deceptive, thuggish, daring, cruel, and prone to commit more and more new kinds of horrible, daring and cruel acts than women. But since you ask I shall explain it a little.

The moment the husband starts disliking his first wife he brings a young woman into his home right in the presence of his first wife. Then he brings a third and then a fourth. At last he becomes her slave and ingratiates himself and enjoys himself. But one does not find in the scriptures of the Arya men any provision that a woman, after finding her husband to be ill-behaved, can marry another man and go on living in the same house. But why talk of it? Who is more partial, betraying and false then, men or women? My child, the Arya brahmans have one measure for giving and another for taking.

Secondly, many men keep their first and second wives at home and do the rounds of prostitutes' houses in the small lanes and by-lanes all through the night and then come home early in the morning and ruminating on the fodder consumed in the night, fall on their bellies and go to sleep right in front of their agitated wives. Even then the Arya men have awarded the title of *patra* to these prostitutes in their books. How would the nihilist men feel anything about the hundreds of women in the zenana of the Muslim emperor, who are torn apart by waves of hatred and anger because their husbands are philandering and their own desires remain unsatisfied? If these nawabs and badshahs honestly and truthfully decided to live with the wives who are caught in their charm, they will have to stay with three women once a month. We will let the reader imagine how these wives should maintain their fidelity.

But for the very few exceptional gentlemen who do not go to dances and concerts, most of the Vedic scholars, shastris, priests, reformers, all being birds of the same feather are so shameless that they watch the dances of the prostitutes and their mistresses in the presence of their wives and make the dancer sit on the lap of respectable men and let her embrace each one turn by turn.[25]

Similarly, most of the men dress up a young boy in a sari and put ornaments on him and make him look like a woman and then make him act in drama and tamasha. Then they make him sing lewd songs and make him dance right in front of the women in the family. Moreover, they make him sit on their laps and frolic about like prostitutes. Each man then gives him a little money and they make him sing the songs they like and feel very proud of themselves.

Why, aren't these men the descendents of the pure brahmans and the impure and ignorant shudra soldiers, who fought against the brave Muslims in the battles at Sonipat, Panipat and Kharde? What can we say to them when they wear nose-rings and dress up and sway their bodies in dance and clap like Narada?[26] Do women ever gather together and make a young, handsome, doe-eyed, strong and robust male singer sing love songs while he gestures with his hands and shoots amorous arrows from his eyes, and do they sit on the lap of this handsome singer one by one and frolic with him like men do? Can any son of his mother[27] amongst us say that he has seen with his own eyes women behave in this way even once since he was born, be it even from the dominion of our Queen Victoria? If he has seen such a thing and writes about it, women, in turn, will have found someone who is not born of woman.[28] [. . .]

Thirdly, everywhere on the surface of this earth it is the greedy rich men (and not women) who find fault with their powerless human brethren and using military forcefully invade and occupy their territory in order to capture it. While all the fierce fighting goes on all the businesses like farming and

[25] These descriptions refer in all probability to the debauchery prevalent in the last years of the Peshwa's rule in Pune, which ended in 1815. [—*Ed.*]

[26] See note 11 on p. 69 of the present volume. [—*Ed.*]

[27] Meaning a man worth his salt. [—*Ed.*]

[28] *Ayonisambhava* is the word Phule uses. It literally means someone who is not born of sexual intercourse. [—*Ed.*]

trading as well as factories close down and the darkness of sorrow pervades. Men become aliens to one another. In some places the merciless Pendhari and Kahiwale[29] loot people and many respectable and rich families become penniless. The cattle of most of the farmers die for lack of fodder. That is why many farmers leave their villages along with their families and cattle and thus many villages become deserted. While huge armies from both the sides fight with each other in wars caused by the selfishness of one or the other, thousands of soldiers lose their invaluable lives and thereby thousands of women become widows and they have to live the rest of their life in great danger and sorrow. Many women mourn the deaths of their only sons and reach the court of Yama wailing for their sons. Many orphan children deprived of food and clothes wander about begging. And here the victorious ruler lets his soldiers loot the unsupported subjects of his defeated opponent and burn their houses and take away everything and divest them of every possession. Then they return home and hold court and award lengthy titles like Uma Rao Bahadur or Jung Bahadur to those soldiers who are extremely cruel, merciless, daring and commit new horrific deeds every day. However, many guileless soldiers who are wounded badly in the battle fall to the ground. But by the stroke of fate there is some life left in them. The porters take pity on them and leave them on the pile of dead soldiers by the stream or ditch. They are not even caught under a landslide and they remain there crying for water. Later even without the doctor's nectar to free them from their pain they ultimately end up surviving. Thousands of such soldiers get meagre pensions and they go to their families or kin moaning and groaning and limping on crutches to spend their final days. During the reign of Julius Caesar, six lakh Roman soldiers lost their lives in order to capture the territories of kings; if it is necessary to have lakhs of soldiers killed, then you can imagine how many Arya soldiers must have died in the tumultuous battle of Parashuram while capturing this area after killing the local kshatriya inhabitants like dasyu, astik, aheer and matang and their children. There

[29] Marauders. [—*Ed.*]

must have been only a few daring women in this unbounded deluge of brave men. I know only a few of those women who have been thrown up in this deluge. Their names are as follows: the first is from mythology, the demon-killer Ambika. The second is Semirame who invaded India, and the third is the wife of the effeminate King of Jhansi who imagined that he was menstruating and therefore kept away from all business during the recent Chapati Mutiny. From this report, who do you think is more daring, men or women?

Fourthly, if we think about how men in Europe and America, who staunchly follow their religion like the brahmans, used to abduct the children of the poor, ignorant and weak people in Africa and take them to their own or other foreign countries and sell them like cattle and birds in order to enslave them and how the religious people who bought these children ill-treated them, we realize the cruel deeds of men and it makes us shiver. One American woman has written a book called *Uncle Tom's Cabin* in order to expose the cruelty of men. Anyone who reads this book, then let him be a stupid, heard-hearted, severe and even the adamant editor of a newspaper, who has deserted his own wife and who is jealous of all of womankind, will have to cry with shame in public like the Marwadi women drawing the pallu of their sari over their heads and will have to sigh and sob. What, then, will be the state of the other compassionate people? Who then is more evil, men or women?

Fifth, when the husband adorned with all ill-qualities dies, a woman has to hold the toe of the husband's dead body and have her head shaven by a barber[30] of the other shudra and impure caste. She has to hand over all her ornaments to her old and dying father-in-law and become like a beggar woman wearing bangles of tulsi wood. She has to give away all her rich clothes to her mother-in-law to wear and show off in her old age, and she herself must prepare to live in a poor cotton sari like that of the mang woman. She has to stop eating delicious food and fast on many days and if she does not even get to eat groundnuts, on those days she has to eat hard and dry rotis and live the rest

[30] This custom was widely prevalent till as late as the 1930s. [—*Ed.*]

of her life like a servant doing all the house work. If she does not have the courage of being called a strict religious woman by doing all these things then, for the greed of attaining immense virtue, she should follow the Arya scriptures and sit down with the husband's head in her lap and then all the utterly soft-hearted men burn alive this living and conscious and ignorant woman.

When the people in France did not like to kill the members of the opponent royal families, their brave lords, the scholarly diplomats, the shrewd and cunning minister and the soldiers with swipes of swords or batteries of guns, they created a machine like the pounding machine of the miller and stuck their necks in it one by one and cut them off. Similarly, let me tell you how the recent Nanasaheb Peshwa[31] who had, in the past, sat with the English lords and consumed liquor and ate meat, bread and biscuits prepared by the mlechhas[32] without defiling his purity, remembered this favour and with what finesse he repaid the English during the Chapati and Cartridge Mutiny of 1857.[33] Here are some examples:

Some 126 scared English people including women, men and children were trying to escape from Fatehgarh by crossing the Ganga in a boat. Nanasaheb promised them sanctuary and brought them to the shore. Now hear what he ultimately did to them. First he separated the men and made them stand on one side. Then he and his men snatched the little infants whom the confused women had been holding to their breasts, and with naked swords in their hands they danced around the infants and very skilfully sliced their heads off like fruit. They cut off the heads of infants who innocently played with their parents. They stabbed the younger children who would be going to school and engaged in all manner of naughtiness. While the children were thus killed and while their helpless parents stood looking at each other sorrowfully the soldiers beheaded all the women. After this they made all the unfortunate Englishmen stand in one line and tied their hands behind their backs by inserting a

[31] The last ruler of Pune. [—*Ed.*]

[32] See note 8 on p. 67 of the present volume. [—*Ed.*]

[33] See note 49 on p. 103 and note 65 on p. 125 of the present volume. [—*Ed.*]

stick through their armpits.

To the Author of *Satsar*

I write to you in connection with the children the people of Mumbai have sent to the school (. . .) in Pune, run by Mr. Krishnarao Bhalekar. If we see what these children have written to their parents regarding the sorry state of arrangements for their meals we would be shocked. Many parents have taken away their children from this school and sent them elsewhere. If you kindly publish this letter in *Satsar*, it would be of great help to a number of parents. We sent our children to this school because Bhalekar, in his advertisement, had mentioned the names of great people and that is why, deceived by all those names we put our children through a lot of pain.

Date 23 September 1885 — A Resident of Mumbai

Wouldn't it indeed be very good if our virtuous friend Bhalekar were to give up preaching on behavioural reform and go around town asking questions like 'What is it that you need'? It is time he gave up such a practice and took his host from Bombay to Vangana and made him administer prayashchitta[34] for his classic good education. Or else like the 'Jack of all and master of none'[35] his tricks will come to light.

[34] Ritual repentance. [—*Ed.*]

[35] This phrase is in English in the original. [—*Ed.*]

From

The Book of the True Faith

Preface: 1 April 1889

Published 1891

Translated by G.P. Deshpande

Sarvajanik Satya Dharma Pustak is almost like Phule's final testament. It is the summary statement of his theology and his view of what a rational and scientific religious system could be for India and the Hindus.

The *Pustak* was published posthumously in 1891. His adopted son Yashwantrao Phule has recorded that Phule did not see it in its final form before he died. The essence of this book and Phule's theological thought was summarized by his colleague and follower, Dr Vishram Ghole:

> [Phule] taught the people to think of religion in terms of what is right and wrong and above all in terms of cause and effect. He placed before them an account of current customs and beliefs in terms of their validity. He attacked idol-worship and made the case for monotheism.

But more important than this is perhaps the fact that the *Pustak* was an attempt at eliminating the middleman between God and man. Brahmans traditionally played that role and thus became an instrument of exploitation. The *Pustak* therefore attempts a reformulation of the Hindu belief-system which would eliminate the priestly class, the brahman. This is a radical position to take even today; in 1891, it must have been more shocking still.

Phule argues passionately for reforming Hinduism into a monotheistic, humane, and benevolent system. That we as a people haven't yet succeeded in doing this, demonstrates the relevance of Phule and his *Sarvajanik Satya Dharma Pustak*. We reproduce here a selection.

Contents

1 The sections included in the present volume are indicated by an asterisk. [—*Ed.*]

Death
Disposal of dead bodies
Memorial rituals of the dead
Author's appeal to all men and women

The Book[2]

BALWANTRAO HARI SAKVALKAR: Does it then mean that there is no religious book that in fact states the Truth, the realization of which would make all living beings happy?

JOTIRAO GOVINDRAO PHULE: All the religious and revelatory books that man has produced on our planet, one and all, do not contain a consistent universal truth. This is so because in every such book are to be seen passages interpolated into those texts by certain groups of individuals as the situation in their view warranted and as their dogmatism and mulishness dictates. Consequently, those religions or faiths did not in the final analysis work towards the good of all. This in turn resulted in sects and sectarianism. Small wonder that these sects hated and turned against each other.

Secondly, the Creator of this universe is also the Creator of human beings. It would not be surprising if He, because He is merciful, would want all human beings to enjoy all human privileges and rights. In reality, however, this does not happen and human beings suffer unbearable miseries of various kinds.

In sum, this solar system and naturally the planet earth which we inhabit are created by one Creator. Why is it then that the human beings living in different states and nations hate each other? How and why are the foolish passions of religions and national hatreds generated? There are any number of rivers on our planet. All of them eventually meet the sea. How and why then can only one of those rivers be sacred? Does that sacred river ever hesitate to carry dogs' excreta to the sea?[3]

[2] The title of the section is '*Dharma Pustak*' which would literally translate as the 'Book of Faith'. What he means here is the Book in the sense of the Religions of the Book. Hence, I have chosen to render it as 'The Book'. [—*Ed.*]

[3] The word pavitra, usually used as a synonym for sacred, also carries the meaning of untouchability. What is 'sacred' is also 'untouchable'. Phule seems to suggest that the river which carries dog's excreta cannot be 'sacred' in the conventional sense. The reference here is to the Hindu belief obviously not

BALWANTRAO: If there is no 'sacred' river, then there should also be no sacred people. How do you then explain that there are certain groups of individuals who are called super-sacred and indeed are worshipped as gods on earth?

JOTIRAO: That is clearly untenable. All human beings on our planet are equipped with similar physical and intellectual facilities. How can some of them be 'sacred' generation after generation? Are they not born and do they not die like everyone else, and do they not have qualities good and bad like everyone else?

Paradise

MANAJI BALUJI MAGAR: It is generally believed by the ignorant that there are heaven and paradise. The faithful and the virtuous reach paradise. They enjoy unlimited happiness in paradise. The sinful and the miscreants, however, go to hell and undergo various kinds of suffering as determined by their sins. What do you have to say on that?

JOTIRAO GOVINDRAO PHULE: In times immemorial when human beings had not yet heard of reform or betterment, some clever people thought of this construct called paradise more to frighten the common people in much the same manner as the peasants use a scarecrow to frighten or scare the birds and animals away from the crops. Later, there were reforms of different kinds. But nobody really thought out the concept of paradise.

MANAJI: Would you then say that there is no such thing as heaven or paradise?

JOTIRAO: Undoubtedly. All religious books talk of heaven and paradise. But can anyone think of a man who has actually seen heaven? Has it ever happened that a certain individual decided not to trust the word of the text unless experience were to endorse it and therefore went in search of paradise and came back to report on its existence? Can you ever find such an experimentalist individual in our midst? The fact is that this concept of Paradise has never been logically thought out.

[. . .]

....

shared by Phule that Ganga is a sacred river. [—*Ed.*]

Woman and man

BALWANTRAO HARI SAKVALKAR: The Creator has created three kinds of beings. Those who move in water, those who move on land and those who move in the sky. Who is the most advanced (or superior) of the three?

JOTIRAO GOVINDRAO PHULE: The human being is the greatest of all beings. Human beings are of two kinds: Woman and Man.

BALWANTRAO: Who is superior of these two?

JOTIRAO: Woman.

BALWANTRAO: Why?

JOTIRAO: The Creator has created in this world sources of pleasure for both man and woman. They also enjoy each other's company. Woman is however self-restrained by nature. She permits a man to make friends with her. The clever man however plays upon the natural desire of the woman. Their closeness grows to the extent that the woman decides to make him her partner and close friend. The laws of nature take their course. The patient woman carries their child without complaint.[4] She does not know what the child is going to be like but it does not matter to her. She does her duty and brings up the child. She teaches it to walk and to speak. Don't we have the proverb that one can repay all debts except the mother's debt? Doubtless woman is superior to man.

BALWANTRAO: What else is special about women?

JOTIRAO: Her brother and sisters like her because (unlike man) she stands by them, supports them. Surely you know that the household is not complete without the woman.[5]

BALWANTRAO: That a woman loves her man more than a man does his woman: what's the basis of this logic?

JOTIRAO: When the husband dies, it is the woman who leads a life of suffering. She has to suffer widowhood for the rest of her life.

[4] While the man does nothing: this is the unsaid. [—*Ed.*]

[5] Phule uses a line from Sanskrit here: '*na griham grihamityahurgrihni grihamuchyate*' ('The house is not a house. It is the woman in the house who makes it a house'). [—*Ed.*]

Surely you know that in times gone by[6] many burnt themselves alive and become a sati on the funeral pyre of their husbands. Have you ever heard of a man burning himself alive in the event of his wife's death and become a sata?[7]

BALWANTRAO: Men's love for their women does not quite match women's love for their men. What is the proof?

JOTIRAO: As much faithful and devoted as the wife might be, men can and do marry again and again. You will never find that women likewise indulge in polyandry.

BALWANTRAO: Why do you think women are subjected to such acts of injustice by men?

JOTIRAO: That's because they are weak. Their lustful and adventurous men push themselves and their desires on to women without their consent. They deprive them of education so as to prevent them from being conscious of their human rights and subject them to oppression. [. . .] The case of the Arya brahman widowers is worse still, who even when advanced in age and in shattered physical condition marry young beautiful maidens and ruin their youth. At the same time they have laid down in their books that a young widow should not remarry. This has the following consequences. These Arya brahmans unashamedly make advances on the weak defenceless widows in their household and greedily seduce them. When these widows become pregnant they are forced to abort. This is quite a common practice. You cannot imagine how many abortions and infanticides take place among the Arya brahmans. [. . .] Now the other castes also follow the brahman's example. They also subject their women to the same miseries and expose them to the same dangers.

BALWANTRAO: But haven't the Vedas, so sacred to the brahmans, banned such practices?

JOTIRAO: Vedas have not laid down that women cannot remarry.

6 Phule specifically says *purvi*, i.e., in times gone by. This means that there was no practice of sati in Maharashtra during his time. Strangely he does not refer to Bengal or other parts of India. [—*Ed.*]

7 There is, of course, no such word. It is an ironical coinage by Phule to suggest a male sati. [—*Ed.*]

Naturally, the question of banning infanticide does not arise.[8] In fact if the elder brother died his wife could marry his younger brother and continue to enjoy life. It is reasonable to assume that there were no practices like abortion and infanticide during the Vedic times.

Sinful conduct[9]

MANAJI BOLUJI PATIL: Hasn't the Creator given any safety devices to the man so that he does not indulge in misconduct and suffer?

JOTIRAO GOVINDRAO PHULE: How can that be? Our Creator is omniscient and merciful. He made these safety devices even before He created human beings. That's not all. These safety devices are the best of their kind.

MANAJI: How is it then that some men have this extraordinary lust for women? Why did not these men use these devices like good and restrained behaviour and save themselves from lust?

JOTIRAO: I am sure that you know the well-known proverb – judge others as you would judge yourself. People who fall victim to lust reject the power of discrimination that God has given them. They give up the code of proper conduct and become sinful. They have to atone for these failures.

MANAJI: I do not quite follow. Please elaborate.

JOTIRAO: Some lustful men who marry more than once, maintain almost a harem; justify their action with reference to some senseless religious text written by equally mulish men. How would they take it if some women were to marry more than one man to satisfy their lust? Would not these men think of right and wrong and be critical of their behaviour?

MANAJI: Indeed if some women were to indulge in such filthy unworldly acts, they must be punished.

8 Since remarriage would legitimize the child. [—*Ed.*]

9 *Paap*, the title of this section, is quite often translated as sin. Sin, however, has a specific meaning in Christianity. Indian or Hindu notion of *paap* is not the same as Christian sin. Phule seems to be using the term (especially *papacharana*, sinful conduct) in the Hindu sense. The notion of absolute or original sin does not exist in Hinduism. The opening section relating to men and women and polygamy is translated here. [—*Ed.*]

JOTIRAO: Precisely. If you do not like such behaviour on the part of women, is it surprising that women would dislike similar filthy behaviour on the part of men? Both men and women are equally qualified to enjoy all human rights in equal measure. How can anyone then have one standard for women and quite another for lustful, adventurous men? It amounts to saying what belongs to women must naturally belong to men; the reverse, however, will not apply![10] Some of them have codified these kinds of selfish formulations about women in their pseudo-religious books.

[. . .]

Caste differentiation[11]

YASHWANT JOTIRAO PHULE: Is caste differentiation natural to human beings?

JOTIRAO GOVINDRAO PHULE: Originally human beings were not divided into castes.

YASHWANT: How does one know that originally there was no caste differentiation among human beings?

JOTIRAO: There is no such differentiation among birds and animals. Why would it be there among human animals?

YASHWANT: Please elaborate on this.

JOTIRAO: Animals, birds, etc., all differ from each other anatomically. Likewise two-legged human beings are different from four-legged animals. It is said that the Arya Brahma has created the four castes.[12] He would have done so for the animals as well. Can you tell me then who are the brahmans among the donkeys, crows, etc.?

YASHWANT: Evidently nobody can prove that there are brahmans among the animals and birds. [. . .] Their scriptures speak of the four jatis having been created from the limbs of the Lord Brahma.

[10] Literally translated, this sentence would go like this: 'Women's [rights] belong to men. Men's rights, however, are Ha, Hu, Ha, Hu!' (Monosyllables. Natural rights do not need elaboration!). [—*Ed.*]

[11] Jatibheda. [—*Ed.*]

[12] Phule means the varnas and the reference to the account in the *Purusha Sukta* of the *Rig Veda*. See pp. 66–70 of the present volume. [—*Ed.*]

[. . .]

JOTIRAO: Have you read the (sacred) books of the brahmans yourself? Have you examined them for authenticity and reliability?

YASHWANT: No. But then the Arya brahmans do not let us even gaze at them. If we asked for the privilege to hear those texts, the Arya brahmans would not let us hear a word of them.

JOTIRAO: Why then do you blindly accept what they say on the fraud of the caste-system? Why don't you examine these texts fabricated by the *bhat* brahmans? A characteristic gullibility of the shudras!

YASHWANT: Brahmans will be brahmans, and shudras will be shudras. No matter what we might try, shudras cannot become brahmans. Nor for that matter will brahmans become the shudras.

JOTIRAO: Indeed, why not? When these very same brahmans, the gods of our planet, join the parties in the Christian houses,[13] they merrily eat meat and consume liquor with anyone – with the untouchable mangs and mahars. Don't they? Aren't these foreigners mlechhas or atishudras for them? But they will have no problem even marrying their young daughters and living happily ever after. I think you should take the initiative and rebel against the advice that brahmans, no matter where, are to be worshipped.[14]

YASHWANT: But then this would mean that the caste groups like shepherds, peasants and horticulturists in our unfortunate peasant-land[15] have no legitimacy. How can that be?

JOTIRAO: You will see that that is not true if you were to think a little about it. Look at it this way. A man has three sons. He assigns the responsibility of his goats and sheep to one. The other works on growing fruits and flowers.[16] The third son cultivates

[13] Phule refers to the brahmans accepting invitations to dinners and banquets with the British officials. [—*Ed.*]

[14] Phule uses a Sanskrit aphorism: *brahmanh sarvatra pujyah.* [—*Ed.*]

[15] *Bali-sthana* is Phule's semi-mythic term for peasant-land. For him the peasant was a Baliraja. [—*Ed.*]

[16] The actual phrase Phule uses refers to the operation of planting trees. I have preferred this simpler expression. [—*Ed.*]

the land and busies himself with grain production. But then you wouldn't argue that these three sons of the same man constitute three jatis. Would you?

YASHWANT: Naturally not. How can anybody do that?

JOTIRAO: Likewise assume that an Arya *bhat* brahman has three sons. One of them became a percussionist. The other became a doctor[17] who treated patients of all castes and performed autopsies and the third became a professional cook. Would you say that the three of them belonged to three different castes?

YASHWANT: Surely not. But wouldn't you agree that the one who does basic cleaning and deals with dirt and filth belongs to an inferior caste?

JOTIRAO: If that be correct, your and my mother would belong to inferior caste. Did not they clean our excreta when we were children?

YASHWANT: Who would say that his mother belongs to inferior caste? I do not think you can find such an ungrateful wretch anywhere in the world. But surely it would be possible to determine the jati according to the qualities of an individual. Wouldn't it?

JOTIRAO: No. That's not possible. People make sure that their children get a fine education. Some of them are bright and intelligent and develop into complete individuals. Some are not as bright. They end up doing all kinds of lowly work. But as you can see good and bad qualities are not hereditary.[18] To argue that a shoemaker's bright son, even when trained properly, cannot compare with a brahman Shankaracharya flies in the face of all natural justice. No fair person would argue that.

YASHWANT: It might be good if you explained how the cruel and out-of-this-world institution like caste differentiation arose in the first instance. How come castes like brahmans, mangs and mahars were created in the first place?

JOTIRAO: In this peasant-land there were kshatriyas, the lords of a given area, kshetra – astik, pishach, rakshas, etc. They were gifted with the martial arts and the use of weaponry. All of them lived

[17] The original has vaidya. [—*Ed.*]

[18] Whereas, of course, caste is. [—*Ed.*]

happily together. In fact there was unprecedented prosperity in this land. At about that time the Iranians,[19] that is the brahmans, invented the bow and the arrow – weaponry superior to the one in use here in India. Then the adventurous, violent and greedy Iranian brahmans, kshatriyas and vaishyas with their eye on the Indian gold, formed a joint front and invaded our peasant-land several times and harassed the local kshatriyas. In the end they even peeled the skin off some of them.[20] This is documented in the Vedas which are their histories. These Iranians then drove the local kshatriyas into the nether-lands, i.e., America, turned the others into their slaves and untouchables for all times to come. [. . .]

YASHWANT: If this is so, why is it that the Lord, the Merciful, does not sympathize with the exploited shudras and atishudras?

JOTIRAO: Indeed, he does. Precisely because of his mercy and his desire to rescue the shudras and the atishudras from slavery he sent the monotheistic Mussalmans who do not believe in caste-system to this land. But then the Mussalmans also betrayed God. They spent their time in banquets, luxurious living and musical concerts. They were busy enjoying the luxuries as if they had almost gained paradise right here on earth. The Creator got annoyed with the Mussalmans. He deprived them of their power and glory.

YASHWANT: And then kept quiet! How could he?

JOTIRAO: No, He did not. He civilized the English primitives,[21] granted them qualities like extraordinary valour. Now he has sent them to our land to rescue the shudras and the atishudras from the slavery of the Arya *bhats*. Some English gentlemen among them following the teaching of a sage of their religion are in all sincerity making every effort to rescue the shudras and atishudras from their unnatural slavery.

[19] Phule believed firmly that the Aryans were the conquering people from Iran. [—*Ed.*]

[20] Phule translates here a line presumably from one of the Vedas: *twacam krsnamarandhayat*. It is not clear to me where the line is from and what incident it refers to. [—*Ed.*]

[21] Phule uses the word *atiranati* which would mean extreme primitives. [—*Ed.*]

[On being asked who this sage happened to be Phule replied:]

JOTIRAO: Their great sage is called Yashwant[22] and his great teaching is: You must love your enemy and do him a good turn.

[22] Phule has turned Yeshu (Jesus) into a Marathi name which means the successful one. [—*Ed.*]

Brief Chronology of Jotirao Phule's Life

Birth (in Bhamburda, Pune)	1827
Marathi education (primary)	1834–38
Marriage to Savitribai	1840
English education (secondary school)	1841–47
Establishes the first school for shudratishudra girls	1848
Turned out of his house by father	1849
Establishment of two more schools	1851
Felicitated by the Department of Education for his educational work	16.11.1852
Establishment of a night-school (for working people)	1855
Attempt on Phule's life	1856
Retires from Schools' Management Board	1858
Establishment of House for Illegitimate Children and their Mothers	1863
Father (Govindrao) dies	1868
Opens the household water-tank to untouchables	1868
Founding of the Satyashodhak Samaj	24.9.1873
Member, Pune Municipal Council	1876–1882
Deposes before the Hunter Commission	19.10.1882
Public felicitation with the title of Mahatma	11.05.1888
Death (in Pune)	28.11.1890

Further Readings

Phule's Works

Play: *Tritiya Ratna* (*The Third Jewel*)	1855
Powada: Chhatrapati Shivajiraje Bhonsale Yancha (*Ballad of Shivaji*)	1869
Powada: Vidyakhatyatil Brahman Pantoji (*Ballad of the Brahman Teacher*)	1869
Brahmanache Kasab (*The Craftiness of Brahmans*)	1869
Gulamgiri (*Slavery*)	1873
Memorial Addressed to the Education Commission	1882
Shetkaryacha Asud (*Cultivator's Whipcord*)	1883
On Infant Marriage and Enforced Widowhood (Comments on Malabari's notes)	1884
Letter to the Marathi Granthkar Sabha (Conference of Marathi Authors)	1885
Satsar (*The Essence of Truth*) No.1 and No. 2	1885
Ishara (*Warning*)	1885
Religious Rites for the Satyashodhaks	1887
Sarvajanik Satya Dharma Pustak (*The Book of the True Faith*)	1889
posthumous publication	1891
Poetry	*written over the years*
Phule's Will	1887

Further Readings

(A) English

Chakravarti, Uma, 1998. *Rewriting History: The Life and Times of Pandita Ramabai*, New Delhi: Kali for Women

Das, Dixit, Paranjpe (eds), 1997. *Western India: History, Society and Culture*, Kolhapur: Itihas Shikshak Mahamandal

Fukuzawa , Hiroshi, 1998. *The Medieval Deccan: Peasants, Social Systems and States: 16th to 18th Centuries*, Delhi: Oxford University Press

Keer, Dhananjay, 1964, 2000. *Mahatma Jotirao Phooley: Father of Indian Social Revolution*, Bombay: Popular Prakashan

O'Hanlon, Rosalind, 1985. *Caste, Conflict and Ideology*, Cambridge: Cambridge University Press

———, 1994. *A Comparison Between Women and Men: Tarabai Shinde and the Critique of Gender Relations in Colonial India*, New Delhi: Oxford University Press

Omvedt, Gail, 1976. *Cultural Revolt in a Colonial Society: The Non-Brahman Movement in Western India (1873–1930)*, Bombay: Scientific Socialist Education Trust

———, 1994. *Dalits and the Democratic Revolution*, New Delhi: Sage Publications

Ranadive, B.T., 1982, 1991. *Caste, Class and Property Relations*, Calcutta: National Book Agency

(B) Marathi

Chausalkar, Ashok, 2001. *Mahatma Phule ani Shetkari Chalwal* (*Mahatma Phule and the Peasant Movement*), Mumbai: Lok Vangmaya Griha

Deshpande, G.P. *Satyashodhak* (a play), Aurangabad: Saket Prakashan

Joshi, Sharad, 1989. *Shetkaryacha Asud – Ha Shatakacha Muzra* (*Cultivator's Whipcord – A Centenary Tribute*), Alibag: Shetkari Prakashan

Narke, Hari (ed.), 1982. *Mahatma Phule Gaurav Granth*, Mumbai:

Maharashtra State Government Publication

Omvedt, Gail, 2001. *Jotiba Phule ani Stree-mukticha Vichar* (*Phule and Women's Liberation*), Mumbai: Lok Vangmaya Griha

Patankar, Bharat, 2001. *Mahatma Phule ani Sanskritik Sangharsh* (*Phule and Cultural Conflict*), Mumbai: Lok Vangmaya Griha

Patil, Sharad, 1987. *Das Shudranchi Gulamgiri* (*Slavery of Dasas and Shudras*), Wari: Prajna Press

Phule, Jotirao, 1969. *Mahatma Phule Samagra Vangmaya* (*Collected Works of Mahatma Phule*), edited by Dhananjay Keer and S.G. Malshe, Mumbai: Maharashtra Rajya Sahitya ani Sanskriti Mandal. Fourth edition 1991, edited by Y.D. Phadke

Punde, Sumant (eds), 1988. *Maharashtratis Jatisanstha Vishayak Vichar* (*Analyses of Caste in Maharashtra*), Pune: Pratima Prakashan

Salunkhe, A.H., 2001. *Mahatma Phule ani Dharma* (*Phule and Dharma*), Mumbai: Lok Vangmaya Griha

Vora, Rajendra (ed.), 2000. *Adhunikta ani Parampara: Ekonisavya Shatakatil Maharastra* (*Modernity and Tradition: 19th Century Maharashtra*), Pune: Pratima Prakashan

Translators

URMILA BHIRDIKAR teaches Sociology in Shiv Nadar University. Her teaching and research interests are in gender and sexuality, discourses of respectability and self-respect and sound and performance. She has published articles on the archive of early modern Marathi musical theatre and music criticism. She translates between Marathi, Hindi and English. They include the translation of the play *Mahapoor* by Satish Alekar (*The Deluge*, in *Collected Plays of Satish Alekar*, OUP, 2009) and with Amlan Dasgupta, translation and critical introduction to *My Life* by Sangit Samrat Khansahab Alladiya Khan (Thema, 2001).

G.P. DESHPANDE (1938–2013) retired as Professor of International Studies from Jawaharlal Nehru University, New Delhi. He was a leading playwright in Marathi and his ten plays include *Udhwastha Dharmashala*, *Andhar Yatra*, *Satyashodhak* and *Raste*. Many of his plays have been translated into multiple Indian languages, including English. He wrote the screenplay and dialogues for several episodes of Shyam Benegal's television series *Bharat Ek Khoj*, including the episode on Phue. He is the author of *The World of Ideas in Modern Marathi: Phule, Vinoba, Savarkar* (Tulika, 2009), *Talking the Political Culturally and Other Essays* (Thema 2009) and *Dialectics of Defeat: The Problems of Culture in Postcolonial India* (Seagull 2006). He was the recipient of the Maharashtra State Award for playwrighting and the Sangeet Natak Akademi Award.

ANIKET JAAWARE (1960–2018) taught in the departments of English in Savitribai Phule Pune University and Shiv Nadar University. He published widely on topics in literary and film criticism, and 19th century Marathi literature and caste. He wrote in and translated between English and Marathi. Some of his publications are: *Simplifications: An Introduction to*

Structuralism and Post Structuralism (Orient Blackswan, 2001), a short story collection *Neon Fish in Dark Water* (Mapin, 2006), a collection of articles in Marathi, *Kale Pandhare Asfut Lekh* (Hermis Prakashan, 2011) and *Practicing Caste: On Touching and Not Touching* (Fordham University Press and Orient Blackswan, 2018).

MAYA PANDIT retired as professor from the English and Foreign Languages University, Hyderabad. Her research and teaching areas include English language teaching, feminism, and translation studies. She has published translations of more than 18 books, among which are English translations of Baby Kamble's *The Prisons We Broke* and Urmila Pawar's *The Weave of My Life*; Marathi translations of Dario Fo's *An Accidental Death of an Anarchist* and Ramu Ramnathan's *Mahadevbhai*; English translations of Jayant Pawar's *The Nowhere People*, Sanjay Pawar's *Pass the Buck on Brother* and Saniya's *Thereafter*. The books she has authored include *Gopal Ganesh Agarkar*, *Adventures with Grammar and Compositions*, *Govind Purushottam Deshpande* (forthcoming) and a poetry collection, *Talkhali*. Currently she is involved in alternative theatre.